D0105325

Dorothy Donnelly

Dorothy Donnelly

A Life in the Theatre

by
LORRAINE ARNAL MCLEAN

McFarland & Company, Inc., Publishers
Jefferson, North Carolina, and London

Frontispiece: Dorothy Donnelly (spring 1905).

Library of Congress Cataloguing-in-Publication Data

McLean, Lorraine Arnal, 1940–
    Dorothy Donnelly : a life in the theatre / by Lorraine Arnal
McLean.
      p.   cm.
    Includes bibliographical references and index. ♾
    ISBN 0-7864-0677-1 (library binding : 50# alkaline paper)
    1. Donnelly, Dorothy.   2. Actors—United States Biography.
I. Title.
PN2287.D523M39   1999
792'.028'092—dc21   99-28403
[B]   CIP

British Library Cataloguing-in-Publication data are available

©1999 Lorraine Arnal McLean. All rights reserved

*No part of this book may be reproduced or transmitted in any form
or by any means, electronic or mechanical, including photocopying
or recording, or by any information storage and retrieval system,
without permission in writing from the publisher.*

Manufactured in the United States of America

McFarland & Company, Inc., Publishers
  Box 611, Jefferson, North Carolina 28640
  www.mcfarlandpub.com

To Robert A. McLean, Jr.

Acknowledgments

I wish to thank Robert Sumpter and John Whitney Evans for reading my first drafts and offering encouragement instead of rightful disdain; Lynn, Bob, and Michelle for welcoming another sibling; Joseph Marchi, director of the Center for the American Musical, for raising the question, "Who is Dorothy Donnelly?"; Thomas McCall for sharing his great-aunt with me; Philip and Nancy Fahringer for taped memoirs from Dorothy's youngest niece and copies of photographs; Sonia Moss of the San Mateo Public Library for many reprints and interlibrary loans; Maryann Chach of the Shubert Archive for making files and photographs available; Michael Morrison for permission to reprint three photographs; Joanne Lafler for wise and critical suggestions; Robert A. McLean, Jr., for his loving support and invaluable assistance.

Table of Contents

Introduction

W hen *The Student Prince* made its first appearance in 1924, *Theatre Magazine* called it the "musical jewel that deserves center place in the crown of this season's successes." It still glitters. Revived again and again, *The Student Prince* continues to play annually in the repertoire of opera companies throughout the United States and the United Kingdom, in summer stock companies, in the castle courtyard of Heidelberg. Given its enormous and enduring success, surprisingly little is known about Dorothy Agnes Donnelly, who wrote the book for the operetta and the words for Sigmund Romberg's memorable songs.

For thirty years Donnelly held every position the theatre has to offer: actress, playwright, producer, director, lyricist, librettist, and benefactor. Although she amassed some important "firsts" during her long career, no one has written her remarkable life story. She left no memoirs to record her achievements in the theatre, no children to perpetuate her reputation and name, no scandals to create a legend. Information about her accomplishments comes to us indirectly through newspapers, magazines, volumes of histories, a few reminiscences, a half-page article in *Who Was Who in the Theatre*, a scrapbook of clippings—many of these with their heads lopped off and their tails truncated—and dusty files in the Shubert Archive that contain correspondence and contracts. Her plays and operettas, as well as extensive interviews with reporters, convey her life's story more immediately. One author used her as the model for the main character in a novel. Relatives remembered her with contagious affection. A parade of witnesses extolled her personal charms: wit, humor, perseverance, and an occasional inclination to fib.

These intermediaries, which speak in her behalf, document her many contributions to the American theatre. Scattered and fragmented, they lie dormant until assembled like pieces of a jigsaw puzzle, when—at last— they reveal the picture of a strong-willed woman, passionately in love with

1

the stage and fiercely determined to keep herself permanently wrapped in its embrace.

Donnelly began her theatrical career as an actress at the turn of the century, when Broadway attracted a host of older, internationally celebrated actresses and produced a bumper crop of young talented ones. "The theatre of the early 1900s was a thriving business," says Herbert Goldman:

> In a world without television. [sic] And where the motion picture had not yet begun to toddle, the stage had the task of supplying entertainment for the masses. The 1906-07 season would prove to be the most active in the history of the American theatre, with hundreds of professional touring shows, more than a thousand active vaudeville theatres, minstrelsty [sic], burlesque, stock companies, and a dozen circuses. More than 30,000 people made their living as performers.[1]

Most are now forgotten, but the names of Julia Marlowe, Margaret Anglin, Ethel Barrymore, Annie Russell, Viola Allen, Sarah Bernhardt, and Eleanora Duse may still remain familiar to us. At a time when the theatre flaunted such luminaries, Dorothy Donnelly's stardom shone less long than theirs but often as bright.

Her exemplary lifestyle may have robbed Donnelly of her rightful place in the history of American acting, as Richard Mansfield's comment suggests. "The stage is the actor's studio and gallery of exhibition," said the actor; "away from it his deeds are of no moment, and many actors would be less known and others more popular if the world judged the actor only by his work."[2] In accordance with his injunction, when writing about performers who departed the stage and the world years ago, today's historians tend to discuss the popularity of their work rather than of their personality. For instance, in assessing the "extraordinary skillful performances by women of the ... era," Ward Morehouse ranks Dorothy among her better-known contemporaries—Laurette Taylor, Ethel Barrymore, Mary Mannering, and Margaret Illington.[3] Most historians ignore Donnelly's acting career, however, because she does not meet what many consider the touchstone of quality in acting—interpreting Shakespeare's heroines. This benchmark for evaluating American actresses evolved during the eighteenth century, since colonists produced few plays of their own and their theatre fare consisted almost entirely of English drama from the Elizabethan (primarily Shakespeare) and Restoration periods. It continued throughout the nineteenth century, when British actors began flocking to the United States to extend their audience. It still persists. In *A History of American Acting*, for example, Professor Garff Wilson relies exclusively on this criterion to judge retrospectively the quality of performance at the turn of the century. Incidentally, film actor Humphrey Bogart once suggested that to keep the Oscars from becoming a popularity contest, the nominees for best actor of the year ought be required to give Hamlet's soliloquy before the voters, members of the Academy of Motion Picture Arts and Sciences.[4] So ingrained has this method of assessing success become that performers are easily and unmistakably identified as "known for his portrayal of Hamlet (or Richard III)." Such thumbnail biographical descriptions require no further elaboration. According to actor Alan Hewitt, this tradition has serious drawbacks. "Histories of the theatre seem to concentrate on the great tragedians, the men and women who played the classic 'great' parts, as if those were all that deserve respectful attention. That may be the test for Ph.D. candidates, but I wonder about the paying public," he says and advocates, instead, the trumpeting of "Working actors—the host of comedians and musical stars who seem to have made theatregoing a delight, not just a respectful obeisance to culture."[5]

Donnelly was indeed a working actress. Her preparation for each succeeding role was deliberate and thoroughly meticulous. Although she seemed simple, natural, and affecting on the stage, her performances were the harvest not merely of genius or talent, but also of discipline and intelligent conception. The Irish playwright George Bernard Shaw acknowledged her as his "collaborator" in creating the title role of *Candida* when she played the part in 1903 in America's premiere professional production of the play. Perhaps the most influential—and hard to please—drama critic of the period, Alexander Woollcott, insisted she was "one of the most brilliant, competent actresses on the American stage."[6] To American playwright Channing Pollock, who thought novelists more fortunate than playwrights since their words remained on the page as printed whereas playwrights must stand helplessly by and painfully watch their lines mangled and altered and misinterpreted, she was a playwright's dream, bringing to each successive part a willingness as well as an ability—each a rare trait—to play the role as the author intended.

Donnelly was also a working writer for the theatre. She revised scripts, penned new ones, adapted plays and novels as musicals and then wrote lyrics for their songs. Her first operetta, *Flora Bella*, led Donnelly into nearly virgin territory. Only three women before her dared to breach the male domain of writing libretti: Anne Caldwell, Rida Johnson Young, and Catherine Chisholm Cushing. None of their musical shows, however, continue to receive the same amount of attention as those Donnelly created.

Both *Blossom Time* and *The Student Prince* gave birth to the revival of operetta, the genre that became the hallmark of the American theatre for the rest of the decade. "In its initial Broadway engagement, *The Student Prince* enjoyed a run of 608 performances, earning status as the longest-running musical play of the 1920s," say Amy Henderson and Dwight Bowers, curators at the Smithsonian Institution. This "bittersweet romance between a royal and a barmaid contains some of the finest compositions in the operetta mold, including "Drinking Song," "Serenade," and "Deep in My Heart, Dear."[7] The *Cambridge Guide to the American Theatre* concurs, noting that it is "considered by many the masterpiece of American operetta."[8] Although *Blossom Time* and *The Student Prince* retain their European origins in settings, costumes, musical compositions, romantic characters, and fairy tale stories, their sad endings contributed to the evolution of the form from "comic" or "light" opera into what is known today as the American musical, marked by well defined characters, vital American themes, developed dialogue, and music that is tightly integrated into the development of both plot and character.

Women in American Theatre, edited by Helen Krich Chinoy and Linda Walsh Jenkins, lists Donnelly as one of the American women writing for the stage early in the twentieth century but devotes no space to her contributions either as a playwright or librettist.[9] In his many comprehensive histories of the musical stage such as *American Musical Theatre: A Chronicle, American Operetta: From H.M.S. Pinafore to Sweeney Todd,* and *The Concise Oxford Companion to American Theatre,* Gerald Martin Bordman offers a few biographical details on Donnelly and brief analyses of her musical plays. Most historians, however, mention only her works. For instance, in *The Making of the American Theatre,* Howard Taubman, a drama critic for the *New York Times* for many years, devotes an entire lengthy paragraph to *Poppy,* one of Donnelly's musical plays. He retells the plot in detail, recalls "Alibi Baby" as the first song written by composer Arthur Swartz and lyricist Howard Dietz, and never once notes the name of *Poppy's* author.[10] Likewise, the illustrated history of the 125 years of musical theatre in New York, published by the Museum of the City of New York and entitled *Broadway!,* offers a brief summary of *The Student Prince* but makes no reference to its author[11]—a glaring omission in view of the fact that Donnelly was a native daughter, and permanent resident in Manhattan. Although Donnelly or her works have been cited in similar histories, neither have received sufficient scholarly attention.

As a writer for the musical stage, Donnelly was doomed to eventual obscurity, since credit for musicals gets assigned by convention to the composer, not to the lyricist or librettist. Musicals are classified by libraries, anthologies, and music shops according to the composer's surname. Nevertheless, "Of a musical's three elements—the book, the music, and the lyrics—the book is the most important," says historian Martin Gottfried. "The book is the basis of the show's existence. It is what the show is *about*."[12] Yet, it is also the least respected element. According to Arthur Laurents, who wrote the text for *West Side Story* and *Gypsy*, the "librettist of a musical usually gets recognition only when the musical fails."[13] The lyricist, likewise, gets shortchanged when bouquets are presented. One frequently repeated story concerns the wife of Oscar Hammerstein II, who quickly tired of hearing "Ol' Man River" referred to as Jerome Kern's song. "Kern merely wrote 'Da-da-da-da,'" she said. "Oscar Hammerstein wrote 'Ol' Man River.'"[14] As Alan Jay Lerner, lyricist for *Brigadoon*, *My Fair Lady*, and *Camelot*, points out, "There is one undeniable fact about the musical theatre. Good lyrics can make a play work, but it is the music that makes it endure."[15] When the orchestra swells, all too often the librettist and lyricist are entirely glossed over.

This book is not a definitive biography. In the first place, in the absence of personal diaries or journals, Donnelly's feelings and motivations cannot be known completely. In the second place, definitive biographies are usually written only about people who are dead. Through her influence on the American theatre, she still lives.

How should I begin to assess the quality of her work? The drama critics spoke long ago, and although their voices must be heard, this book makes no attempt to judge their opinions.

How should I presume to tell the chroniclers of American theatre that their histories remain incomplete? They cite or omit her name all the while placing her musicals in the context of what preceded them and especially what followed. Theirs is necessarily a myopic view. They are interested only in the product and not in the process or the manufacturer.

I have dared; the fruit is the story of Dorothy Agnes Donnelly.

CHAPTER 1
Beginnings

The year was 1880; the setting, New York City. Engineers installed electricity in the form of arc-lamps to illuminate a mile-long strip of Broadway. The *New York Daily Graphic* published the first reproduction of a photograph to appear in a newspaper. The subway extended its route along Sixth Avenue, from downtown's Rector Street all the way past Central Park, now completed—just in time for the grand opening of the new Metropolitan Museum of Art. Notices heralded the premiere of the latest Gilbert and Sullivan musical, *The Pirates of Penzance*. On February 26 the drop curtain caught fire just as the audience were taking their seats for Steele MacKaye's *Hazel Kirke*; firemen quickly extinguished the flames, and the highly successful play (486 performances) went on as scheduled. These were the events that received banner headlines; the birth of Dorothy Agnes Donnelly on January 28, by contrast, went virtually unnoticed.

Nothing at the time save speculation could link such disparate milestones. Yet, someday those Broadway lights would blaze the name "Dorothy Donnelly" on billboards throughout the city's theatre district. Who could foresee that pictures of her, often in costume, would brighten the pages of American newspapers and magazines with routine frequency? Enthusiastic about their first jaunt in goat-drawn carriages, children boarded the subway bound for the woodlands of Central Park; as adults, eager to see Donnelly set the theatrical world afire, they crowded subway cars crammed with theatregoers en route for the premiere of *Candida* or *Madame X*. No one could predict that marquees would light up the title of not one, or two, but three of her musicals—all during a single season. Nevertheless, anyone who knew anything about the history of her family might not have been entirely surprised.

Dorothy Donnelly "came from a long line of theatrical folk. Of generations of theatrical folk."[1] Her family on both sides were mostly Irish Catholics, who fled their homeland during the great emigration of the

1840s. During this decade tens of thousands annually sought escape from the centuries of misery under harsh British oppression and the consequences of the famine caused by potato rot. To Roman Catholics, the Penal Laws—enacted as early as 1692 and 1695 to prohibit ownership of land by Catholics, to exclude them from office, and to eliminate most of their civil rights—had been especially galling, for they effectively "ensured a Protestant preeminence in finance, the professions, and most fields of commerce and industry long after those statutes were repealed."[2] During the nineteenth century the British government generally "favored Irish emigration as good riddance to a troublesome population,"[3] and deliberately relaxed restrictions on emigration. Moreover, glowing reports of opportunities abroad—"the panacea for every ill and untoward difficulty in the old country"[4]—also induced people to leave the shores of the Emerald Isle. As Thomas Colley Grattan, the Irish-born British Consul in Boston, explained at the time, "in Ireland among 'the small farmers, artisans, and peasantry, the United States are considered as a sort of half-way stage to Heaven, whither some of the kindred have already repaired' and sent back descriptions of the new land as 'the very El Dorado,' in comparison with Irish hardship."[5] Typically, one family member would send for another, often a younger sibling, mailing money for the passage.

Dorothy's maternal grandparents, the Williamses, settled in Boston, the coastal port whose Irish population trebled during this decade.[6] There Mrs. Williams joined the Boston Museum's stock company, established in 1843 by two brothers, Moses and David Kimball. Housed on Tremont, between School and Court streets, it ranked as one of the leading theatres in America for 62 years.[7] To shield the godless theatre from puritanical eyes, the company kept the house dark on Sundays and crammed it with stuffed animals, wax figures, and any sort of natural and scientific paraphernalia. Mrs. Williams resumed her acting career, setting an occupational precedent for her children and grandchildren. Indeed, "for an entire generation, the Irish immigration had a profound effect upon the development of the American theatre," notes historian Carl Wittke. "On the vaudeville stage and in the regular theatres," he says, "the stage Irishman had, by 1850, become such a full-grown giant that he threatened to dwarf all other stage types, including the Yankee."[8] He describes a typical Paddy, the stock Irish character, "as a bizarre individual, preposterously dressed in a red-flannel fireman's shirt, effecting a swagger, and with a shillelah in hand to knock out all others in the cast at the proper moment; and he spoke with a brogue that seems to have been especially appealing to the risibilities of the audiences of Civil War days."[9] The character, incidentally, brought William Jermyn Florence his first recognition as an actor.[10] This stereotype, however, did not constitute the sole contribution of the Irish to the American theatre. More important, they provided the stage with talented performers.

Dorothy never knew her grandmother, who died young. Her grandfather Williams moved to New York City and remarried after his wife's death, rearing the two children from his second union, Annie and Robert, in his Protestant faith.[11] His firstborn son and daughter, however, remained ardent Catholics and "theatrical folk." From his beginnings as an actor, Dorothy's uncle, Fred Williams, who would play a decisive role in shaping her career, gradually developed an interest in directing. He married a fellow member of the Boston Museum company, and during his tenure as stage manager of the Ideal Opera Company, their home became the fashionable gathering place on Sunday nights for Boston's artistic community. His reputation as a sound adapter, who could convert novels into plays or foreign plays into good American versions, eventually reached New York City. When Augustin Daly wrote to him, Fred Williams replied on July 3, 1879: "I shall be most happy to enter into the collaboration you have suggested."[12] Negotiations between the two were soon settled. On July 8, Williams sent Daly another letter. "If you consider the position worth the salary I expect, namely, sixty a week, I see no obstacle to a satisfactory arrangement." He reminded him, "You remember I presume that I have told you I am ignorant of German, the adaptations I have made from that source were all in conjunction with Dr. Harris" (who provided Williams with literal translations of plays).[13]

Augustin Daly numbered among the handful of impresarios that commanded the New York stage during the last half of the nineteenth century. He began his theatrical career as a drama critic and later wrote a highly successful play, *Horizon*. However, "it was as a producer and director that [Daly] made the greatest dent in the theatre, and this not merely with the variety of his productions but with his large reliance on realism in stagecraft and scenic effect."[14] Moreover, he struggled to ensure that his casts would adopt a "natural" style of acting, omitting the extraneous "ah" and "er," sticking to the text, and performing all types of roles. From 1870 to 1890, Daly's stock company boasted "the finest troupe in New York" and the "brightest stars of the era"—Clara Morris, Ada Rehan, Fanny Davenport, Otis Skinner, Maxine Elliott, and John Drew.[15] His cronies, meanwhile, bragged that Daly "always ordered his friends seated down front on the aisle, so they could exit easily for cocktails at intervals."[16] Another theatrical manager, James William Wallack, established a resident company at Wallack's Theatre from 1852 to 1887. It included his actor-son, Lester Wallack, and "such celebrities as Rose Coghlan,

Charles Coghlan, Edward Hugh Sothern, and Maurice Barrymore," all lured from the London stage.[17] Albert M. Palmer's company at the Union Square Theatre presented Rose Eytinge, Maude Granger, Charles R. Thorne, McKee Rankin, Stuart Robson, and James O'Neill, "who became well known as touring stars."[18] A 25-year-old English-American performer, who danced well, sang beautifully, and already had some experience in minor Gilbert and Sullivan companies, sailed from Boston to New York in 1882 and applied to them for work. "No, no," Daly, Wallack, and Palmer told Richard Mansfield; "they didn't want a singing comedian."[19] Two brothers also acquired reputations as astute managers; Daniel and Charles Frohman individually created companies respectively at the Lyceum and Empire Theatres and made stars of Maude Adams, Ethel Barrymore, Henry Miller, William Faversham, Margaret Anglin, May Robson, and Henrietta Crosman.

These celebrated actors and actresses collectively dominated the American stage for nearly a century. The list of their names is necessarily lengthy because the foremost contribution of the impresarios to the American theatre was the creation of resident theatres with "experienced actors, who were used to playing together and meshing their talents" and capable of providing stars with competent support.[20] The producers also adopted technical innovations, such as overhead lighting developed by Steele MacKaye, and used realistic scenery and set designs. *The Playbill*, which would evolve into a slick magazine with editors in every major city, began as a one-page flyer inserted into New York's *Dramatic Chronicle* in 1884 by a local printer, Frank V. Strauss, to offer a brief synopsis or a commentary on the play. German comedies, French melodramas, British drawing-room comedies, and Shakespeare's plays constituted the usual fare. Sometimes the audience saw an occasional American social drama based on the Civil War, the issue of slavery, the problems of economic realities, or the western movement. The producers, however, much preferred imported plays and foreign dramatists. The prolific playwright Dion Boucicault added an Irish ingredient to the stew of American theatrical offerings. When actors Minnie Maddern Fiske and Richard Mansfield originated their own repertory companies, they starred in and respectively introduced the plays of Henrik Ibsen and George Bernard Shaw. Then and now, New York City was the live entertainment capital of North America.

After joining Augustin Daly's company, Fred Williams wrote the words for all of the songs in the musical comedy, *Zanina*, which opened January 18, 1881. He starred in its 1882 production of *Odette*, staged a comedy in four acts by John Oliver Hobbs called *The Ambassadors*, and translated a French play that the company performed as *Tiote*. For ten years he had his hand in the company's productions, variously as translator, writer, performer, and director. In March 1890 Williams left Daly's company to succeed David Belasco as stage manager and director for Daniel Frohman at the Lyceum Theatre. The Lyceum hosted a school for acting, founded principally by James Morrison Steele MacKaye to promote the theories of François Delsarte, whom he had met in Paris. A French actor, drama coach, and mentor, Delsarte taught actors to use movement and gesture to convey thoughts and feelings, then—and only then—to confirm them by delivering the lines. Furl the forehead to suggest disapproval, for instance, or raise the eyebrows to insinuate surprise: such gestures comprise body language that communicates wordlessly. A trained elocutionist and noted orator, he also taught actors to use their diaphragms properly and to control their breath so that they could project their voices without gasping for air. Delsarte's ideas fueled the growing conviction in America that acting constituted an appropriate academic discipline. For this reason, the Lyceum invited Harvard to become affiliated with the school. When Harvard declined, Professor Franklin Haven Sargent left the university to head the school. Renamed the American Academy of Dramatic Arts, it became the first institution of its kind to win accreditation by the Regents of the University of New York. Sargent appointed a teacher with impeccable credentials as dean of faculty: Fred Williams.

"The great value of my uncle to me was that he was a scholar as well as an actor," said Dorothy. "He knew the stage both historically and practically. He has prepared the 'prompt' copy for more productions than I can remember—Mr. Sothern's 'Hamlet' for instance. He added an appendix in that instance of seventy-four pages of stage business and details from nearly every famous production of 'Hamlet.'"[21] At the Academy, Williams produced plays by Ibsen, Strindberg, and Maeterlinck, but his adjunct duties paled by comparison with his primary job—coaching budding actors. He was "considered the greatest student of his day in the mechanical acting of the roles. By this I mean the presentation of characters aside from the personal equation of the individual player,"[22] said Dorothy, in a fumbling attempt to explain what would become coined as "method acting." Acting was the product of analysis and deductive reasoning, Williams believed, not the expression of autobiographical experiences and emotions.

Fred's son, named for his father but known to the family and the public as Fritz, made his debut at the age of six months, when carried on stage in the farce *Seeing Warren*. While a teenager, Fritz appeared in *H.M.S. Pinafore*, produced and staged by his father. Later, in New York, he played

Cradling the skull of Yorick, E. H. Sothern makes his first appearance as Hamlet. Dorothy Donnelly's uncle, Fred Williams, prepared the prompt copy for this 1901 production. (Courtesy Michael A. Morrison Collection.)

the violin in the orchestra pit of Tony Pastor's theatre on East Fourteenth Street and partnered Lillian Russell in vaudeville sketches presented by Joseph Weber and Lew Fields. However, he became better known for his roles in straight plays, particularly *On and Off* by Alexandre Bisson, *A Japanese Nightingale* by Winifred Reeve (Onoto Watanna), and Somerset Maugham's drama *Rain*, based on the life of Sadie Thompson. At the time of his death in 1930, the papers bemoaned the loss of a 67-year veteran of the stage and more than a thousand mourners attended his funeral. Other entries in the family's "book" of "Who's Who in the Theatre" include Fritz's wife—Katherine Florence—with whom he often costarred, and his sister—Sally Williams—also an actress.

Dorothy's mother, Sara D. Williams (her first name sometimes appears with an added "h"), quit the stage after her marriage to a fellow actor, Dublin–born Thomas Lester Donnelly, and the arrival of their children. The eldest was born in Lancaster, Ohio, in 1862, while his parents were on tour. He was christened Henry Victor Donnelly in honor of the Union's first major success in the Civil War, when Ulysses S. Grant defeated Confederate soldiers at Fort Henry.[23] Next came Thomas Frederick Donnelly, born December 13, 1863, and named for his father and uncle in a family tradition that makes it difficult to differentiate succeeding generations from one another. Nora Donnelly's birth took place the following year. Then there was a long lapse before the arrival of Dorothy and, scarcely nine months later, of Christina Donnelly, who lived only fourteen days and lies buried in her parents' grave.[24]

An exhaustive list of his credits would fill several pages and only confirm that Dorothy's father was in constant demand as an actor, first in Boston, then in New York City beginning July 1861. Three aspects of his stage career deserve some mention. He played mostly comic roles, often in parodies of serious works, and built a wide reputation for his impersonation of women in burlesques. In tribute to his national heritage, Donnelly also appeared in plays like *Xion* and *Lilies of Killarney* that catered to Irish audiences. When Dion Boucicault's *The Colleen Bawn,* the first play to depict Irish life realistically,[25] was scheduled to open at the Academy of Music in Brooklyn in January of 1874, Donnelly successfully coaxed his wife out of her early retirement. Sara's name surfaced on the bill along with his. In addition, he costarred with well-known vaudevillians like "Dizzie" Davey, mother of actress Minnie Maddern Fiske (Mary Augusta Davey), and Tony Pastor, the father of American vaudeville. Pastor earned his title, incidentally, by eliminating bars, prohibiting smoking, presenting inoffensive works, offering matinees for women, and adding comic sketches and short plays to a variety of acts that might include juggling, clowning, singing, and dancing—in short, by making vaudeville respectable.

From Pastor, Donnelly acquired practical lessons in theatrical management. Beginning in 1870 he successively managed the Brooklyn Opera House, the Neptune House and Summer Amphitheatre at Rockaway

Beach, and the Olympic Theatre on Fulton Street in Brooklyn, where his ventures gave impetus to a family story:

> He brought there a singer of whom no one had ever heard, and he advertised her as "The California Nightingale." She drew good audiences, notwithstanding some of his friends twitted him on the quality of her singing.
> "Keep still," he used to say, "don't you know there are no nightingales in California?"[26]

By 1874, Augustin Daly's financial resources, spread among diverse theatres in New York and London, had worn thin, and the impresario felt forced to abandon the Grand Opera House, located at the corner of Eighth Avenue and Twenty-third Street in lower New York City. With playwright John L. Poole as a business partner, Donnelly leased the newly renovated and remodeled house in 1876. On Sundays, since blue laws were still observed, the Grand Opera House offered concerts. On weekdays, it promoted new plays and revived popular operas and dramas. Donnelly regularly booked the most celebrated actors of the period: Mr. and Mrs. W. J. Florence, E. H. Sothern, Fanny Davenport, Edwin Booth as Hamlet, and Joseph Jefferson in his most famous role as Rip Van Winkle in the dramatization of Washington Irving's short story. Since admission was cheap (orchestra seats cost 75 cents), and the playbill changed weekly, the Grand Opera House quickly became a mecca for families living on the west side of Manhattan. "A regular patron of that house," in George Odell's opinion, "saw more good acting and more notable stars and more established plays than did the patron of any other theatre in New York."[27]

The popularity, and profitability, of the Grand Opera House enabled the Donnellys to move from what Alexander Woollcott described as "the top floor of a shabby lodging-house in Spring Street" to the "comparative elegance" of a home at 264 West Twenty-fourth Street.[28] They paid a tutor 50 cents an hour to ensure that young Tom became fluent in German and kept the girls out of the kitchen, seating them instead at the piano bench or parading them on the dance floor, saying, "They had better things to do than to cook."[29] Unfortunately, neither Thomas nor Sara Donnelly lived long enough to enjoy their newly acquired financial security. Dorothy was not yet six months old when her father died unexpectedly at half past six on the evening of July 3, 1880, at the age of 47. The grieving widow maintained the partnership with Poole at the Grand Opera House for two more years, but gave up the business in 1882 when Poole retired. The public version of the partnership's dissolution differs from family legend, however. Their story says that Poole "rooked" Sara Donnelly

Coached by her family, 18-year-old Dorothy Donnelly launches her long career in the theatre as an actress. (Courtesy Philip Fahringer Collection.)

"out of her money" by selling the lease in his name only and that all she managed to salvage from the sale was a rosewood couch. She had asked the house's stagehands to haul it out of the greenroom (a term in the trade for the common parlor where actors collected between scenes—a forerunner of a time clock, noting the early arrival and late departure of the

cast) and carry it around the block to the Donnelly's home.[30] Barely two
months after Dorothy's eighth birthday, a freak storm struck the East
Coast. Known ever since as "the blizzard of '88," it came on the heels of
the mildest winter New York had enjoyed in the previous 17 years and
followed a warm spell that found most of Central Park's flowering trees
in full bloom. It halted trains, closed shops and factories, and isolated
Washington, D.C. Two hundred ships north of Chesapeake Bay were
either lost or grounded. Horses froze to death on the streets of Manhattan. A hundred seamen perished, and the "Great White Hurricane"
claimed an additional four hundred lives. Despite the adverse weather,
Sara Donnelly left her home on a goodwill mission to pay the rent for
some of her late husband's impoverished relatives.[31] She contracted pneu-
monia and never recovered.

A few days before her death on March 17, she dashed off an affectionate, newsy letter to her son, currently on tour with a company of actors.
She addressed the envelope "Henry V. Donnelly, Natural Gas Comedy
Company, Detroit, Michigan," dated the enclosed letter "Mar. 6th, 1888,"
and began, "My Dear Henry":

> Sunday after you left home was really a most depressing day. For some
> unknown reason Mary had dinner at half past twelve and so the after-
> noon seemed years long. Then it was bitter cold and there was nothing
> in the papers so in the evening we all went to the Williams'es [sic] had
> a very dull evening but coming home Joe Shannon stood treat so we
> had a very good supper at O'Neils on Little Av [sic] ... and were quite
> jolly ... Doll [referring to Dorothy] has got another chapter of her story
> done and two illustrations. One of them is good enough but stiff and
> just what any twelve year old girl with a triate [sic] for drawing would
> do but the second is wonderful. It's a Lady in full dress seated and the
> Face, Head, dress, and Pose of the figure is simply great. I wonder in
> what other direction my wonderful children will branch out. Senator
> Covert went to see you act out Saturday last and tells Tom [referring to
> Henry's brother] that you are the coming light comedian. Your Brook-
> lyn appearance has sent touring stock up in the Office. Your Loving
> Mother. [some punctuation and capitalization supplied]

Henry saved the letter and savored the satisfaction he felt in having
recently sent his mother a picture of Harlequin, posed atop Columbine's
rose and fan.[32] He had bought the painting while on tour in Lancaster,
Ohio, as a romantic reminder of his birthplace; the large crate attracted
the neighbors' attention, and the gift thrilled his mother when it arrived.[33]

Dorothy went to live with her aunt and uncle, Mr. and Mrs. Fred
Williams, after her mother died. The older Donnelly children were perhaps

too young, and certainly too unsettled, to serve as her surrogate parents. Henry, who began his acting career in vaudeville before undertaking comic and serious roles in straight plays, was still costarring with Eddie Girard in *Natural Gas.* This farce opened in May of 1888 in New York City, enjoyed fifty performances during its first season there, and then toured the country for the next six years. Originally called "effervescent" and "humorous," by 1894, after the actors as well as the audience "had plenty of time to grow weary of the play," *Natural Gas* was described as one of the "frothy confections so popular in the days of the decline of the 'legitimate' theatre."[34]

Henry's long and frequent absences contributed to Dorothy's enduring resentment of road tours. To distract herself and dim the pangs of loneliness, she added new chapters to her illustrated story, mentioned in her mother's letter. Gradually her childish scrawl filled blank sheets of paper as she quickly peopled them with prim characters. Then she laboriously copied the manuscript onto closely written pages. When Henry returned for a brief visit, Dorothy gathered her family around her, perched on a short three-legged stool in the center of the semi-circle, and read aloud "this premature literary outpouring." Having detected no "gleam of anything save encouragement in the eyes of her auditors," she presented Henry with the completed novel. It was tied with a red ribbon and weighed a pound.[35]

Dorothy's brother, Thomas, had attended the College of the City of New York and graduated cum laude from Columbia Law School. Admitted to the state bar in 1885, he had just begun to practice law. Meanwhile, their sister Nora was busy with plans for her forthcoming marriage to Ambrose O. McCall of Albany. For the wedding, she wore a gown of white brocaded silk and the Irish point lace veil her mother had bought for her. (It would become a family heirloom, worn eventually by Nora's children and grandchildren or their brides.) Dorothy, dressed in yellow surah, served as maid of honor; Ambrose's two sisters (Mamie and Jennie) and a friend, Jennie Curran, wearing pink crepe de chine gowns, as bridesmaids; Thomas, as best man; and Fritz as an usher. Following the ceremony, which took place at St. Leo's Church on June 11, 1889, Henry hosted a catered reception at his spacious, tall-ceilinged home for the 300 wedding guests.

Although her brothers had attended New York City's public schools, the family sent Dorothy to the expensive and exclusive Academy of the Sacred Heart, housed in a four-story building on Seventeenth Street.[36] It was staffed by members of a French religious order that had responded to Bishop John DuBois' plea for educators when a flood of Catholic immigrants from Ireland, Italy, Austria, Hungary, and Russia descended on New York City. The local press promptly dubbed them "Ladies" when they arrived in 1841; Western alumnae of Sacred Heart Schools still affectionately refer to them as "Madams."

The academy offered a rigorous curriculum: English, history, religion, logic, psychology, a little German and Latin, "some math, a dabbling of science."[37] According to the Plan of Studies that mandated the curriculum, "In teaching literature the mistresses will aim at giving the children an intelligent appreciation of great masterpieces."[38] Thus, the teachers presented a broad selection of literature, including American poetry, Greek and Roman classics, the poems of John Milton, Dante's *The Divine Comedy*, and Shakespeare's plays. Each Monday morning at eleven o'clock, Dorothy and her classmates, wearing white gloves and freshly laundered uniforms, assembled to curtsy to the Reverend Mother and receive from her one of three report cards—"tres bien," "bien," "assez bien." They wore long dresses with full, sometimes loosely pleated, skirts, topped by jackets that featured leg-of-mutton sleeves and small pointed collars or round banded ones atop floppy sailor collars, which the schoolgirls bought at Best and Company. At table, during the one o'clock dinner hour, all conversation took place in French. At the academy Dorothy acquired a taste for reading that became a lifelong habit and developed a good ear for foreign languages.

After classes that lasted from nine o'clock in the morning until three-thirty in the afternoon, Dorothy would practice the piano. Her instructor was William Mason. He "was sweet and very kind," Dorothy later recalled, "but a lesson never passed without my crying. For he never leaves much to your imagination as regards your deficiencies."[39]

Mason had all the qualifications required for being a demanding teacher. He was the son and third child of Lowell Mason, a renowned composer, organist, and conductor. After his debut as a pianist at the age of 17, William Mason pursued his studies in Frankfurt, Prague, and Weimar, where he became the protégé of Franz Liszt. He gave concerts in Europe and England, then settled in New York City. Mason gained celebrity as the first pianist in America to give recitals unaccompanied by either a singer or another instrumentalist. His reputation grew as he began writing music for the piano and textbooks for learning to play it.

"I remember going to him once feeling very blue," said Dorothy, "because I had played a piece by Chaminade at a party and everybody had talked while I was playing." Mason consoled her. "'Never mind,' he said, when I told him about it. 'I have had similar experiences myself. The real artist plays to hear himself, not to please others.'" Dorothy found comfort in his words: "I felt very much complimented when, after the lesson, he asked me to play the Chaminade piece for him,—very much complimented, that is, until I had played it, and he remarked in a dry way, 'I don't wonder they all talked.'"[40] Once her mind was made up, Dorothy never let anything, not even disapproval, derail her. So she persisted: "I practiced Schumann's 'Grillen' four hours a day for three months, until my family rose in rebellion against me, against Schumann, and against 'Grillen' in particular. But I had the satisfaction of being told by Mr. Mason, 'Now you play it perfectly.'"[41]

She planned to become a concert pianist. This early ambition, however, could not prevail in the atmosphere of the theatre that permeated the Williams' household. By taking his young niece to see "Bernhardt, Bartet, Rejane, and Hading in their greatest roles,"[42] Fred Williams undoubtedly influenced her decision to become an actress. Then he trained her to be one. He cast Dorothy as Lady Macbeth, Juliet, and Portia in student productions of Shakespeare's plays. He showed her how to define the heroine's desires and motivations, scene by scene, then in the play as a whole, and, finally, in relation to the other characters. He encouraged her to substitute skilled observation and hard thinking for personal experience when playing someone much older or more powerful or temperamentally different. These were the lessons taught, but not yet learned.

CHAPTER 2
On Stage

A ny lingering thoughts of devoting her life to music vanished completely in 1897, when Dorothy's brother leased the Murray Hill Theatre. Located at 162 East Forty-second Street on the southeast corner of Lexington Avenue, it was a large house, capable of seating 1,400. Henry Donnelly's decision to form a stock company handed him fewer odds for success than a three-legged horse in the Kentucky Derby, for by this time all bets lay on the long-running show and its stepsister, the star system.

Beginning about mid-nineteenth century, European actors began coming to New York, eager to repeat their success abroad. A few like Maurice Barrymore remained permanently; others like Mrs. Patrick Campbell, Eleonora Duse, and Sarah Bernhardt—the famous divas of the era—made repeated visits. Gradually their American counterparts realized that they, too, might lengthen their engagement—and boost their salaries—by taking productions on tour. For example, James O'Neill, father of the playwright Eugene O'Neill, played Edmund Dantes in *The Count of Monte Cristo* more than 4,300 times, and William Gillette became known as Sherlock Holmes through countless performances. Theatre owners and producers jumped aboard the long-run bandwagon as soon as they discovered they could reap more profits by mounting one successful show than by experimenting with a number of new or unfamiliar plays. So, for example, when Dion Boucicault's *The Colleen Bawn* became well received in New York, the playwright decided to take the play to London, but, beforehand, to take it on tour throughout the United States.[1] Then they even resorted to various gimmicks to stretch a play's run. "During [the] fall of '98 souvenirs were given, in accordance with the custom of the day, to playgoers at the time of the fiftieth and one hundredth performances," writes historian Ward Morehouse. For example, "hand-painted and imported Chinese teapots were distributed on the occasion of performance Number 100 for *The Village Postmaster*" at the Fourteenth

Street Theatre.[2] In another instance, just eight years later, although the ticket lines for *The Little Gray Lady* were already long, the Shuberts publicized free admission to one performance of the show for those blessed with gray eyes or sporting gray gowns; the advertisement caused some consternation for ticket takers, brusquely brushed aside by women who claimed free entry because of their gray hair. "By the end of the nineteenth century dramatic production in America had shifted ... to long run plays, cast in New York and sent out to tour the country," note Toby Cole and Helen Krich Chinoy,[3] and "the once common stock company had all but disappeared."[4] Finally, the expansion of railroads accelerated long-runs and, conversely, undermined resident troupes. Trains made travel easy, cheap, and speedy, and when they crisscrossed the country transporting plays and players, local amateurs found they could not compete with "name" stars from Broadway. "With the advent of the booking syndicate in 1896," says Kenneth Macgowan in summary, "the long-run system of Broadway and the touring system of the Road became the fixed economic form of the American theatre ... as characteristic of America as mass production and the skyscraper."[5]

The rise of the star system gained additional impetus as women actors enjoyed the patronage and support of their husbands. During the first decades of this century, for example, Harrison Grey Fiske produced plays in which his wife, Minnie Maddern Fiske, could shine; J. Hartley Manners wrote *Peg O' My Heart*, the play that catapulted his wife, Laurette Taylor, to prominence with its 608 performances; and Jane Cowl counted on favorable reviews from her spouse, Adolphe Klauber, for several years the drama critic for the *New York Times*. When long-running productions and the star system became the norm, they made the founding of a stock company as challenging as launching a space missile and the acting profession as hard to crack as a Brazil nut.

Because the Murray Hill Theatre's survival would rely exclusively on its repertory, Henry refused to gamble on new or little known plays. He selected them shrewdly, guided by two criteria—their prior popularity and their variety. He "refused to cater to the debased taste of the day, and instead of claptrap his audiences were treated to the best plays that could be obtained."[6] These consisted of French melodramas, classical British comedies, contemporary American plays, sentimental plays, farces, and an occasional Shakespearean drama, all presented for one week only. Nearing his fortieth birthday, Henry had broken the theatre's dictum for actors: he lost his hair and grew a belly. Nevertheless, Henry often played the lead in comedies to warm reviews and shared the male roles with Robert Drouet, William Redmond, Walter Allen, Emmet C. King, Charles D.

Waldron, E. T. Stetson, Ned Singleton, Edwin Nicander, Herbert O'Connor, Willie Lambert, and Litta Nowothny. He installed Harold E. Allen as business manager, Walter Burridge as set designer, and William Dooley as musical director. The position of director, whose job primarily involved the blocking of shows, Henry sometimes assigned in rotation to each of the actors but mainly reserved for William Redmond and later George Henry Trader. He hired six actresses: Hannah May Ingram (Mrs. E. T. Stetson), Laura Hope Crews, Alice Johnson, Frances Starr, Edna Phillips, and one novice who argued her way into the company—Dorothy Agnes Donnelly.

"Well, if that is what you want," Henry replied dubiously when his sister informed him that she now wished to be an actress.[7] His hesitation did not depend on the novelty of her proposal, since every woman in their family spent some years on the stage, and even their mother had, in Dorothy's words, "acted whenever she couldn't get out of it."[8] Nor did his reluctance rest, as well it should have, on the precariousness of the profession. Rather, it stemmed from her desire to make acting a career. "In every family," Dorothy said, "there is a strong feeling against the girls' going out to make their own living in any way."[9]

Her first professional appearance came in *The New South* as a walk-on servant in the company's first production, which opened August 27, 1898. Two weeks later, in *Young Mrs. Winthrop*, she delivered her first (and only) line. Then, in Tom Taylor's *The Ticket of Leave Man*, she performed her first song and dance routine. She determined it would also be her last. The *New York Times* called her "comely and sprightly enough" and added, "You get your money's worth."[10] Even though she was the only member of the cast singled out for praise, Dorothy felt she shortchanged her audience by her performance and could never recall it without chuckling.

By the end of its opening season, the Murray Hill Theatre showed a net profit.[11] Tickets were sold by subscription to guarantee a loyal and steady patronage. And they were cheap—only 25 cents for a matinee.[12] Yet, wages were fair. The principals like Frances Starr earned 50 dollars a week; those who played utility parts like Laura Hope Crews and Dorothy, 30 dollars. These salaries, incidentally, compared very favorably with the weekly sum of 35 dollars that Tony Pastor paid Lillian Russell when she was already well regarded as a comedienne, or the yearly salary of 40 dollars that Katherine Cornell received in two payments nearly a decade later, during her second season with the Washington Square Players.[13] Considered a "metropolitan success" by any standard,[14] the company was more frequently referred to as the "Henry V. Donnelly Company" in acknowledgment of Henry's competent leadership. "My father was strongly inclined to managerial ventures, and I suppose my brother inherits the tendency," said Dorothy.[15]

To limit expenses, the company used costumes and props more than once. Dorothy could fool regular patrons into believing they were looking at a new costume by having a dressmaker add a bow, shorten a hemline, or redesign the neckline: "I have a treasure, two treasures in fact; sisters they are, who do all they can to oblige me.... I tell them what I want and they make the purchases," she said; "The luxury of trotting around the shops to match a sample of lace or ribbon is denied me."[16]

Like a student liberated from the classroom, Dorothy welcomed summer as a relief from a grueling schedule—two performances and one rehearsal, six days a week. When fall arrived, Henry told her "that whereas she might now be described as an actress who could walk on and off without falling on her face, he could not say much more for her than that."[17] This was no deterrent but a spur for Dorothy. She enjoyed a reputation in her family for being, in the words of her grandniece, "a brilliant student in everything she attempted."[18] This ability to learn quickly would prove the central key to her career and success. Thus, while she began her second season cast in juvenile and bit parts, before long she played principal roles and captured critical attention. The *New York Times* gave her "credit due for good work" in *The Girl I Left Behind Me*, for instance, and called her "sincere and forceful" in *Men and Women*.

The stock company suddenly faced a crisis on January 15, 1900, when its veteran leading actress, Hannah May Ingram, died quietly and without warning at the table while lunching with her husband and her cousin. She had performed the night before and completed a rehearsal of *Never Again* that morning. Since she considered her indisposition only temporary, Ingram resisted her husband's advice to rest. "It is small business to try to hurt the repute of the stock company system," editorialized the *New York Times*, "by attributing her death solely to the overwork their routine requires." Nevertheless, some nine years later, *Theatre Magazine* did just that. Ada Patterson titled her article "Martyrs to the Stage":

> Every stock company player cites in support of his theory that the stock actor will eventually collapse from the long continued strain, the case of Hannah May Ingram, the actress member of the Henry V. Donnelly's company in the Murray Hill Theatre. From that company graduated Frances Starr and Dorothy Donnelly into eventual stardom, and Laura Hope Crews into the "featured" state of recognition. But these were younger women, and stronger. They had not served so long the Moloch stock.[19]

The brown-haired, blue-eyed Starr never considered herself a martyr, nor the tyrant's victim, however. "Constant professional practice, not merely 'the divine spark' or laboratory exercise, is what stimulates and nourishes the actor's interpretive imagination." And David Belasco did his best trying to stir that imagination into a higher pitch, casting her in *The Music Maker, The Rose of the Rancho,* and *The Easiest Way.* Starr eventually pitied her successors: "It's much harder now. *We* had so much more security."[20]

Out of respect for Ingram, Henry promptly canceled the scheduled afternoon performance. By the next day Dorothy was asked to replace her. "I took up her work as best I could," she said.[21] The *New York Times* reviewed Dorothy's succeeding roles and variously pronounced them "convincing and true to life," "excellent work," "good impersonation," "entirely satisfactory." When the troupe presented Shakespeare's *Romeo and Juliet,* one critic noted that it lacked the handpicked cast and spectacular sets of a high-price theatre but insisted "there is not a hint of amateurishness or gaucherie" in the production.[22] He found Dorothy's delivery too colloquial but nevertheless thought she read well. "Her ability to act was so conspicuous," said another reviewer, "that she has been retained for leading parts in whatever the Donnelly Stock Company has produced at the Murray Hill." Commenting on Dorothy's interpretation of Juliet, he added, "and no woman who ever attempted the part had more sincere admirers."[23] The reviews were necessarily skimpy because the papers allocated only a column inch to stock companies, reserving most of their space for first-class houses and plays with "name" stars. This string of favorable notices suddenly snapped when she played Fay Juliani in Arthur Wing Pinero's *The Princess and the Butterfly.* With its clever lines but little dramatic substance, this melodrama lent itself to overacting, and Dorothy fell into the trap. She delivered her lines vehemently like an "Italian fruit seller," declared the *New York Times*' critic, softening the attack with a gratuitous addition: "But her vigorous portrayal is still effective and the sentiment of the role is not missed."[24] When her name failed to appear on the cast list of the company's next production, the critic reported, "Dorothy Donnelly is taking a rest this week, and she certainly deserves one."

Facetious, but true. In her last two years with the company, she had learned 57 new leading roles. That represented "sixteen thousand lines, or 160,000 words, absorbed by one brain within a period of twenty-nine weeks," reported Jane Gordon after coercing Dorothy to do some quick arithmetic.[25] Her memory was prodigious. According to family legend, when an entire script had once been lost, Dorothy rewrote it word for word, even recalling all the playwright's directions.[26]

Scripts were distributed and parts assigned on Saturdays. Dorothy read the play on Sunday but did not study the role until Tuesday, after the first rehearsal. She memorized one third of her lines each night following the evening performance, and by Thursday, she was "letter perfect," as she put it:

> If I am tired or stupid or not in the mood, I give it up and try it between performances the next day. I never force myself to study.... I never sit up all night, or resort to a wet towel around my head. I can "swallow" it, as we say, very "quick study," and if a part is interesting I can "swallow" it very readily.[27]

Dress rehearsals were never held. There simply was no time. The company therefore relied on the properties manager to explain any complicated stage business such as the Murphy beds in *The Girl and the Judge*. These were hinged beds that could be folded or swung into a closet for concealment. Tucked away, they freed the stage; lowered, they instantly converted the set into a bedroom. Enamored with their usefulness, the props manager, Charles V. Lord, demonstrated them to his fellow crew members so frequently that one of the beds became impaired. Dorothy and the actress who played her mother were unfamiliar with any of the props until just moments before the opening curtain. "There was not much of 'mother'—she weighed a little over one hundred pounds," she said, "but 'Props' assured her that if she was careful there was no danger of accident." Dorothy's story continues.

> We disposed ourselves in our respective beds and the curtain rose. Everything went smoothly and I, watching "mother" out of the corner of my eye, decided that all danger was over. "Mother" decided so too and began to throw a little fervor into her acting. In the throes of remorse she began to roll around the bed, and, to my horror, "mother" began to disappear.
> The room was lighted by the pale rays of the moon. "Mother's" bed was in semi-darkness, and neither "mother" nor the audience realized what was about to happen. I jumped out of bed and ran frantically to the door calling, as I thought, in a stage whisper, "Turn off that moon." Evidently the electrician misunderstood me, for it began to shine with redoubled force, slowly revolving until it finally rested full on the horror-stricken face of "mother" who at the sight of me shrieked in piercing tones, "Save me, save me!" I sprang for the slowly ascending footboard and, to a chorus of giggles from the audience, plumped myself upon the foot of the bed, giving thanks for the first time in my life that Nature had been kind to me in the matter of flesh.[28]

To the occasional mishaps, long hours, and demanding schedule, she raised few objections:

> I remember my three years in a stock company happily. I had reduced my work to a system. I ate a hearty, old-fashioned breakfast, then rehearsed from ten to twelve. After that I invariably took a brisk walk for a half hour. I drank a cup of cocoa and went to the theatre and played the matinee. We had a sitting room at the theatre, where I rested and dined between the afternoon and evening performances.[29]

Since most of her time was spent at the theatre, she brought the comforts of home to her dressing room. Framed etchings and engravings covered the walls. In one corner stood a gilded cage with a canary. She added rose-colored shades to lamps to soften the glare of the light bulbs. Wicker armchairs and a couch piled high with cushions invited relaxation. "I catch forty winks now and again, between performances, and sometimes during a long rehearsal when I have a 'wait'."[30]

Even after the final curtain dropped, she did not rush home. "After playing an evening performance one is wide awake and has no inclination to go to bed," she noted: "It is a time most players like to get together and talk." Dorothy often used that time to study. She read Sir Henry Irving's *Lectures on Acting* and called it "the best epitome of the art of acting ever written." She read Anna Brownell Murphy Jameson's analysis of Shakespeare's women, *Characters of Women*, "although every one who knows it calls it *Shakespeare's Heroines*," she noted and termed it "indispensable." She stocked her book shelves with plays, old and new, and also with novels "in which the characters are well drawn." "For instance," she said, "if one wants to do character work, what is better than Dickens?" Given free rein to mention what else she found helpful, Dorothy expounded, perhaps even exaggerated. A painting of a Spanish dancer became "a picture of youthful poise, of insouciance," to recreate in a future role. A piece of music that "stirs and keeps alive temperament and the understanding of temperament"[31] could be used to recapture fleeting moods, evoke unconscious thought, give color and texture to crucial scenes.

Asked about her favorite roles, she replied, "I like to make people laugh and forget their troubles. I like to laugh and feel light-hearted myself." She defended her preference for comedy: "Emotional parts are depressing, and when played twice a day, they drag your spirits down to the very depths," she said, citing the title role in *Fédora* as a particular strain.[32] *Fédora* teems with plots and counterplots, love and deception, death and revenge. The Russian heroine, a princess, plans to seduce the man she mistakenly believes has murdered her husband and hand him over to the secret police. Instead, she "falls madly in love" with him, and "rather than have her lover discover her attempted treachery the lady takes poison."[33] Widely heralded at the time in France as a master craftsman and admired for his light comedies and historical melodramas, Victorien Sardou gained immense popularity in the United States as a playwright. He wrote both *La Tosca* and *Fédora* specifically for Sarah Bernhardt, whose "writhing death scenes ... were the Bernhardt specialty."[34] Sardou retains some vestiges of his turn-of-the century popularity. Brennan's Restaurant in the Vieux Carré section of New Orleans still serves "oeufs Sardou," a famous breakfast dish named for the fecund French playwright, and English-speakers use the term "fedora" to designate that soft felt hat with a marked crease in its low crown and a brim that can be turned up or down. Although Sardou's most dramatic theatrical works are now more than a hundred years old, they remain perennially fresh set to music as operas— *Tosca* by Giacomo Puccini and *Fédora* by Umberto Giordano.

To a young actress like Dorothy, scarcely out of her teens, it must have been a daunting experience to undertake a role first created by Sarah Bernhardt, of whom Cornelia Otis Skinner, her biographer, says—only partly tongue-in-cheek, one suspects—"In her prime, [Bernhardt] was known as The Eighth Wonder of the World and even in her declining years as the greatest personality France had had since Joan of Arc."[35] Someone less precociously successful than Dorothy would have been accused of reckless brashness; Dorothy was merely self-confident. Calling the title role in *Fédora* a strain was putting it mildly. On the whole, however, Dorothy seldom complained:

> I am young and strong. Besides, congenial work is always a blessing. Work becomes hard labor when it is all against the grain. I am under the watchful eye of my fond manager-brother, and no harm can come to me. This life is exacting, but things are made as smooth as possible, be sure of that. And I am very happy.[36]

Her professional life spilled over into her personal and social ones. For fun, she joined the Twelfth Night Club, founded in 1891 as a mutual aid society for actresses. In 1901, Dorothy became its president—an indication that, despite her youth, she already demonstrated qualities of leadership and garnered the respect of her peers. Like its male counterparts, The Lambs, the oldest theatrical society in America, and The Friars, founded specifically for comedians some ten years later, Twelfth Night Club offered its members opportunities to meet informally, to enjoy a spirit of conviviality and animated conversation. Every month the club invited a leading man to be guest speaker. Its name derived from the club's tradition of celebrating Christmas on the twelfth day following the holiday, since the twenty-fifth of December was a regular workday unless it fell on a Sunday, the only day of the week on which the theatre went dark. The actresses decorated a tree and laid out an impressive buffet with "two kegs of ale and a boar's head on the table, and a large Yule candle ... burning in the centre." After dinner they presented silly skits, invariably funny and elaborately costumed. In "The Heroines of Shakespeare," for instance, Hamlet dismisses Ophelia, thinking her crazy, while Macbeth rejects Lady Macbeth for instigating murder.[37]

She formed a lasting friendship with another member of the Twelfth Night Club, a mid–Westerner, Louise Closser Hale, who never forgot their first meeting:

> She was coming down the wooden steps which led from the old Savoy stage door to the pavement of 33rd Street. Her hat was wide and her dress was gray silk, very shimmery—a smiling silk like herself.... It was her technique to make me feel at once that meeting me was the most important thing in the world to her. I didn't know it then that it was going to be the most important thing in the world to me.

Dorothy was already well acquainted with Louise's husband, Walter Hale, who shared the stage with such notables as Fanny Davenport, Sol Smith Russell, William Crane, and Julia Marlowe, but gained greater recognition as an etcher, lithographer, and illustrator. Years later, Dorothy laughingly confided to her youngest niece that he was her first beau.[38]

Most of her recreational time she spent with relatives, who usually called her Dolly. She moved to 327 West Twenty-second Street to live with Henry and his wife, Catherine, nicknamed Kitty. Her brother Thomas had won election to the State Assembly in 1896 and to the state senate three years later. Currently he spent more time in Albany than in New York City, serving as minority leader and drafting anti-trust legislation that remains in force today as the *Donnelly Anti-Monopoly Act*. Consequently, she saw him only occasionally. She called often on her sister Nora, whose husband—Ambrose McCall—was now a clerk for the Supreme Court of New York (his brother, Edward Everett McCall, served as a justice), and their children. Whether Dorothy infected her sister with the acting bug, or Henry drafted Nora, "who could play the piano and sing very well,"[39] to help out in a pinch, Nora's name occasionally appeared on playbills of the stock company. On Sundays the family might gather at the Donnelly country home in Babylon, Long Island, or drop in on friends.

Tagging along with Henry, Dorothy became a frequent guest of the English actor, Maurice Barrymore. Born Herbert Blythe, in India, and educated at Cambridge, he married into a family of distinguished actors: John Drew, an Irish comedian who managed a stock company at the Arch Street Theatre in Philadelphia; his wife, Louisa Drew, famed for her role as Mrs. Malaprop in Sheridan's *The Rivals*; and their son, John Drew, Jr., noted for his parts in Shakespearean plays and modern comedies. Barrymore and his wife, Georgiana Drew, produced another theatrical dynasty—Lionel, Ethel, and John. One year following the death of Georgiana, Maurice married Mamie Floyd. Now, estranged from his children and separated from his second wife, who objected to his growing menagerie of dogs, he bought a farmhouse in Coytesville, New Jersey. To endear himself to his new neighbors, he had signed up as a volunteer fireman. When a fire broke out in town one Sunday, with Henry's help Barrymore dragged a hose cart to the blaze, while Dorothy bellowed words of support from the front porch. On August 11, 1900, several weeks later, the Donnellys returned to Coytesville and performed an impromptu play at the Fort Lee Town Hall to raise money for firemen's uniforms.[40]

Such busman's holidays were the only social outlet her schedule afforded her, but she reveled in them. When Fred Williams invited her to attend the graduation held at the American Academy of Dramatic Arts on March 27, 1900, she promptly accepted. The featured speaker was Madge Robertson Kendal, an accomplished British comedienne who had made her American debut six months earlier in Sardou's *Scrap of Paper*. "You must be a marvel of patience, have the figure of a Greek statute, the temper of an angel (that's very necessary), the face of a god, and the skin of a rhinoceros,"[41] Kendal began. She alluded to the social consequences of life in the limelight; she referred to the public's jaundiced view of stage folk and pleaded for moral behavior, saying that the action of one actress reflected on the entire profession; she suggested the hardships encountered in combining marriage with such a demanding career.

This address impressed Dorothy so profoundly, even indelibly, that she began repeating it almost immediately. When reviewing her experiences at the Murray Hill Theatre, for instance, she talked of having "made many sacrifices to hold my position, which I dearly love"—without mentioning a single one. Whether she had acquired a tough skin by the time she left the stock company in 1902, it was too early to tell. She did, however, have some of the other attributes Kendal mentioned. A 62-inched beauty, Dorothy had long slim arms and a tall graceful neck rising from light olive shoulders. Her face was round and full, though her chin, set off by a slight crease, looked firm. Her teeth were white and even. She had well-defined wide lips that curved into a winsome smile, and a straight and finely sloped nose, which Dorothy found too large. Dark eyebrows, ample and symmetrically arched, framed her gray eyes.[42] These were round, wide-spaced, and deep set, with prominent circles below. Topped by long, sweeping black eyelashes, they hinted of mystery and impishness. The tangle of dark brown hair flecked with gold, she wore swept back, with curls that clung to her neck, just below the ears. Anyone who looked at her imagined "*señorita*," not "*colleen*."

The years ahead would try her patience and temper. And she believed herself willing to pay the personal costs of a career on the stage.

CHAPTER 3
Breakthrough

An invitation to replace Maud Hoffman in *New England Folks* ended Dorothy's apprenticeship at the Murray Hill Theatre. She undertook the part of Rose Dunham on November 11, 1901. New York's *Evening Journal* announced the substitution, declaring her, at age 21, "the youngest leading woman on the New York stage." Next, she costarred with Robert Edeson in *Soldiers of Fortune*, based on the book by Richard Harding Davis, originally serialized in *Scribner's Magazine*.[1] This was the period, says Ward Morehouse, "of stage success for popular novels turned into plays."[2] Producer Charles Frohman first invited Davis to dramatize his own novel. The results, however, left Frohman "vaguely dissatisfied"—"too talky" and insufficient focus on the heroine, he said—and, much to Davis' disappointment, Frohman then arranged for a more successful adaptation by Augustus Thomas.[3] He engaged Henry B. Harris to produce *Soldiers of Fortune* at the Savoy Theatre. It opened March 17, 1902, and ran for 88 performances. Edeson, who was making his Broadway debut as a star, received top billing; Dorothy, the publicity. Newspapers carried full-length photographs of her as Madame Alvarez, dressed in an elaborate lace gown with a long ruffled train, bought at one of New York's most exclusive shops—Henri Bendel[4]—that reputedly cost 950 dollars. "Miss Donnelly's reputation as an actress of finished methods is well sustained throughout the production," commented one reviewer.[5] The play closed for the summer, then reopened August 30 for another 41 performances. Pleased with her portrayal of the woman who can scarcely disguise her affections for an officer in her husband's command, Davis gave Dorothy an autographed copy of his novel, illustrated with photographs from the play that were signed by the cast, to keep as a memento.

The family's celebration of Dorothy's new roles was suddenly cut short by the unexpected death of Ambrose O. McCall. Thomas Donnelly, still a bachelor "with exquisite manners" and "such consideration for others' feelings,"[6] moved in with his sister Nora to help raise the McCall children: Sara (referred to as Sally, now aged 12), Nora Donnelly (called Junie by the family), Ambrose Victor (nicknamed Buddy), Kathleen O'Neil (known as Cassie), John Ambrose (named for his uncle, John A. McCall, president of the New York Life Insurance Company), and the latest arrival, Dorothy Donnelly, Dorothy's namesake and third godchild, born in 1901. Dorothy came to the Donnelly-McCall home at 151 East Ninety-second Street, sometimes with colleagues to discuss their roles, sometimes alone to read to the children. Herself an orphan, she found it easy to be sympathetic to those who had lost a father at so young an age. In fact, she taught young Dolly to read.[7]

Dorothy's tastes in literature rested more on her personal response to a writer than on cold objectivity. For instance, she admired Robert Louis Stevenson "for his wonderful optimism in spite of all he went through [and] for being so cheery, so merry, so spontaneous."[8] She respected his ringing defense of Father Damien, the Flemish priest who established the leper colony in Hawaii not for its quality, but for its ability to evoke memories of her school days when she and her classmates packed cartons of donated goods for shipment to Molokai. While she liked the work of Rudyard Kipling, especially *Kim*, she dismissed Robert Browning outright: "For how can one take seriously letters in which the lover addresses his beloved as 'Dearest Baa'!"[9]

She tolerated novels and poetry but thrived on scripts. Yet, the rest of the 1902-1903 drama season came and went, and not a single stage manager thrust a blue bound book typewritten on half sheets of paper into her hands, telling Dorothy to memorize the sides. Then, just as her future looked bleak, serendipity intervened, disguised as two playwrights, eventual winners of the Nobel prize in literature. Products of the Irish literary tradition, William Butler Yeats and George Bernard Shaw became the foremost contributors to its rebirth when the long Irish struggle for self-governance gained renewed impetus. The death of Charles Stewart Parnell (Ireland's uncrowned king) in 1891, the revival of Irish (often mistakenly identified as Gaelic) as a spoken language in 1893, and the Irish Parliamentary Party's reorganization in 1900, all fueled the rebellion against British domination. Armed with money and sympathy, immigrants in the New World joined the battle for Irish freedom. In 1901 John Redmond, leader of the Irish Parliamentary Party, made a fund-raising tour of the United States and founded the United Irish League of America to generate support and solicit donations for the home-rule movement. Two years later, on June 2, 1903, the Irish Literary Society filed incorporation papers in Albany. The organization designated as their objective the promotion of the knowledge and the study of Irish language and literature. The next day, in New York City, they presented a single, premiere performance of Yeats' *The Countess Cathleen (Kathleen ni Houlihan)*. Yeats based this nonsectarian, nationalistic play, completed in 1899, on an ancient Irish myth. The heroine is a countess who returns home after a devastating war to find her people suffering, donates food and money to rescue them from starvation, and rallies them in battle against demonic merchants who would buy their souls with gold. The society chose Dorothy to create the title role, and the *New York Times* described Dorothy's portrayal of Cathleen as "simple, unaffected, and entirely satisfying."

Unlike Yeats, Shaw was already familiar to Broadway. *Arms and the Man* opened in 1894, and *The Devil's Disciple*, in 1897, both with Richard Mansfield in the lead. Encouraged by their success, Mansfield wrote to Shaw, requesting additional works. The playwright sent him *Candida* and Janet Achurch, a British actress, to play the lead. *Candida* focuses on a self-possessed wife, free of illusions and capable of running the household all the while appearing submissive to her husband. He is the Reverend James Mavor Morrell, 15 years her junior, a likeable Christian Socialist clergyman and a popular guest speaker, long in name but short in charisma. Onto this scene of complacent domesticity bursts the poet, an 18-year-old infatuated with Candida, who rants and whines, raves and wails—always to excess. The climax comes when Candida is forced to choose between the two: the reverend, stung by jealousy, or the poet, Eugene Marchbanks. To Candida, the choice is clear. She has been mother, wife, and sister to her husband; his weakness demands her strength; of course, she must remain. Who else would peel onions for him? At the end of the play, husband and wife achieve a fuller understanding of each other and of their marriage. Obliged to seek his inspiration elsewhere, the poet leaves, not empty-handed, according to Shaw's directions, but with "a secret" in his heart.

"The woman's part divides the interest and necessary genius with the poet's," Shaw explained: "There are only two people in the world possible for it. Janet Achurch, for whom it was written, and Mrs. Kendal."[10] After a few rehearsals, Mansfield returned both Janet Achurch and the script. "*Candida* is charming," he wrote to Shaw, "it is more than charming—it is delightful, ... but—pardon me—it is <u>not</u> a play.... Here are three long acts of talk-talk-talk—no matter how clever that talk is—it is talk-talk-talk."[11] In yet another letter to Shaw, Mansfield discussed the role of Marchbanks. He declared, "To be frank and to go further, I am not in sympathy with a young, delicate, morbid and altogether exceptional young man who falls in love with a massive, middle aged lady who peels onions. I couldn't have made love to your Candida," he said, referring to Janet Achurch, "if I had taken ether."[12] He dashed off a note to his biographer, William Winter, saying "There is no change of scene in three acts, and no action beyond moving from a chair to a sofa, and *vice versa*. O, ye Gods and little fishes!"[13] Mansfield's wife, Beatrice Cameron, raised another objection: "The people here are not ready for 'Candida'—they would not have understood it."[14]

Their assessment was partly true, as Shaw readily acknowledged on the play's forty-third birthday. Shaw admittedly borrowed both the theme and technique for this play from Henrik Ibsen's *A Doll's House*. Ibsen's play focuses on the marital madness of Nora and her husband, Torvald Helmer, who treats her like a plaything on display to the world. *Candida* reverses this theme, making the husband his wife's doll and suggesting that a female-dominated marriage, cleverly masked, might produce happiness. The exposition and analysis occupy the first act. The climax comes, not in the last act, as might be expected, but in the one before it. Then, the characters invite the audience to remain while they spend the final scene drawing a moral from the action. Shaw deliberately spread discussion throughout *Candida*, "thus bringing the drama back to the classic practice of Shakespeare and the ancient Greek playwrights." He used three acts filled with talk and devoid of much action to make his point, namely, that a husband need not be a cad in order to become the household's lapdog. Then he sat back, smugly gloating at the reaction:

> That is why *Candida* made me many women friends and a few male enemies (among the less generous of their sex). I have no fear of its proving out of date, though some of its first audiences were certainly in that condition. A play that will not last forty years and be all the better for it is not worth writing.[15]

Candida initially failed twice in London. After seeing one production with Janet Achurch playing the part he had written expressly for her, Shaw remarked dryly, "She did not play it: she kicked it around the stage. But she was wonderful in the second act."[16] In America (with very limited authorization), it was produced first in 1899 by pupils of Anna Morgan at the Fine Arts Building in Chicago and again in 1903 by the Browning Society in Philadelphia. *Candida* captured the attention of a struggling actor, Arnold Daly (Peter Christopher Daly), who first read the play in 1898.[17] Spurred by the favorable reviews the two amateur productions received, and convinced of its dramatic possibilities, Daly determined to stage *Candida* professionally. "Restless, aggressive, difficult," Daly experienced a turbulent youth. He was expelled from four public schools and dropped out of school at the age of 11.[18] His education, he believed, conflicted with his ideas of individual freedom. Nevertheless, Daly found employment as a cashier in a department store in Brooklyn. Each day, on his way to work, he passed by a theatre and impulsively decided to enter the profession. He started as a messenger boy for Charles Frohman, served for a short period as a dresser for John Drew, slipped into a minor role when an actor took sick suddenly, then, undaunted, leapt into production. He chose Hilda Spong and then Annie Russell for the title role of *Candida*, but Daniel Frohman, their manager, initially balked. Daly refused to give up. According to Dorothy, he "played in *The Girl from Dixie* just to make money in order to put on this play."[19] In all, Daly scraped together $350 of his personal funds, enticed playwright Winchell Smith to contribute $400, and with him borrowed an additional $600.[20] He hired Hilda Spong as Candida, Dodson Mitchell as James Morrell, and kept the role of Marchbanks for himself.

He also cast Louise Closser Hale as Miss Proserpine (Miss Prossy— the secretary, saucy but sensitive), thereby atoning for the trick he had once played on her. "A few years earlier, Mrs. Hale had come to the Frohman office and was told by Daly that the magnate was out," wrote historian Lloyd Morris, recounting the anecdote. "May I wait for him?" Louise asked. "Yes," said Daly. Three hours passed before Louise worked up the courage to inquire, "Where is Mr. Frohman?" Daly imperturbably replied, "He is in London."[21] Louise's persistence eventually paid off, however, gaining her the part of Miss McCullagh in Frohman's production of *Arizona* and a husband, Walter Hale, an actor she met on the set.

After the first week of practice, when Daly rehearsed only the scenes in which he appeared, Spong quit *Candida* in disgust. One rainy afternoon in November, Daly telephoned Dorothy. "'Of course you know the play,' he said casually." Thus begins Alexander Woollcott's story:

> "Who doesn't," exclaimed Miss Donnelly enigmatically, thereby concealing the fact that she had never read a line of it. Well, then, Daly would come around immediately and talk it over. At that unfortunate suggestion Miss Donnelly managed to remember six pressing engagements and could not promise to see him before the next day. In the interval she swathed herself in a mackintosh and padded over to the bookstore, so that by the following morning she not only read *Candida* through and through, but could give a tolerably good imitation of an actress who had loved and yearned to play the role for years.[22]

Why did this Shavian expert, who had seen the famed Mrs. Patrick Campbell and Mrs. Fiske bring Shaw to life on the stage, choose as his leading lady the little-known Dorothy Donnelly? Did Louise Closser Hale, who knew of Dorothy's reputation as "an actress successful in melodrama,"[23] forcefully nudge him?

The title role was awesome. Even the celebrated and highly versatile British actress, Ellen Terry, told Shaw it was impossible.[24] "Candida, between you and me," Shaw responded, "is the Virgin Mother and nobody else."[25] (Shaw's directions during Act I indicate, "A wise observer, looking at her, would at once guess that whoever had placed the Virgin of the Assumption over her hearth did so because he fancied some spiritual resemblance between them, and yet would not suspect either her husband or herself of any such idea, or indeed of any concern with the art of Titian.") According to her youngest niece, Dorothy's education in a Catholic school lent her a spiritual quality, making her capable of projecting purity and goodness,[26] a sentiment confirmed by Gustav Kobbe, who noted, "her charming personality seemed to … fit her especially for a role in which great charm of person and sweetness of manner absolutely were essential to success."[27] Although one day's notice was all the time Dorothy needed to memorize Candida's lines, delivering them well presented problems. She studied the playwright's guidelines. The stage directions were explicit and copious, but she found them hard to execute—especially for a 23-year-old, very young for the role of a matron. "What would you do with this one for instance?" she asked. She was referring to the scene in which Marchbanks, seated at Candida's feet, rests his head against her knee and says he is doing wrong now but is perfectly happy. Then she quoted Shaw's accompanying directive: "Quite nobly, without the least fear or coldness and with perfect respect for his passion, but with a touch of her wise-hearted maternal humor, she is to lay her hand upon his head."[28] When she looked to the producer for help, she found him sympathetic. Daly himself tried to follow "every one of Mr. Shaw's stage directions to the letter," he said, but stopped short when called upon to "trot" across the stage: "I'm too heavy … I don't dare risk it."[29]

When Dorothy approached Daly with suggestions, she found him receptive. Believing that "incidental music properly subservient to a situation is sometimes of great assistance," she persuaded Daly to use a song by Tchaikovsky during the final intermission. "The most beautiful story of spiritual love ever written in music," she said: "We thought it excellent preparation for the last act, in which Candida's love for her husband and Eugene Marchbank's love for her are the theme."[30] Deriding what he called "emotional acting," Daly refused to be "consumed with internal contemplation about external expression," as he told the drama critic Adolphe Klauber. "I'm usually thinking whether it's snowing outside."[31] He encouraged Dorothy to adopt the same attitude. "There never was another such stage director as Mr. Daly," she said:

> He does not say, "Play the part like this," and show you how he would play it, and inject his personality into the interpretation instead of your own. On the contrary, he will say, "Subdue this or that feature of your personality that is not attractive, and make prominent this other that is." The interpretation is your own, and your own is best when he has finished.[32]

It helped that she liked Candida "as a play and as a part and as a woman," calling it "one of the finest tributes to the domestic woman that has ever been written."[33] Dorothy saw Candida as intellectually superior both to her husband and the poet. "The common belief is that the domestic woman is incapable of anything but domesticity. Candida is in direct opposition to this idea. The little red onions and paraffine [sic] oil and the deadly round of domestic drudgery which she voluntarily chooses do not dull her ability to think for herself."[34] In fact, "her serenity, courage, and dignity ennoble what in smaller women would be mere cunning."[35] Dorothy also recognized the character's affectionate nature: "My desire is to drive the fact home to my hearers that Candida's bigness of heart equals the largeness of her mind."[36]

At last she was ready. "I understand her," said Dorothy, "or perhaps it would be less egotistic to say I have tried to understand her."[37] To underscore the heroine's virtuousness, she played Candida in a long-sleeved white blouse, buttoned high on the neck and edged with a lace collar. Her gray skirt dropped in soft folds from the waist and swept the floor with its hem. She wore a pair of plain gray pumps.

Candida opened for a trial matinee on December 8, 1903, at the Princess Theatre in New York. Louise Closser Hale felt a "strong inclination to run" and wondered whether Dorothy shared her jitters:

> I peeped at her in the mirror of my dressing shelf. She was again in gray, a yielding color. I thought if we both ran there couldn't possibly be a show. She was deadly quiet, but she was wearing her gray like a coat of steel. It was a coat of her own fashioning. It was not inherited—this courage. Not that she was without fear. For fear is a driving force if it is not craven.

"I see that one Arnold Daly is playing *Candida* in New York," Shaw wrote to Sir Johnston Forbes-Robertson, a British actor known for his portrayal of Hamlet. "If he plays anywhere within your reach, ask Mrs. Robertson to go and see it and tell me what it's like. There is a sort of snivelling success possible for *Candida* if the right cast could be got for it."[38] According to Adolphe Klauber of the *New York Times*, the cast was decidedly wrong. His review began well: To have missed *Candida* "is to have missed a literary and dramatic event of the highest delight." Dorothy's grin dissolved into grimace as Klauber continued: her performance was "the single and almost insuperable blight" on the production; she should be replaced by "a Julia Marlowe with the spiritual intentions and refinements of Annie Russell."

Just as the play was about to begin its regular run, disaster struck. On December 30, 1903, fire broke out on the stage of the Iroquois Theatre in Chicago, where the owners, Klaw and Erlanger, had booked *Mr. Bluebeard*. It starred Eddie Foy, who yelled "Play!" to the orchestra and tried to calm the audience. "Keep quiet! Take your seats! There is no danger. Plenty of time to go out quietly."[39] A stagehand opened a back door to clear the air of smoke, but the wind swept in, fanning the flames. Another member of the crew began to lower the curtain, but it jammed partway down the roller. Suddenly people were trapped. Those in the balcony jumped from the fire escape, many more were trampled, and in all, 578 (or 602, for records differ) lost their lives. Theatres throughout the country closed immediately until cities adopted stringent codes and seriously enforced them. Patrons were subtly alerted to potential dangers. A 1908 program for *The Lion and the Mouse* at the Chicago Opera House contains this notice: "red lights above exits, operating on independent gas system." Panic doors that open outward, curtains made of asbestos, and evacuation plans posted on walls—these are today's visual reminders of the Chicago catastrophe.

As a consequence of the fire, Daly's company found themselves scrambling for a place to stage *Candida*. A make-shift town hall erected above a livery stable provided one solution. Other, better scented, lodgings were found at the Madison Square Theatre on January 4, 1904, at the Vaudeville Theatre on January 11, and finally at the hastily renovated Berkeley Lyceum Theatre, rented from Charles Frohman.[40]

Klauber's demand for substitutions did not go unheeded. When the play reopened, two minor characters—Ernest Lawford and Herbert Standing—were replaced. Dorothy, however, remained. Klauber saw the play again and resumed his attack: "With the possible exception of the Candida of Dorothy Donnelly," begins his review.[41] Archibald Henderson, Shaw's official biographer, also delivered a retrospective blow: "The Candida of Dorothy Donnelly, although better at the end than at the

Dorothy Donnelly wears a simple, modest costume to emphasize the heroine's purity when creating the title role in the first professional American production of Candida. *Drawn from life, the illustration accompanies an interview published in 1904 by* Theatre Magazine.

Introduced to road shows by her triumph in Candida, *Dorothy Donnelly* (left) *appears in a traveling production of* Daughters of Men. *(Courtesy Philip Fahringer Collection.)*

beginning of the evening, was not memorable, being marked as much by affectation as by engaging sweetness," he wrote: "there was no suggestion of the personification of the maternal instinct."[42] But Dorothy was her own worse critic:

> I hear a little gasp from a woman in the audience now and then when I speak the lines: "How can you talk to me of goodness and purity? I would give them both to Eugene as willingly as I would throw a shawl to a beggar who was dying of cold if there were not other things to restrain me." People seem to miss the last saving clause…but it's a mighty clause. For she does love her husband. She will always love him.[43]

These gasps told Dorothy that she had failed to convince the audience of Candida's love for her husband.

Was the fault in the stars, in her performance, or in the audience, as Shaw himself suggested? So persuasively does the play reveal Morrell's moral and intellectual limitations, that many theatregoers rejected Candida's crucial line: "Put your trust in my love for you, James." They believed, instead, that Candida remains with her husband because she prefers the security and financial comfort of marriage. Furthermore, many refused to accept her attraction to the poet as morally justifiable. Others, however, understood Shaw's message. "I have seen several women in the audience nudging their husbands," said Dorothy, "when I have been telling the Reverend Mr. Morrell how I have been mother and sisters and everything to him."[44] Nevertheless, she shouldered the blame for having "wronged" Candida, to use her own expression, and generously admitted, "It hurts me to hear any one say that there is even a suggestion of materialism in her nature, for I feel then that I haven't shown the character aright, that I haven't done her justice."[45]

If she sought absolution, Dorothy received it. Most critics reviewed her performance favorably: "A delightful Candida," wrote one; the "serene womanly archetype," said another; a convincing portrayal of a "prudent wife and motherly friend," claimed James Metcalfe. Zona Gale declared, "Seldom have such uniformly excellent players been met in one piece as [Daly] secured for Candida." *The Evening Sun* commended her "fine impersonation" and added, "This is by long odds the best work that Miss Donnelly has ever done." Still another critic concurred: "They have given such a promising young actress a chance to show in exceptional surroundings the intelligence and the sense of character that are in her. She has added to her reputation, and few actresses have brains enough to make Shaw's paradoxical heroines as plausible as does she."[46] (As early as 1906, the *St. Louis Star* identified her as one of the most intellectual actresses on stage.) Gustav Kobbe, who wrote extensively about actresses, composers, and operas and whose *The Complete Opera Book*, published posthumously, remains in print today, gushed like a geyser. He required five full pages in his book, *Famous Actresses and Their Homes*, to extol Dorothy's Candida. Here's a snippet: "There are two Candidas. George Bernard Shaw himself has one,—a charming wife.... The other Candida is, of course, Dorothy Donnelly.... No one more exquisitely suited to it can be thought of—now that we all have seen her play it."[47]

On February 11, 1904, *The Man of Destiny* was added to the bill. Shaw wrote this one-act play in 1899 for Richard Mansfield and Ellen Terry, a cast, he hoped, that would predetermine its success both in America and England.[48] This work paints an unheroic picture of the emperor Napoleon, trying to wheedle a packet of letters from a female spy. Known only as the Strange Lady, she successfully outwits his cunning. Again Arnold Daly and Dorothy took the leads. And again Dorothy received mixed reviews. John Corbin of *The New York Sun* looked for a little more "fire" and "allurement." Arthur Hornblow, editor of *Theatre Magazine*, wrote that she "lacked some of the exquisite charm which Shaw's brilliant stories called for, but it was an agreeable and careful effort." Archibald Henderson, however, reversed course; this time he criticized Daly's makeup and "painfully strident and harsh" voice but thought that Dorothy's "Strange Lady was much more able and effective than her Candida."[49] Interestingly, despite all her efforts to prepare for the parson's wife, Dorothy found the Strange Lady a harder role. "My part in 'The Man of Destiny' is more trying than Candida. Not only must I … deceive Napoleon, but I must convey to my audience the fact that I am deceiving him," she said. "This requisite is the greatest task of the player's profession."[50]

Dorothy's reputation spread far beyond the confines of New York City in April, when both Shaw plays hit the road after 131 performances, stopping in Boston, Toledo, Chicago, San Francisco, and Toronto, winning "its way to complete success."[51] Minutes before the call boy yelled "beginners, please," Dorothy would often pop out of her dressing room, head for the wings, sit at the piano, and play a succession of trills. She used music to arouse her emotions and to keep them honed and intelligible. Bizet's *Carmen*, Puccini's *La Bohème*—"one of the most temperamental things ever written"—Grieg, and Tchaikovsky now topped her list of favorites. "In music, as in other things," she said, "you lose your academic taste as you grow older and go in for color."[52] She was 24. Whether repeated performances bolstered Dorothy's self-confidence, reinforced and increased her understanding of the character, or sharpened her portrayal of Candida, clippings, mostly laudatory, mounted like slips of straw in haystacks.

The *Chicago Sunday American* published a lengthy interview by Forrest Arden, entitled "A Talk with Miss Dorothy Donnelly," and illustrated it with several photographs and even more amusing ink drawings. Peter Robertson reviewed the play for the *San Francisco Chronicle*, subtitling his article, "Arnold Daly Introduces the Crazy Poet and Some Other Queer People." He summed up *Candida* in a single word—"tommyrot." He treated the cast a little more generously, noting, for example, that Louise Closser Hale "gave a clever bit of character work in the typewriter"; but spent his wad on Dorothy:

> A better cast could not have better brought out Mr. Shaw's meaning, if anybody could feel perfectly sure, from the intrinsic evidence of the lines and business, what that was. Of Miss Donnelly, it is only just to say that she gave a charming and even, as far as could be, a logical performance of Candida. Gentle and sweet in nature, refined and reposeful, a trifle too deliberate sometimes, but with a good, strong will behind it, she made Mr. Shaw's play attractive.[53]

Rodney Lee of the *Toledo Blade* singled her out in *The Man of Destiny*: "She displayed any amount of virtuosity—what a blessing it is that Shaw himself used that word; it fits Miss Donnelly to perfection. She invested the character with rare charm, and if the other members of the company had equaled her, the bit of bravura would have been much more satisfying."[54]

Whatever tributes her performances reaped, Dorothy assigned to others. She never mentioned her start in the theatre without giving credit to three teachers: her brother, Henry, who coached her in modern comedies; her cousin, Fritz, whose technical suggestions she found helpful; and her uncle, who trained her to use her head rather than her emotions to shape a part.

To commemorate her success in *Candida*, Henry gave his sister an expensive, handsomely bound volume that contained the complete set of the Murray Hill Theatre's playbills. Dorothy stored it beside photographs of their father in his favorite roles and near the pile of rare books left to her by Fred Williams. Still mourning the recent death of her uncle, Dorothy sailed for Europe in July 1904 with Fritz Williams' wife, Katherine Florence, as her companion.

This was the first of many successive summer trips abroad and of regular stops in England, where she called on Bernard Shaw and his wife, Charlotte Townsend-Payne. On one such visit Shaw handed her a copy of *Candida*, his favorite play he still maintained many years later.[55] Shaw had reason to be grateful. As one critic noted, "Miss Donnelly in *Candida* set a standard for the interpretation of Bernard Shaw that is likely to remain for a long time."[56] Moreover, "American audiences made him successful and rich at a time when in England he was merely admired by intelligent people who crowded short runs at the Court [Theatre]."[57]

"Shall I write something in it for you?" Shaw asked. "Oh do," Dorothy answered. "Well," he said, venting his tendency to tease, "how would this do: 'To Miss Dorothy Donnelly who says she has made a great success as Candida, but I have not seen her.'"[58] When she opened the book, she found the following inscription on the flyleaf: "Candida. A Mystery by Bernard Shaw. Also by Dorothy Donnelly, who brought Candida to life in her own person in New York. In acknowledgment of which the author subscribes himself as her grateful collaborator." It was dated "1906 28th June" and signed "G. Bernard Shaw."[59]

CHAPTER 4

Beyond the Footlights

Following a brief revival (eight performances) of *The Man of Destiny* at the Berkeley Lyceum beginning September 26, 1904, Dorothy left Arnold Daly's troupe to accept a five-year contract tendered by Maurice Campbell. As a producer, Campbell had scored a big hit when he arranged for David Belasco to produce and stage *Sweet Kitty Belairs.* Based on Agnes and Egerton Castle's book, *The Bath Comedy*, this four-act play opened in December 1903, ran the season, then reopened in August 1904 for an additional 25 performances. It starred Henrietta Crosman, Campbell's wife, and introduced Jane Cowl to Broadway. (Theatregoers were less likely to toast Campbell, however, when he became the Prohibition Administrator for New York City in 1927.) Whether he had acted on his own in extending Dorothy a contract or at the direction of Henry B. Harris remains uncertain—and unimportant. Pudgy and aggressive, Harris had learned theatrical management from his father, William Harris Sr., one of the founders of the Theatrical Trust. Then he left the syndicate to produce plays independently.

For Dorothy, bent on acting and determined to be self-supporting, their offer proved too tempting to refuse. As an independent actress, she had already tasted, if only briefly, the bitter unease of being without a script. The contract would guarantee her steady engagements for a long stretch of time. It would eliminate the need to beg before managers' doors or to repeat nerve-wracking rounds of auditions unfamiliar to her. Having feasted on success at a tender age, she could not foresee that her acceptance could nearly capsize her career.

At the outset this seemed a dumb decision, destined to drive her from one dismal play to another. She appeared in *Friquet.* Produced by Charles Frohman at the Savoy Theatre, *Friquet* opened January 31, 1905, but folded after a mere 23 performances. Most reviewers considered the Parisian comedy unworthy of translation. The critic for *The Evening Sun* minced no words when he wrote, "*Friquet* is bound to take rank from every point of view as the most puerile production of the season."[1] Campbell next produced Henrik Ibsen's *When We Dead Awaken*. It played three matinees at the Knickerbocker Theatre and moved on March 27, 1905, to the Princess Theatre for a three-week run. This American premiere, however, did not escape unscathed. It "has interest as the final work in the author's series of studies in social pathology," noted the *New York Times*: "Of actual dramatic value it has none."[2]

Of practical value, however, *When We Dead Awaken* had plenty for Dorothy. Cast as the wronged wife of a sculptor, who finds his artistic inspiration in another woman, she learned to stir the mind without stifling the heart. According to the *Times*, "In the acting more than in the reading—although it prevails to an extent even there—the character of the wife is the only one which makes a particularly sympathetic appeal... The best acting of the afternoon was contributed by Dorothy Donnelly, who conveyed with a considerable degree of skill the restless longings of the entirely human Maia, not withholding unduly the phases of her pleasure-loving nature, but indicating very well the occasional deeper note of the woman's longing for her husband's wanting sympathy."[3] In brief, Ibsen's play released Dorothy from unnatural restraint, from that tendency to clamp down too tightly on the expression of emotions.

She appeared next with Hassard Short in *The Proud Laird* at the Manhattan Theatre on April 24, 1905. Its plot revolved around a Scottish lord's attempt to marry a wealthy American heiress to save his family's estate from falling into further ruin. "Trivial" declared *The Evening Mail*[4]; "Benedick and Beatrice in Kilts" proclaimed *The New York Sun*, alluding to Shakespeare's *Much Ado About Nothing*.[5] Meanwhile, the *New York Times* reviewer found no point or purpose to the play, noting that the title provided its only local color. "Dorothy Donnelly, technically precise and generally competent throughout, is temperamentally unfitted for the role," the critic added, insisting that the role of the heiress called for "girlish simplicity."[6] Drama critics were hard to please: at 23 Dorothy was considered too young to capture "maternal instincts" and two years later, too old for "girlish simplicity."

A few more flattering notices greeted her performance in *Mrs. Battle's Bath*, in which she again costarred with Hassard Short.[7] This one-act play, penned by the British writer Cosmo Hamilton in collaboration with Charles Cartwright, was added as a curtain raiser on May 9 during the final week of *The Firm of Cunningham*'s run at the Madison Square Theatre. It recounts the experiences of two young people who meet in the bathroom at midnight on Christmas Eve. The Earl of Bedford saunters into the bathroom, slams the door shut behind him, and turns around to find the widow, Mrs. Mildred Battle, in the tub. Locks that fail to work, romantic conversations that take place in a most unconventional setting, and plans for escape that include constructing a rope of towels to which Mrs. Battle offers to add a frill from her skirt contributed to the humor and risqué quality of the farce. According to one reviewer, the play's merits depended exclusively on "Dorothy Donnelly's ankles, encased in silk stockings."[8]

On May 29 Dorothy appeared at the Hollis Street Theatre in Boston in Ira B. Goodrich's dramatization of the novel by Dwight Tilton, *On Satan's Mount*. She should have stayed at home, however, for the play never made it to Broadway.

The *Brooklyn Eagle*, on November 16, 1908, noted that Dorothy "has suffered no failure on the stage in the past six years." It may have been more accurate to report, however, that her parts in these three inconsequential plays called into question her budding reputation as an accomplished actress in the minds of critics—and perhaps even the audience—who remembered her interpretations of Shaw's Candida and Ibsen's Maia Rubek. "From Ibsen and Shaw to *Mrs. Battle's Bath* is a heavy fall," said one anonymous critic, "and it is no pleasure to record that Miss Donnelly took it without a tremor."[9] Dorothy may have quivered when chastised for accepting roles in plays devoid of artistic quality, but she must have trembled mightily when the reviewer stepped beyond his professional bounds to "record" her reaction. Dorothy never underestimated the value of publicity to an actress. Therefore, she freely shared her thoughts and opinions about plays and parts with the press and the public. However, she was scrupulously careful to keep her feelings private. Only Louise Hale, who knew her best, could safely speculate about her joys or disappointments. Few others dared.

Fortunately, the following season gave her yet another opportunity to prove her mettle. While costarring with Julia Dean in *The Little Gray Lady*, she again tested her skill at handling dramatic confrontations without underplaying. The play takes place in Washington, D.C., mainly in a rooming house owned by Captain Henry Jordan and his wife. One of their boarders, Perriton Carlyle, says he loves Anna Gray, whom he affectionately refers to as the "little lady in gray," but he squanders his salary on their daughter. When he runs out of funds, he steals a $100 bill from the Department of the Treasury, where he and the Jordans are employed. Written by Channing Pollock, and produced by Maurice Campbell at the Garrick Theatre, the melodrama aimed to prove the thesis that a single misdeed could not condemn a person to a life of evildoing. It set its sights on a young man attracted to a beautiful lamebrain but redeemed by a "noble, plain, true-hearted woman," as the playwright described her. (Rumor has it that Pollock, press agent for the Shuberts, was about to propose, and his intended was only moderately comely.) But it was Dorothy who hit the bull's eye.

She prepared for the role of Ruth Jordan, the landlady's seductive daughter, as she always did, first by carefully examining the character:

> Ruth's type is common and sordidly familiar enough to every one. You see her in the streets, behind the counters in the big stores, and in the homes of hard-working mothers. With all her prettiness she is selfish, shallow, incapable of deep feeling either of pleasure or pain. Yet, the fact remains that she is eternally attractive to men, and you have somehow got to suggest that attractiveness as well as the hardness and vulgarity.[10]

Next, Dorothy probed the relationship between Ruth and the other characters:

> It seems to me men like that kind of girl mainly because of her shrewdness and her absolute poise. She knows exactly what to do on all occasions, and her feelings never get in the way of her instinct for the main chance. In dealing with men, therefore, she has a big advantage over her sisters who are apt to lose themselves in their own simpler emotions. The general run of men are immensely attracted by a girl who always knows just what to do and say and who never seems to drop out of her bright, gay, calculating manner.[11]

Finally, Dorothy considered the audience:

> It is a curious fact, though, that one can rarely play unpleasant people quite true to life. Usually you have to take care not to make the characterization utterly repellent—particularly when the character is supposed to be in any way attractive to the other people in the play.[12]

To develop a multi-dimensional character, she deliberately elicited the playgoers' sympathy for Ruth by capitalizing on the character's assets. "To me this lightening of the actually unpleasant is the most interesting problem of the landlady's daughter," she explained: "Accordingly I have tried to make Ruth's ease and sureness of manner a little overbalance her ignorance and her vulgarity."[13] By the time Dorothy felt she understood the character, she created an imagined portrait of Ruth Jordan as sharply and cleanly etched as any engraving of Albrecht Dürer.

When Alice Rohe of the *New York World* popped into Dorothy's dressing room to discuss the play, she had already written the lead—"This interview is about cats." Rohe toyed with Dorothy, hoping to elicit her support for the preconceived theory that all women are felines. Dorothy settled back into her chair, neither touching up her hair nor fingering her jewelry to stall for time, and calmly pretended to play the game. "The catty woman is generally the woman who has missed opportunities," she began: "She is jealous and envious to the last degree, and she hopes to level comparisons between her bitter, disappointed life and others, not by building up her own, but by scratching and tearing down the others." Then she popped the critic's balloon by adding, "Ruth Jordan is much too shallow and vain and superficial to be a real cat like that."[14]

Robinson Locke, who filled scrapbooks with clippings and photographs of the most prominent performers during the first decade of the twentieth century and devoted one volume exclusively to Dorothy, forwarded her copies of the tryout's reviews. Dorothy responded from the Claypool Hotel in Indianapolis:

> Thank you very much for your note and its enclosures. I <u>had</u> read the criticism and also had secured several copies for my family and friends so I shall keep the one you sent me for my own scrapbook. As I told you Wednesday night it made me very happy to think my words had pleased so able a critic and I trust I may always continue to do so. Much renewed thanks.[15]

He also sent her an encouraging telegram before the Broadway opening of *The Little Gray Lady* on January 22, 1906. She replied to him a few days later on monogrammed stationery: "It was kind of you to think of me— and I assure you I appreciate it. If it weren't for the good wishes of our friends I don't see how we could get through those dreadful first nights."[16] Locke captioned her photograph as Ruth Jordan with a single word: "Success."

Dorothy's performance received twenty-one curtain calls, ten minutes of applause, and reams of approving notices. "Remarkably capable," wrote *Theatre Magazine*. "Wonderfully bold and buxom … selfish and designing to the limit," noted the January 23 *New York Times*. The *Providence Bulletin* admired Dorothy's "convincing picture of realism" and added that she "spares none of the coarseness necessary to make the role effective." *Vanity Fair* devoted its front cover to one of her scenes in the play,[17] and noted, "She has made the part 'rich' with points and showed herself a real comedienne—a word that is constantly misapplied to May Irwin, Marie Dressler, and a few others."[18] Alan Dale (Alfred J. Cohen), reporting for the *New York American*, wrote, "Here is the best example of training that we have on hand."[19] *Everybody's Magazine* insisted that "nothing could be further from her performances in *Candida* and Ibsen plays, and yet, in its way, it is as fine as those."[20] Acton Davies of *The Evening Sun* wrote, "To Miss Donnelly perhaps, the first honors belong, not only on account of her excellent performance but because of the contrast which this tough character affords to her previous work as Candida."[21] The *Toledo Blade* summed up the consensus of the critics: Rodney Lee called Dorothy a "consummate actress" who "embellishes and accentuates till the character fairly radiates actual life." Then he launched into a summary of the plot and an analysis of the play before returning to his favorite subject:

> Dorothy Donnelly is a delight, pure and simple. Her Ruth Jordan is a work of art, finished and perfect in every minute particular, and she invests it with a thousand details that would never occur to an actress less talented than Miss Donnelly. It is impossible to even attempt an enumeration of the many bits of by-play, the deft touches that she continually gives the characterization to make it not only effective but real. With the sure instinct of an artist and with the perfection of technique that is her great charm, she has seized the essential points of Mr. Pollock's creation and vivified it with life and truth. It is a remarkably fine piece of acting in every way.[22]

Even the playwright applauded. Asked to comment on the current state of the acting profession, Channing Pollock noted that "modern performers are little more than a parade of personalities."[23] Even after lengthy rehearsals, Pollock added, they generally chose to play themselves rather than the character the playwright intended. "Three performances I have considered brilliant," he said: "the Ruth Jordan of Dorothy Donnelly in *The Little Gray Lady*, and the Edward Ramsay of Grant Stewart and Mag Monohan of Helen Ware in *In the Bishop's Carriage*"—a short honor roll indeed, as Pollock himself pointed out.[24]

The *New York Times* revisited *The Little Gray Lady* again on February 4. "In the acting of this play," began the review, "Donnelly is chiefly to be commended for the disclosure of an ability at variation of effort much less common in women players than in men." High praise indeed, but there was more. Noting that Dorothy gave a "commendable exhibition" in *Soldiers of Fortune*, the review continued, "there was nothing in the part to suggest such capacity as her Candida developed." Her successive roles showed steady progress, said the anonymous critic and, in conclusion, noted, "That she has succeeded admirably in these varying roles indicates very clearly that she is capable of that rare quality—character differentiation. Our actresses so generally play themselves, and themselves only, that such an achievement as Miss Donnelly's justifies more than the mere word of adjectival praise." This review dismissed forever any remembrance of Klauber's accusation—"insuperable blight"—and confirmed Arnold Daly's claim that "there never was a greater fallacy than that great parts make great actors."[25]

Another drama critic who appreciated Dorothy's versatility was Acton Davies, who wrote, "In these days of long runs it is a very rare thing to find a woman artist who can jump successfully from a straight part into character work!"[26] But Dorothy pooh-poohed this notion. "I think all parts are 'character' parts," she argued. "What is it that fascinates one in the work of almost all the French actors and actresses? Characterization," she insisted. "Whether they are interpreting the fashionables or the people of the half world and the under world, each person becomes a separate and distinct personality, or, in other words, a character."[27]

Dorothy also deplored the confusion between skill and personal traits. Talent "is something within and independent of that without," she added, citing as example an actress already past her fortieth birthday: "Ada Rehan is too tall and large for a girl, and she is no longer young, yet she is the best player of girl parts in America."[28]

The contention that Dorothy displayed an "ability at variation of effort much less common in women players than in men" acknowledges her success in overcoming two obstacles: sexism—on the part of these two critics, at the very least—and typecasting. Another by-product of long-running shows and the star system, typecasting encouraged actors to exploit their personal mannerisms and idiosyncrasies rather than interpret a broad range of characters. For example, if you needed a swashbuckler, you cast E. H. Sothern, who played that role in a series of plays. Sometimes, as director J. C. Huffman suggested, you chose actors for their appearance: they looked the part even if they could not play it.[29]

Dorothy easily explained the appeal of typecasting:

> What audiences want is something and somebody they can always recognize and be sure of. They love to see an actress they know doing parts which they have learned once and for all to associate with her. They make up their minds that a particular artist is always to do a certain kind of role, and it somehow disappoints them if she appears on the stage in an unexpected character. Therefore, from my point of view, it is far better to identify one's self with a certain well-defined class of roles than to experiment with a score of varied characterizations that only bewilder the public and blur the artist's individuality. As long as audiences continue to be interested in persons more surely than in parts, specialization rather than versatility is the actress's safer line. I don't mean, of

course, that one's roles need necessarily be always pleasant; they may perfectly well be just the opposite. But to be associated in people's minds with doing one sort of thing and doing it pretty well is the surest way of becoming secure in the real interest and affection of your public.[30]

Versatility delivered mixed reviews, specialization brought raves. Could she who once spoke of wanting to be "liked on the stage and loved off"[31] have meant the opposite? Apparently.

Dorothy easily resolved the apparent contradiction between her assessment of the French actress' ability to bring characterization to each role and the public's clamor for the familiar. Henceforth she would play the part of the "not so nice" woman, sensual as opposed to intellectual, and bring her to life on the stage as an individual rather than a type. Arthur Hobson Quinn, who wrote the history of American play writing from colonial days through the first quarter of the twentieth century, says, "We think we know tragedy and comedy, but we do not know what to do with the vast body of plays which lie between these categories. We call them all melodrama," he adds, admitting to the temptation to classify and characterize.

> Tragedy exalts; comedy entertains. But there are times when we wish neither to have our souls exalted nor to have our weaknesses exposed. We wish to have our attention caught and held by interesting situations and capable dialogue, and we wish to have above all the element of intense suspense which is the heart and soul of melodrama....We are willing to forgive the writer of melodrama if he heightens the sentiment or even exaggerates the passion. But not only must he make the ending satisfactory to us; he must also provide situations that are well knit together—the action must be sustained, and the illusion of probability preserved. [Melodrama] attempts character drawing and even concerns itself with the social problems of the day.[32]

If her triumph in *The Little Gray Lady* persuaded Dorothy to abdicate dramatic parts in favor of romantic or melodramatic roles, it was her determination to master these that led her once again to a stock company. Practice surpassed any school of acting when it came to training and study, she thought: "The best teacher an actor can have is the audience. You can learn all the teachers have to give, but that won't make an actor out of you. It is the stage, and the place to begin is in stock."[33] So, from April to June 1906, she played in summer stock repertoire at the Harlem Opera House, where William J. Kelly was presenting revivals of popular American melodramas originally produced by Charles Frohman. In *The Masqueraders*, the company's first production, Dorothy appeared as Dulcie

Larondie in a sold-out performance that received many curtain calls, a demand for the director to address the audience, and a brief critical review, announcing the short season and characterizing Dorothy's performance as charming.

Regrettably, the Murray Hill Theatre company had ceased operations two years earlier. In all the years her brother managed it, the house offered only one revival—*Never Again.* Henry never lost sight of his goal: "After months of discouraging box office returns he saw the tide turn in his favor and thereafter his playhouse became the center of attraction for many of the most distinguished literary men as well as a high grade clientele of regular patrons,"[34] three-fourths of whom he could address by name. Even though it was considered "one of the most famous stock companies of the period,"[35] in 1904, when he could no longer find worthy plays to present, Henry closed it. He nevertheless maintained his career as an actor, taking to the road once again.

After her brief stint in summer stock and a two-month European vacation, Dorothy accepted another role as the *femme fatale.* In *Daughters of Men* she played Louise Stolbeck, a revolutionary who vents venom and hurls accusations at the oppressors of the common man. Perhaps prompted by the creation in 1905 of the Industrial Workers of America, a radical union of unskilled workers, Charles Klein wrote this play to explore the conflict between labor and capital. It received due credit for its social commentary on political corruption and developed sufficient popularity to enjoy a run in London with Edward Breese and Margaret Illington in the leads. Once again the hero is forced to choose between two women—one his social superior from a wealthy family, the other a child of anarchy—and once again feminine demureness triumphs in the end. Most reviewers saw the play as a formula melodrama, and many sided with the *New York Telegraph* critic, who called it "long-winded" and "dull,"[36] or with Frederic Edward McKay of the *Evening Mail*, who deemed it "bombastic" and "boresome."[37] *Daughters of Men* premiered in Springfield, Massachusetts, held a trial run in Boston, with Mr. and Mrs. Charles Klein in attendance at the opening performance, then began its New York run at the Astor Theatre on November 19, 1906. That same evening—perhaps prematurely?—the Twelfth Night Club held a congratulatory reception for Dorothy.

Although the reviewer for the *New York Telegraph* did not like the play, he praised Dorothy's interpretation: "From start to finish her work is much more worth while than anything she has done previously, even with her brilliant record quite unforgotten." The *Philadelphia Record* found her voice unpleasant at times but thought the character study outstanding. "In her comely lines, many of which were cleverly introduced at the moments when the strain was reaching the limit of coherent emotion, she was excellent and carried the audience with her headlong," read the *New York Times*.[38] Other reviews were less favorable. Acton Davies of *The Evening Sun* found her "stagy and artificial for the first time in her career." Although usually complimentary, this time Alan Dale considered her voice "raspy" and panned the hysteria in her delivery. So did John Corbin of the *New York Sun*, who also thought her speech indistinct. Being labeled by the "Matinee Girl" as the "cleverest of young American actresses"[39] provided Dorothy with scant immunity to criticism.

The real test of whether her interpretation of Louise Stolbeck was genuinely convincing or mere overacting did not rest with the critics, however—not, that is, if you place any credibility in the *Toledo Blade*. The paper dutifully quoted Dorothy, as she reported, "Every day I receive from ten to twenty-five letters from Socialists and other radicals, offering me positions as Socialist leader, or as writer of some Socialistic paper... And I am besieged at the stage door by all sorts of radicals, who insist upon congratulating me or asking me to join their societies." Then it reprinted a letter she received from Maxim Slokowsky, identified by the *Toledo Blade* as "one of the leading Socialists of Russia":

> We need you here in this great demoralized country of ours. We have heard how every night on the stage of a theatre you preach the cause of socialism. We, great thinkers in this country, believe you would make a great leader for our cause. We have lost faith in Maxim Gorky. We sent him as an envoy to America, and he was literally cast from your shores. Therefore, we believe that an American woman could incite sympathy for the cause of the masses of this country.[40]

Dorothy declined all invitations, however, even the promise of a trip to Russia with all expenses paid in full. Despite her acquaintance with Bernard Shaw, she was no socialist.

Like an infatuated teenager, she viewed Shaw with an uncritical eye. She praised his simple home life (made complex by "infidelities and villainies of all kinds," Shaw admitted[41]), his methodical approach to work, and, especially, his support of women's suffrage—although he stood by waving a flag instead of marching in a London parade to promote women's right to vote. She appreciated his irrepressible wit and enormous self-confidence, summed up in the three-line motto that hung above the door to his library: "They say—What they say—Let them say."[42] She enjoyed hearing him laugh at his own unpopularity on the British stage and watching him shrug off with a grin the mixed reception his newest play, *Major*

Barbara, received in London. Aware of his reputation as a nonconformist, she steadfastly denied that he was a "poseur" or an "eccentric." No, Dorothy argued: "He is tremendously in earnest," adding that he would "rather be known as a thinker than a playwright."[43] Nor did she flush when confessing "Bernard Shaw is my idol. I worship him and his love of truth and his way of getting at the truth." The playwright presented her another autographed copy of the play, this time inscribing it "To Dorothy Donnelly, who made America fall in love with Candida. From G. Bernard Shaw, 11 July 1907."[44]

With Shaw's blessing and encouragement, she accepted speaking engagements to explain his techniques and objectives. In Washington, D. C., while addressing the faculties of Trinity College and Catholic University, Dorothy insisted on the cultural importance of drama. "I believe in it as an art with its special place and its special mission in the development of national character," she said: "I believe, too, in the final judgment of the public. That which the public really takes to heart will endure and live."[45] Her words would echo in Daniel Frohman's autobiography, *Memoirs of a Manager*: "It is the multitude that makes a stage work valuable."[46] When they realized Dorothy was articulate as well as lovely, knowledgeable as well as talented, women's clubs sent her an honorarium along with a request to lecture. "The independence of making your own money is something that I wouldn't miss for anything," Dorothy volunteered.[47]

What she prized most was the independence, not the money. Once, when an interviewer asked about her hobbies and discovered that she liked playing the piano and reading, Dorothy quickly recanted. "Please don't say that," she implored: "Every actress that has ever been written about is invariably described as domestic in her tastes." The idea of being pigeonholed made her feminism shudder. Yet, she expressed sincere sympathy for women who preferred to stay home and "who must repress their real feelings, and go on and work because some one is dependent on them."[48]

Although she objected to being categorized, she nevertheless confined herself to "a certain well-defined class of roles" like that of Marion Manners in *The Movers*. In this new work by Martha Morton (Coheim), Dorothy portrayed the elder of two sisters, abetted by their callous parents, who are anxiously trying to break into the ranks of high society. Marion Manners marries a Wall Street broker and then runs up the household's bills, forcing her husband to embezzle funds to cover his growing debts. When he commits suicide, she begins to realize the waywardness of her extravagance and seeks to redeem herself through gainful employment. Assuming the role of a trained nurse, she moves into her sister's home to care for the baby fallen ill from neglect. Her family is shocked and, they believe, socially disgraced by her willingness to work as a commoner, but Marion steadfastly urges them to renounce the materialistic life.

Produced by Henry B. Harris and staged by Maurice Campbell, *The Movers* opened at the Hackett Theatre on September 3, 1907. Two days earlier, in its Sunday edition, the *New York Times* published a photograph of Dorothy. Wearing Mona Lisa's enigmatic smile and a pearl choker, she looked confident about her forthcoming appearance, even though she had only three weeks to prepare the lead. She always made acting seem as natural as slurping vanilla ice cream from a cone. "There never had been a period in her life when she was aware of her thumbs sticking out aloofly from her other digits as she made a gesture; ... crossing the stage was to her never a breathless trip, unending and stiff legged; ... her voice passed over the footlights with no effort of curving it, like a buttonhook, from the diaphragm over the back of the mouth, out to the waiting audience," wrote Louise Hale. While the mechanics came quickly to Dorothy, "living breathing characterization comes to me more slowly," she acknowledged. Her grasp of character appeared intuitive, but she preferred "a week or two of thinking the character out more closely and of developing the details and side lights that reveal such a character."[49]

Her performance in *The Movers* garnered high marks from Acton Davies of New York's *Evening Sun*, who noted that she "scored the one real success of the evening," and the *Chicago Register* that declared it the "best emotional work of her career." *Theatre Magazine* had even more to say:

> Dorothy Donnelly, who gives greater promise in every role she essays, was excellent in the part of the wife, which she played with much charm, naturalness, and force. The frivolous, restless character of the young wife, as well as her unhappiness and repentance, were indicated with a sureness of touch and authority that ranks Miss Donnelly among the most successful of our young emotional actresses.

Adolpe Klauber of the *New York Times* dissented, however; he labeled her as "a promising young actress," who reached for and failed to grasp "Bernhardt's emotionalism." To measure the quality of her interpretation, the critics used the same yardstick—emotionalism. Moreover, they used the term liberally without bothering to explain it. It's hard to define an emotional actress, acknowledges Willard Holcombe. "Shall a player merely act, or really feel his part? Which is truer to art and nature?" One thing is certain: the portrayal must "contain [the] touch of truth."[50] Whether the head or the heart predominates and clarifies the characterization, the actress must persuade the audience that the emotions they witness are genuine, not merely simulated.

Although the critics differed in their assessment of Dorothy's performance, they concurred on one point: the structural weakness of the play. Too much purpose and too little drama, they said. *The Movers* closed after 23 performances for revision. By the time it was ready to reopen six months later, Dorothy had another job. Harris had assigned her to play the lead in a touring company (Company C) of *The Lion and the Mouse*. This play, a thinly disguised exposé of John D. Rockefeller (the male lead, John Ryder, bears the same initials), reflected antipathy towards monopolies and may have hastened the break up of the Standard Oil Company. Although born in England, Charles Klein wrote about contemporary themes in American life during the first decade of the twentieth century. His dramas gained popularity through their serious treatment especially of political problems or finances. *The Lion and the Mouse* was no exception; it opened in November of 1905, played two full years on Broadway for a total of 686 performances, then traversed the country with six different casts, often playing simultaneously.

In *The Lion and the Mouse* Dorothy was cast as Shirley Rossmore, whose father, a supreme court justice, is threatened with financial ruin and professional disgrace by the capitalist John Ryder. Hoping to thwart his plans for unseating the judge, Rossmore insinuates herself into the Ryder household as "Miss Green," author of Ryder's biography. The family's son, Jefferson Ryder, falls in love with the young woman, who initially refuses to marry him. Dramatic confrontations with her future father-in-law ensue, but the plays ends happily. Company C's first opening on the road, attended by Klein and his wife, took place in Baltimore, her "good-luck city" Dorothy called it, for it was there that Harris had "discovered" her. Another of her "good luck" charms, incidentally, was a favorite pocketbook, carried so often it became tattered and shredded into ribbons, but she couldn't bear to part with it and repeatedly took it to a shoemaker to have it stitched.[51]

"To differentiate my various roles is a delight to me," Dorothy once said.[52] Restricting their variety, however, seemed to her the surer and quicker road to rapidly growing popularity. Just at the time when it appeared that she had found her niche as a dramatic performer in some of the most progressive plays in this formative period of American theatre, she flirted briefly with comic parts, all too frequently in insignificant plays. Through trial and an occasional error, par for any actress' course, she discovered a better fit—emotional roles in melodramas. "When you are liked," she said, "you take your hearers up and do your best work."[53]

CHAPTER 5
On the Road

Touring had became a necessary part of Dorothy's career as early as 1904, beginning with *Candida* and *The Man of Destiny*. "I like to have a place of my own, where I can feel perfectly at home,"[1] she said, but her calling card likely read, "have part, will travel." She performed in Baltimore, Rochester, Buffalo, Philadelphia, Toledo, St. Louis, Columbus, Chicago, Spokane, San Francisco, Los Angeles—all the major cities and countless in between.

From her perspective, road shows were ledgers whose liabilities tended to outweigh their assets. For one, they set a relentless pace. Sometimes the train would pull into town about six in the evening, disgorging the troupe just a couple of hours before the opening curtain. As soon as each act ended, the stage crew loaded the sets and sped them across town to the railroad platform. When the applause ceased, the company would race back to the station and board again. The cast often played one-night stands, especially in small towns, where they slept in shabby hotels, performed in unfamiliar theaters, and survived on unpalatable food (unless, like Fanny Brice, they chose to prepare their own meals on a 25 cent alcohol stove).[2] Park City, Utah, for instance, boasted only two hotels with accommodations so miserable that Dorothy opted to stay in a rooming house instead. That night, as she tossed back the coverlet, she noticed the absence of bed linens and spoke to the landlady. "You're going to put some sheets on this bed, are you not?" she asked. "My, do you want sheets?" came the reply. "I never use any because all the miners that have ever slept in that bed prefer to sleep in blankets."[3] Sometimes even dingy theatres were unavailable. In 1908, when the Shubert brothers sponsored another of Sarah Bernhardt's habit-forming "farewell tours," they encountered fierce opposition from the Theatrical Trust. Finding the doors to legitimate theatres barred to them, the Shuberts scheduled her appearances in skating rinks throughout the South, then in a circus tent in Kansas and

Texas.[4] The pace was no less brutal in large cities. The bill for *The Lion and the Mouse* at the Chicago Opera House, for instance, advertised daily evening performances, and matinees on Wednesday, Saturday, and Sunday. "Don't you think it is dreary to live at hotels for any length of time?" asked Dorothy rhetorically.[5]

Traveling was also dirty, tiring, and worrisome. Soot settled everywhere—on faces, clothes, and luggage. Squeezed into tiny cubicles, hunched over cracked basins, the players washed it off as best they could in cold water. The clackety-clack of metal wheels jostling along iron rails often kept them awake rather than lulling them to sleep. Whenever they did doze off, the forlorn whistle of the locomotive invariably punctuated their dreams. Very early one morning, a porter sauntered past while the exhausted cast lay sprawled among their baggage stacked haphazardly on the platform—many asleep, some yawning, Dorothy rubbing her eyes open. The bewilderment on his face demanded an explanation: "Those are the 'Sins of Society'—don't they look it?" acknowledged Joseph Brooks, the company's manager. The porter nodded, "They sure does, boss."[6] Any late arrival created unduly long hours. Case in point: when the train finally pulled into San Francisco late on February 3, 1906, the curtain rose, not fell, at 9:30 for the evening performance of *The Lion and the Mouse*. Dorothy may well have forgotten the delay while basking in the glow of Colgate Baker's review that appeared in next morning's *San Francisco Chronicle*. The critic had seen an earlier production of the play at the Old Columbia Theatre in San Francisco; this one opened at the Van Ness Theatre, recently rebuilt following the devastating earthquake of April 1906 and the ensuing fires that flattened most of the city. Baker lavished praise on the timeliness and political authenticity of *The Lion and the Mouse* and of the cast assembled by Henry B. Harris:

> Surely the immense popularity of this clever comedy, which flays the great money kings who have acquired their wealth by illegal means with a merciless hand, is a sign of the times. Last night every time that Shirley Rossmore scored in her battle with John Ryder, who may be easily identified with John D. Rockefeller, the audience was thrilled. It is a remarkable scene, this duel of wits between a wonder girl and such an intellectual giant as the American Croesus.... It is a scene of such power and scope that even if it were indifferently acted, it would still hold the audience in its spell. Last night it was superbly played. In my judgment it was better acted than it was even in the original production, and it carried the performance to distinctive success.
>
> Dorothy Donnelly, whom I have always considered one of the most brilliant of our modern-day actresses, makes an ideal Shirley Rossmore.

Left: *Vigilant of her appearance in front of the public and the press, Dorothy Donnelly sports the latest hairdo, fashionable in 1906. (Courtesy Philip Fahringer Collection.)* Right: *"Earnest gray eyes with occasional, unexpected gleams of roguishness, curling dark brown hair flecked with hints of bronze—that is Dorothy Donnelly,"* reports Theatre Magazine, *one of the numerous publications that regularly published pictures of the photogenic actress. (Courtesy Philip Fahringer Collection.)*

> She gives the role the same keen study that made her Candida such a satisfying performance. She is the mistress of every situation and realizes the full acting value of every line. Miss Donnelly is always distinguished for her excellent technique, and last night, in the matter of mere mechanics, her acting was also faultless.[7]

Timetables played havoc with the scheduling of shows, and weather with timetables. The heavy snowfalls of winter sometimes buried the tracks, making passage impossible. During the torrential rains of spring, railroad bridges faced the threat of collapse, as the roiling waters of swollen rivers mercilessly battered their supports. While making her first United States tour, "Sarah Bernhardt came near to being lost to the world and the rest of her company along with her" somewhere outside New Orleans by the Bay Saint Louis, or while crossing the Ohio River, or in yet another altogether different state, for the French troupe placed little premium on their knowledge of American geography. "As the 'Sarah Bernhardt Special' was going along at its customary clip," continues Cornelia Otis Skinner, "the brakes suddenly went on and the train came to a full stop at a small station located near a river which was overflowing its banks." Edward Jarrett, the company's manager, with the help of 2,500 dollars in gold coins contributed by Bernhardt, persuaded the train's engineer "to try for a dash across the weakened bridge."[8] In the interest of safety, delays were unavoidable.

Long hours and delays were an inconvenience, but the danger that lurked round the next bend was a frightening possibility. While Minnie Maddern Fiske and her company were en route from Salt Lake City to Los Angeles, touring with *Mis' Nelly of New Orleans*, the train struck an open switch. The impact threw the locomotive and four cars off the rails. "The car in which Mrs. Fiske and her principal players were riding was not overthrown, but all the persons in it were thrown out of their seats, and it finally came to a stop with a terrific jolt."[9] Railroads could not eliminate entirely the hazards of potential derailments and collisions. Sam Shubert, for instance, died on May 12, 1905, of injuries sustained during a fiery wreck on the Pennsylvania Railroad. He was traveling with his attorney, William Klein, to Pittsburgh "to close the lease on the Duquesne Theatre," when their passenger train crashed into a freight train just outside Harrisburg, Pennsylvania.[10] His sudden death at age 28 shocked everyone, including Dorothy, who promptly wired condolences to the family.

Touring kept performers exposed like goldfish in a bowl, first and foremost with advance notices and reviews, then with innocuous tidbits of gossip. Columnists flaunted their every observation. Dorothy was spending all her salary on furs this winter, including a full-length black coat and a muff "quite large enough to house seven kittens and a squirrel or two, boas, tippets galore."[11] She frolicked with Richard Harding Davis and his wife, Cecil, in parodies of his plays; sported a hairdo in the latest fashion—a Pysche knot fastened at the nape with a wide barrette; met interviewers with a "hearty handclasp;" displayed "spinal spasms when a street piano struck up Mendelssohn's 'Spring Song' the other day"[12]; and ran "financial risks on the relative speeds of equines at the Belmont track."[13] Columnists also noted that she spoke French to her maid—an important piece of information since, at that time, "having a maid was more than just a luxury and comfort; it was a symbol of stardom."[14]

Even the most trivial incidents found their way into print as actors themselves helped the press fuel the public's appetite for titillation and their own need for publicity. Thus, Dorothy mentioned one occasion when a woman seated in front of her at a theatre repeatedly turned back to stare. No longer able to restrain herself, she finally blurted, "I beg your pardon, but you look so much like Dorothy Donnelly." Dorothy kept a straight face and solemnly responded that she'd been told that before.[15] While attending yet another play, Dorothy found herself seated behind her fellow cast member, Elsa Payne. During the first act she noticed that the man and woman sitting to the left of Elsa never exchanged a word. Thinking that she might swap seats with him at intermission, Dorothy leaned forward and tapped him on the shoulder. "Are you married?" she asked. "Get wise, get wise," he whispered in reply: "My wife's with me."[16] Such innocuous "human interest" items, freely reprinted—only slightly changed—in other newspapers, increased Dorothy's marketability as an actress in demand.

Racing to fill column inches, sometimes the press placed small premium on accuracy and analysis. The *Los Angeles Times* critic, for example, praised Dorothy's "thorough perception of the trying role" in *The Lion and the Mouse* and "her charming sense of adroit use of technic"— whatever that means—but he variously misspelled her name "Donnell" and "Donneli" and closed his review with a delicious logical fallacy: "That she is an artist is proved further by the fact that she is a strong personal friend of Bernard Shaw, a man who bothers with no one who is not worth while."[17] Often their predictions of her forthcoming roles proved wrong. If reporters did not know the identity of her companion, they tried to guess. If she inadvertently called attention to herself, they rarely failed to notice. To give an example, when she attended *Minstrel* and its star, Lew Dockstader, invited the audience to join him in a reprise of the chorus, Dorothy tittered, unwittingly interrupting the performance and forcing the vaudevillian to ask for an end to the giggling. The only report they failed to mention was the alleged loss of her jewelry, a sometime, most always erroneous, ploy to call additional attention to a celebrity.

While road shows kept performers in the public eye, they did little to enhance their social status. On the contrary, they reinforced the perception of actors as vagabonds. (The stigma attached to the theatre persisted for centuries—as late as 1910 rooming houses in Los Angeles bore signs reading, "Rooms for rent—No dogs or actors allowed," but its history is too long to retell in all its fascinating detail.) To counter this perception, when Daniel Frohman assumed the presidency of the Actor's Fund of America, a position he held from 1904 to 1940, he recruited the support of people prominent in the political, social, and business world to lend an aura of respectability to the profession. From May 6 through May 14, 1907, Actor's Fund held a fair to augment its endowment, and Dorothy spent the week selling souvenirs at the Metropolitan Opera House. The Fund also contributed $125,000 to the victims of the San Francisco earthquake, thereby creating a continuing tradition of championing worthy causes.

Frequently, touring companies raised eyebrows and questions of impropriety. "The public thinks that what may be termed the 'huddled living,' the close quarters of players behind the scenes, makes for a peril to the actress," reported Lillian Russell. She dispelled this and other myths:

> Again in this, as in all errors, there is a semblance of truth, but over against this is the truth that there is "safety in numbers." … It is [also] the rule that the actress does not admire—often she does not respect— the man of her own profession. It is another general impression that the love scenes played on the stage are an index of what happens between the players off the stage. That is by no means true. Under the spell of acting, in a love scene, the pair, while playing, may actually feel the scene, but when the curtain drops with a thump and they have gone to their dressing rooms the spell vanishes with the slam of the dressing room door.[18]

In England, "drawing-room doors are open wide to actors, and many of the stars build the foundation of their popularity upon cups of afternoon tea," wrote Louise Closser Hale.[19] By contrast, in America the Puritan tradition of considering actors as lower class citizens or libertines endures. Speculation regarding the sexual lives of actors and actresses and "the illusion of promiscuity have been inseparable since theatre began," write Stuart Little and Arthur Cantor in *The Playmakers*, a book touted as an "insider's view" of Broadway producers. Their penultimate chapter, "The Sexual Ethic," deliberately fuels, rather than dampens, such speculation and illusion. In it the authors mention by name New York psychiatrists but quote more liberally from unidentified sources to bolster their arguments that among actors proximity and opportunity inevitably lead to casual sexual encounters and that homosexuality runs rampant among male dancers.[20]

Road shows imposed additional social costs—the more personal ones. Dorothy caused quite a stir, for example, by remaining an extra day in Chicago to see her brother Henry open in *The Dream Waltz* while the rest of the cast of *The Lion and the Mouse* moved on to Springfield for its next scheduled performance. Road shows curtailed her leisurely meals with friends that "grew from a simple dish on narrow strips of toweling to great feasts on wide strips of lace," as Louise Hale described them. They confined visits with family and friends to the theatre's off-season, to summer months when she would sail to Europe for a few weeks of vacation, occasionally bringing along a niece, as she did in 1908 to commemorate Sara McCall's eighteenth birthday.[21] Or they limited visits to revivals.

Following a lengthy road tour, *The Lion and the Mouse* reopened at the Grand Opera House in New York City, and Dorothy seized this rare opportunity to invite her sister and youngest niece to a matinee performance and to dinner with the family afterwards at the Waldorf-Astoria. After the grown-ups had placed their orders, Nora asked her six-year-old daughter what she would like. Dolly piped up: "If you all are going to eat all that, I guess I'd better not have anything. I don't want to make Aunt Dorothy awful poor."[22] Nora's daughters, incidentally, each attended the Sacred Heart Academy in Kenwood, near Albany, within visiting distance of their grandmother McCall, but even farther from their doting aunt.

Constant traveling, furthermore, obliged the cast members to socialize mainly among themselves. Consequently, Dorothy acquired an intimate though not necessarily happy view of leading men:

> I don't think I would fall in love with an actor unless he was among the "great" big ones. There is something repugnant to me about the attention that an actor gives to his personal appearance. His make-up, the constantly thinking about how he looks and acts, and what everybody thinks of him—well, it makes him less masculine. It *seems* all right in a woman to do those things, but if I should marry I think I would want to marry a business man, and if I did I should expect to leave the stage and stay with him.[23] [Emphasis added.]

Whenever popular actresses met someone new, they had to wonder if they were being collected like trinkets on a social charm bracelet, valued more for the prestige of their names than for themselves. In any case, they rarely met business men. "I don't expect to marry," Dorothy concluded:

> I think a woman wants to be with her husband and I don't think successful marriage is possible with separation. I don't think anybody can buck up against an absence, no matter how charming and beautiful they are. Nature abhors a vacuum, you know—there, that is a horrible trite thing to say, but she does, and you can apply it to marriage.... What is the use of being married if you cannot be together? It is better for the woman, *or one of them*, to give up the profession when marriage comes.[24] [Emphasis added.]

These comments on masculinity and marriage reveal Dorothy's growing struggles to develop her own values—to reject stereotypical perceptions of gender behavior and conventional expectations of roles for men and women, and to insist upon equality between the sexes. She readily accepted Madge Kendal's pronouncement regarding the difficulties of merging the roles of wife and actress, a warning reinforced by her Catholic upbringing. However, Dorothy resisted the notion that woman's work was merely a temporary stopgap between school and marriage and that it was the woman's exclusive duty to stay at home and raise children the moment she began sporting a wedding ring. Moreover, despite the rigors of constant travel demanded by her career, Dorothy was not ready to relinquish it for marriage; she continued to relish both her independence and the limelight.

This independence exacted financial costs. Although producers might pay for the most elaborate gowns, performers generally bought their own make-up, costumes, and accessories. Thoughtfully chosen and well executed, costumes conveyed considerable visual information to the audience about a character's personality, profession, and social standing even before the actor delivered his opening line. To an actor, they constituted an additional expense. Consequently, some fifty years earlier, "Nobody was shocked," writes historian Lloyd Morris, when W. J. Florence purchased the theatrical wardrobe from the estate of a deceased predecessor, actor William Evans Burton, and wore the very same costumes in identical roles.[25] For their parts in *The Sins of Society*, for example, Dorothy needed eleven evening dresses and nine pairs of shoes; Louise Closser Hale, nine outfits and six different pairs of gloves. Louise lugged along so many hats that they scarcely fit into the dressing room. She resorted to stashing them in drawers marked "flour" and "sugar" in a small kitchen cabinet that stood in the corner of the room. Fortunately, she did not have to pack any wigs, for her hair by now was silvery white, "intensely becoming to her"[26] and befitting her role in the play. "On a hot matinee day," wrote an interviewer, "it might strike you that changing one's gown twenty times in the course of an afternoon and evening—shoes, stockings, gloves and sometimes underclothing—is not particularly conducive to the joy of living."[27] Three dressers, crowding into an already crammed room to help the costars with the costume changes between scenes, added to the swelter. Dorothy, eager for her next call, ignored the conditions. "I always know as soon as I go on, just what the feminine verdict is concerning my gowns, because there is a little murmur all over the house, and a swish-swish of voices, in case they approve," she said. "It always reminds me of the sea-shore, when waves are washing gently onto the beach—it is very much the same, and a very soothing sound in either case."[28] The outlay for clothing was not limited to costumes, however. Performers also had to maintain a second wardrobe, a personal one, suitable for appearing successful before the public or for business meetings with managers and producers. They also had to impress the press. At one interview, for instance, Dorothy wore a kimono of the palest green over a dainty mass of white muslin skirts. At another, she entered "wearing a gown which a bachelor would describe as all white and fluffy."[29] She knew that reporters liked devoting at least a few words to describe her dress—"quietly elegant," most interviewers noted—to lend their articles a setting. So she obliged them.

Road shows filled the coffers of theatre owners, who moved their "hits" from Broadway to one of their own houses in other cities, scheduling them north to south or east to west, in as straight a route as possible to minimize travel and thus curb costs. By contrast, they drained the pockets of performers. Since the regular drama season was only 28 weeks long, actors had to exercise fiscal wizardry to make their salaries last a full year. Salaries were small—as little as $10 a week for walk-ons during 1908[30]—but expenses loomed large. When producers insisted on Pullman sleepers so that the cast would arrive well rested for their next performance, the actors picked up the tab. Like Dorothy, who had an apartment of her own by now in lower Manhattan, other members of the troupe had to retain a permanent residence in New York City, thereby incurring an additional expense: rent. Finally, the future of their personal finances always remained uncertain. Actors could be fired at a whim, even during rehearsals, and a play might fold at any time, leaving them stranded with neither salary nor severance pay unless the producers had obtained adequate fiscal backing.

Other factors contributed to the monetary instability of the profession. As the 1908-1909 drama season opened, the United States had not yet recovered from the financial panic that had struck a year earlier, and the country sweltered during an usually hot spell. Even well-known actresses like Julia Marlowe and Annie Russell were out of work. Moreover, not many producers could afford the weekly sum of 250 dollars that major stars commanded for each show.[31] In their search for parts, stage actors faced a new, formidable rival—the cinema. After the first motion picture house opened in 1905, in McKeesport, a suburb of Pittsburgh, Pennsylvania, eager entrepreneurs began filling empty storefronts with wooden chairs and benches, some borrowed from catering services and mortuaries, and offering 12 to 18 short films a day.[32] By 1908, there were some 8,000 nickelodeons that attracted a daily audience of two million people, one-third of them children.

This lean season offered Dorothy only a single role—the lead in *The Sins of Society*, a British play by Cecil Raleigh and Henry Hamilton. Cast as Lady Beaumont, she played the part of a smart young widow with a passion for playing bridge and an addiction to gambling. When her debts and those of her sister mount up, Lady Goldbury, acted by Louise Closser Hale, lends her a diamond tiara, suggesting that she take it to a pawn-broker. Lady Beaumont promptly substitutes lumps of coal for the head-piece, hands over the box to her unsuspecting victim, accepts his check for 7,000 pounds sterling, and immediately squanders it in bets. Subse-quently, she drugs the hapless pawnbroker and steals the box before he can uncover her duplicity.

The Sins of Society opened for a trial run at the McVicker Theatre in Chicago, described by Walter Eaton as a harrowing ordeal: "In America the New York (and of late years in Chicago) verdict on a play, almost invariably means its success or failure, and an opening in either of those cities is a nervous strain of the first magnitude, for seldom enough is the first night verdict reversed."[33] Two circumstances eased the strain for Dorothy and Louise: the pleasure of sharing a suite of rooms at the Virginia Hotel and the recent release of Louise's new novel. *The Actress* ran as a serial in *Ladies' Home Journal* before being published in book form by Harper's in 1909. Louise was in England, playing in *Mrs. Wiggs of the Cabbage Patch*, when she began writing the story. To create its main character, she freely borrowed many of Dorothy's convictions. She chose the first person point of view, thereby allowing the unnamed actress to express her thoughts and feelings directly without restriction.

When the book opens, she has fallen in love with a financier. "Next to my art, there is nothing in the world so attractive as a perfectly clean, perfectly sound New York business man in a dinner-coat," she says, shar-ing Dorothy's expressed penchant for businessmen.[34] She compares her career to those of stockbrokers, who have nothing to lose but their money when they make an investment:

> They do not have to stand for three hours before a body of men and women to be judged critically of their appearance, their manner of deliv-ery, their personal appeal, and their ability to act—according to each auditor's standard—nor do they have to realize, as the actors do when they go through this ordeal, that their bread-and-butter depends upon the passing of these tests. And yet, like the financier who scents a con-test, we derive a certain fearful joy in this strain that is put upon us. We do not know it at the time, ... but ... any kind of keen emotion, even a miserable one, is a pleasurable sensation to the actor.[35]

It was the risks offered by the theatre that consistently enthralled Dorothy. "I like the work—I like the game outside of the art of it," she said.[36]

Louise's actress, like Dorothy, values her career for the personal freedom it provides ("In our capacity as actors we are allowed liberties that the young unmarried men and women of the upper class are not."[37]) and the financial independence it affords:

> When I go out with a member of the company I expect to pay my share. Every actress feels as I do; that's one of the joys of being an actress. Why, if we allowed the men in the company to buy our late suppers, for instance, we wouldn't be able to go out with them when we wanted to, but have to hang about looking hungry, and wait for an invitation just like those poor, dependent females who don't work for a living.[38]

The actress conveys the very claim Dorothy made when insisting, "I couldn't allow anyone to support me."[39]

Above all, Hale's actress thrills to the exhilaration of acting. The conclusion of an evening performance might find her tired, "but I was not ready for bed," she says: "That would end this lovely time of kindliness, of rapturous ease, of chaffing among my comrades, to lie between cold sheets and, with this new fear of critics overcoming sleep, toss about until the roll of morning papers I had ordered the night before clumped at my door."[40] Saying "I was born to the stage, and I did not intend to leave it,"[41] she readily rejects a proposal of marriage: "My dear work, with all its misery but all its joy. To think a man could ask a woman to give it up for him—for *him!* And to get what in exchange? A place behind his coffee-urn, a house to play in through the day, and through the night—"[42] She wants nothing more than "to be left alone, to always have a fair part in an agreeable company, and a dressing-room near enough to the others to borrow rouge and exchange gossip."[43] Most of the action and "argument" take place in London, during a road tour, giving the actress distance and time to review her position. A sudden fainting spell in the middle of a performance prompts her further reconsideration. She marries, abandons her career, and presumably lives happily ever after. The fainting spell provided the deus ex machina Louise relied on to make the book a romance and to eliminate the need for explaining why a woman would replace such a satisfying career with marriage.

If road shows dished out hardships, they also served platters of advantages, especially constant publicity, waiting audiences, and more or less steady employment for the better known performers. Some actresses actually liked them—Eleonora Duse, Maude Adams, Minnie Maddern Fiske, and Sarah Bernhardt, who rode in her private "'Palace Car,' the *dernier cri*, the *ne plus ultra* in travel luxury"[44]—to cite a few. Like Hale's actress, they believed that "it only takes a half a dozen photographs on the mantel-piece, a special one on the dresser, and the trunks unpacked to the bottom to be at home."[45]

To be sure, Dorothy had some lighthearted moments on the road. She enjoyed shopping and delighted in buying prints and native textiles for friends and family. In Chicago, she gladly accepted an invitation to dine with her colleague, Mabel Dixey, appearing as one of the stars in *Texas.* "But Dorothy Donnelly was a born Manhattanite," said Alexander Woollcott, "hungry for home, sick with a nostalgia for a house where her pictures, her piano, her books, her capacious old chairs would be around her all the day and her friends could come in for dinner and talk around the fire until the edge of midnight."[46] Dorothy admitted, "I envy the artistic or literary woman who can carry out her plans surrounded by her pictures and her books. My volumes, my china, my drawings, are all in my apartments in New York and I can only see them a few weeks in the year. We who play and travel miss so much."[47] When a starry-eyed girl, bedazzled by the glamour of the stage, sought her advice, a verbal reply was superfluous, or so thought Alan Dale. "Ask Miss Donnelly for advice," he said, neatly summarizing Dorothy's experiences with road companies, "she can give it from the sweat of her brow."[48] Yet, Dorothy did respond. "Unless you have the beauty of Venus, the hide of a rhinoceros, the constitution of a horse, the diplomacy of a Machiavelli, and unbounded influence and impudence," she said, freely paraphrasing Madge Kendal, "put out of your mind the thought of adopting the already miserably overcrowded stage as a career."[49]

While Dorothy's first decade on the stage ended uneventfully, it imparted important lessons. She had cut her milk teeth on French melodramas, sampled the wares of European dramatists, but feasted on native playwrights: "Why should it be necessary to look for plays on the other side, when Americans are capable of producing equally good ones, I cannot see."[50] She also toughened her hide. By applying the soothing lotion of favorable reviews, she could withstand such blistering blows as Adolphe Klauber's write-up of *The Movers,* when the critic accused her of having been "overpraised for her acting which thus far lacks the firm touch of complete self-possession" and of possessing "the means of excellent mimetic expression without their full command." More significant, these ten years reconfirmed her belief that acting was not a natural talent, but an art to be mastered. They convinced her that the part she played ought not be full of herself; rather, she should be full of her part.

Although Dorothy would be the first to admit that versatility greatly enhanced her skills, she found it a hindrance to rapid advancement. At the very moment of escaping the stultifying limitations of typecasting, she embraced it. By forsaking the intellectual heroines of contemporary European dramatists and confining herself to the emotional roles of

American playwrights, Dorothy was a product of her period. By her performances, however, she was clearly ahead of her time. Before the theories of Freud became blueprints for American drama, Dorothy showed a rare aptitude for psychological analyses of both characters and audiences. Her performances revealed an increasing ability to stress the subtext beneath the dialogue and move not from speech to speech, but through an entire experience. Nor did she wait for relaxation, concentration, imagination, and perfection to become buzz words before applying them. A few minutes at the keyboard, for example, enabled her to focus on the coming performance and stretched her ability to repeat a role again and again, convincing the audience that each performance was the first. Although there was talk of Harris' starring her in Arthur Wing Pinero's *The Second Mrs. Tanqueray*, Charles Klein's *The Third Degree*, and Martha Morton's *On the Eve*, the five-year contract had expired. Now, at age 29, in her prime, she faced the future with confidence. "The tide is at the flood for every player at least once," announced the *New York Review* on August 29, 1909. "Dorothy Donnelly will have her big chance soon."

CHAPTER 6

The Limelight

T he novelist and essayist E. M. Forster once remarked that "failure or success seem to have been allotted to men by their stars. But they retain the power of wriggling, of fighting with their star or against it, and in the whole universe the only really interesting movement is this wriggle."[1] During the next ten years of her life, the stars allotted Dorothy one major triumph, a few minor successes, and some dismal failures. Her "wriggling" continues to fascinate. She assiduously prepared for the limelight, persevered in her career as an actress when it began to fade, and eventually sought new and different ways to achieve it once again.

In May of 1909, after a six-month trip abroad, Henry Wilson Savage sailed home on the *Auguste Victoire* with a copy of a new French play tucked in his trunk and proudly announced, "*Madame X* is Bisson's first serious work, and I have arranged to have the leading role played by one of our most talented emotional actresses."[2] He meant Margaret Anglin. A graduate of Charles Frohman's Empire Dramatic School, Anglin had created Roxanne in the American premiere of *Cyrano de Bergerac*, toured for one season with Henry Donnelly in *The Eternal Feminine*, and costarred with Henry Miller in William Vaughn Moody's *The Great Divide*. Reviewers admired her keen intelligence, delicate sensibility, and sure instinct. Anglin, they said, "could wring emotion from a keg of nails."[3]

When Anglin declined the stellar part, the names of many leading actresses were proposed to Savage. These included Ethel Barrymore, Chrystal Herne (Dorothy's successor as Candida in the 1905 production of Shaw's play), and Laurette Taylor. Yet, in a burst of inspiration he could never regret, the producer cast Dorothy in the role of Jacqueline.

"I got the script in June," Dorothy remarked, "and read it to my family. We all wept."[4] The play was an unabashed tear-jerker. In the first act, restless and bored with her very busy and highly proper husband, Louis Floriot (played, incidentally, by Robert Drouet, who also began his acting career in the Murray Hill Theatre Company), Jacqueline abandons him and their infant son to join her lover. When the child becomes ill, she returns to visit him, but her husband denies her permission to see the boy, having convinced the son that his mother has died. Jacqueline begs Floriot to forgive her, but he cold-heartedly refuses. The second act opens twenty years later, with Jacqueline old and despondent, the model of years of addiction to absinthe and ether. Her current lover is a ne'er do well adventurer named Laroque (Malcolm Williams), who delves into her past and discovers that Jacqueline has bequeathed to her son money held in her own name. His unscrupulous friend encourages him to persuade Jacqueline to ask for the return of her dowry. They scatter hints of blackmail. Driven by worries regarding the boy's possible disinheritance, she kills Laroque. The final act takes place in a courtroom. Since Jacqueline refuses to talk following her arrest, even to the point of not revealing her name, she becomes publicly known as "Madame X." She is looking for peace of mind, expecting—and hoping—that she will be executed as a criminal. Raymond (William Elliot), the twenty-four year old lawyer appointed to defend her, however, grows increasingly convinced that someone else bears ultimate responsibility for Laroque's death. Through an impassioned speech he brilliantly obtains her acquittal. Meanwhile, Jacqueline's husband attends the trial. As president of the court, he has been invited to sit on the bench along side the presiding judge. Realizing who she is, he finally reveals Madame X's identity to the lawyer, who rushes to his mother's side. Overcome by shock, she collapses and dies as Raymond poignantly wails "too late, too late."

Madame X, noted Alan Dale, "was delightfully simple and deliciously improbable." Dorothy was equally mesmerized. "It takes hold of the spectator and forces his admiration and interest, in spite of certain rather melodramatic passages and typically French costumes and surroundings," she said. "The appeal it makes is such a strong human one, the eternal theme of mother love, and the play is so well constructed around this theme, that it becomes one of unusual power."[5]

The role of Jacqueline was also unusually demanding. Chaste, sexually inexperienced, and drug-free, Dorothy had to portray a realistic picture of a libertine—her diametrical opposite in both temperament and behavior. She had to make the sins contemptible, the sinner sympathetic and worthy of salvation. Moreover, she needed to show the extent of Jacqueline's dissipation and, simultaneously, the noble qualities of the woman whose love for her child prompts her action, at once both sublime and despicable. With remarkable insight, Dorothy noted:

> The chief characteristic of women like Madame X is their absolute indifference to what is happening around them. They seem dead to every influence but that of the drug. This is shown very clearly in the hotel scene of the play. Merely acting that scene brings out all the phases a drug fiend passes through. Dull, stupid at first, she awakens gradually as the drug begins to take effect. She sees everything in the worst light; she is sad and feels miserable, but as she drinks more freely the bad humor wears off, while reminiscences begin to crop up. Gradually roused to violence, she finally bursts into a paroxysm of passion, in which she kills her lover. The horror of her deed brings about a sudden realization of what she has done, and when the curtain goes down she is perfectly sober. Just in such a way do the symptoms follow one another in real life.[6]

"Yes, I suppose that one must have seen such characters to understand them," said Dorothy.[7] To prepare the role, she sailed for France in July aboard the "St. Louis." En route she stopped briefly in England, at their invitation, to visit the Shaws at their country home in Sussex. This was primarily a working vacation, however, since Savage had arranged for Dorothy to visit Salpetriere, an institution for female addicts in Paris. "It was very interesting and awful at the same time," she recalled, giving a graphic description of her keen observations:

> We came first to the Pavillion Charcot, I think it was, where a long row of people were waiting to be examined. Merely remnants of human beings some of them seemed to be. Some old, some young, all weak and tottering. It positively pained my eyes to look at them. Yet even vanity had its place here, and their ideas of their own importance were pitifully amusing. They discussed their symptoms with such animation! "Oh, I have such a pain in my head," one old woman would say, drawing her arm over her forehead, while another would rub her knees and tell how it hurt her to take just one step. Oh, they were proud of their suffering, and each one was persuaded that her case was the most serious of the lot, and that thought kept up her spirits.[8]

She used her fluent French to speak with them: "But I gained practically nothing. Their indifference, their torpor, made them act like creatures without will power or intelligence.... They seemed unable to grasp my meaning, and they made no effort to understand what I said."[9] While Dorothy may have culled little from her conversations with the patients during her four visits to the hospital, she paid meticulous attention to their every gesture, every posture, every movement.

Her imagination and intellectual curiosity still not yet satisfied, Dorothy loitered in Montmartre and at night clubs like the Moulin Rouge, Maxim's, and the Follies Bergere—any place social outcasts might frequent. She translated an old, dull French medical treatise entitled "The Ether Subject" and studied it. Next, she journeyed to Vienna and Berlin to confirm her observations of addictive behavior. "My most amusing experience," she reported, "was with a German specialist with a name almost impossible to pronounce and a long black beard falling to the waist."[10] She simulated all the symptoms of an addict so convincingly that the doctor pronounced her case hopeful and prescribed treatment. Only then did Dorothy confess to her deception. "You should have seen his disgust—and heard him."[11]

She returned to New York in August, (just in time for the New York City opening of *The Sins of Society* with Laura Nelson Hall as her replacement in the lead). Since she knew that most addicts die of heart failure, she rehearsed the death scene with a physician until she had mastered the shallowness of breath and the peculiar death rattle characteristic of heart stoppage. Because Dorothy did not smoke at the time, she trained herself to handle cigarettes:

> You can't imagine all the trouble I've had to master certain tricks that I must do with my cigarette. Have you noticed when speaking to tobacco fiends that one never seems to see them smoke?.... Well, Mme. X was a woman who smoked incessantly, and her smoking ought not be remarked.[12]

Even after two months of practice, however, she never "got quite the knack of the inveterate smoker."[13]

Mindful that the addict retains her vanity, masks her age, and uses clothing to call notice to herself, Dorothy took pains with her costumes. She ordered copies of those worn by the French actress Jane Hading, who created the role of Jacqueline in the Paris premiere, but shopped locally for others. She had a wig made, "and we keep it so unkempt looking by giving it no attention at all." She bought a bright red ribbon and wore it high around her neck as if to hide those ropes of skin older women eventually develop beneath the chin. She found a non-descript hat at the end of the season in a Sixth Avenue shop for thirty-one cents and added some cheap red roses to match the neckband. "I did this to carry out the note of red, and again to be consistent in trying to attract attention." On Division Street she purchased an old calico sack and a skirt. Her shoes were worn and bursting at the seams:

> They are the shoes I wore in *Candida*. Being Irish makes me superstitious, I suppose. I felt that having worn them in one success, I should like to wear them in another. Besides it would have been hard to find more disreputable ones anywhere.[14]

Dorothy made one additional concession to superstition: during every rehearsal and on all first nights, she wore a gold bracelet, now battered and thin,—a souvenir from her childhood.[15]

Madame X premiered at the Globe Theatre in London on September 1, 1909, with Lena Ashwell in the title role, and on the thirteenth in Rochester, New York. Dorothy received glowing reviews: "Miss Donnelly has never done anything that approaches her work as Madame X," reported the *Rochester Democrat*: "She plays the repentant wife with marked strength, but it is as the drug stupefied woman whose heart is full of mother love that she excels."[16] Henry Savage and George Marion, the producer and director who were in the audience, could only smirk like Lewis Carroll's Cheshire cat and nod approvingly after reading the *Rochester Post Express*:

> In the hands of a playwright less continent [sic] than M. Bisson—in those of the author of 'La Tosca,' for instance—the trial scene in 'Madame X' would have been unendurable. But Bisson is never hysterical and the actress who played Jacqueline, Miss Dorothy Donnelly, bore in mind the counsel of Hamlet and kept the empire over herself in the torrent of passion.[17]

The play next moved to Toronto, then began its formal tryout in Chicago, on September 9, 1909, where at first it received a cool reception from playgoers. This was a typical response, explains Arthur Hornblow, editor of *Theatre Magazine*:

> Many plays have become great successes in other cities after a brief and very uncertain tryout in Chicago…. The truth is that the theatregoing public in Chicago, as elsewhere, avoids a play until it is known to be really successful. There is only a very small coterie of real first nighters in Chicago who go to everything, irrespective of results. The remainder wait cautiously, are suspicious of every new play and are inclined to resent the fact that Chicago is used as a tryout town.[18]

Some of the local reviewers panned the acting and expressed a preference for Margaret Anglin or even Helen Ware in the lead. *Madame X* also came under attack on artistic grounds, thereby infuriating drama critic Alan Dale. "This play, I am told, was a tremendous success in Paris," he wrote; "Yet, when it opened in Chicago, the critics of that city went for it, tooth and nail—at least they set it down as mere melodrama, which was meant as a squelcher."[19] *Tips and Tales*, Henry Savage's trade magazine, naturally defended the play and praised the lead:

PHOTOGRAPH BY MOFFETT STUDIO, CHICAGO.

Dorothy Donnelly poses for a 1909 studio portrait during the trial run in Chicago of Madame X.

Dorothy Donnelly creates the title role in Madame X *in 1909. Insert shows fortune-telling card scene from Act II of the play.*

If it be theatricism to lay bare the human soul, to show how even the gravest sin may find expiation here on earth—then let there be more "theatricism" but less cynicism. If it be melodrama to prove anew the wondrous quality or that greatest of all human powers, mother love—then let there be more melodrama and less dramatic dishwater. If it be sensationalism to picture the terrible consequence of wrong-doing, then let there be more "sensationalism" and less gliding [*sic*] of evil.... To Dorothy Donnelly ... falls the main burden. From the opening scene where the young wife returns to beg forgiveness for her transgression and is driven forth, to the ultimate moment, when she dies with the first smile of happiness she had had on her lips in a score of years, this talented actress held her audience, so to speak, in the palm of her hand. All the gamut of emotions is hers and she plays upon the hearts of her spectators with a delicacy and reserve, but also power and authority, that stamps her as one of the very first emotional actresses of her time.[20]

To Dorothy, also, fell the burden of refuting moral objections to the play—an historically unending task. "We might as soon attempt to reform the gambler, by teaching him fair game, or the thief, by teaching him concealment, as attempt to reform the stage; its reform, from its very nature, is impossible," wrote Timothy Dwight as early as 1824 in "An Essay on the Stage." Does a clinically correct physiological study of addiction have any place on the stage, the critics questioned and the public wondered. "Soften the realism," recommended the *Rochester Post Express*. These misgivings arrived too late to stem the tide of growing realism in the theatre, however. Towards the close of the decade, this realism manifested itself in performance, like Dorothy's portrayal of Madame X during the second act, in setting, and in the selection of plays produced. For the production of *The Easiest Way*, to cite one example, David Belasco, (whose theatrical career began as an usher at San Francisco's Bush Street Theatre), dismantled a cheap boarding house and reconstructed it on stage.[21] This play by Eugene Walter, incidentally, featured Dorothy's former colleague at the Murray Hill Theatre, Frances Starr, in her biggest role as the mistress of a Wall Street broker who struggles futilely to reform and to establish an honest relationship. Other plays that broke ranks with conventional offerings included Clyde Fitch's final work, *The City*, (the American playwright died in France in September, 1909) which explores the virtues of urban life versus living in the country and contains the then-shocking line, "goddamn liar," and Edward Sheldon's *The Nigger*, a provocative play about a Southern governor, elected on a white-supremacy platform, who discovers he has "mixed blood."

The growing realism raised new controversies, or, more accurately, raised old ones anew. *Green Book*, an illustrated monthly devoted to the theatre, published Dorothy's rebuttal in its December 1909 issue as "Bad Women in Plays." This scholarly essay, remarkably well argued and amply supported by examples and metaphors, makes several cogent points. "Whether bad women should or should not be depicted upon the stage had long been a mooted question," she begins. "Perhaps I can indicate my position in this matter quite clearly by saying this":

> If any woman were wholly good, or if any woman were wholly bad, then neither one would have any place on the stage. She would—whether wholly good with nothing bad about her, or wholly bad, with no redeeming trait—be such a strange creature to all the rest of us that our only interest in her would be the same interest we might have in any freak. She would be unreal, and no amount of acting, scenery, talking, or thinking could ever convince us that she existed anywhere except in the too vivid imagination of the wildest, most untrammeled dreamer of utopian dreams. Consequently, she would have no place on the stage, since the object of the stage is to reveal people and scenes and tell stories that might happen in real life, or that have happened in real life.
>
> There is where the appeal of theatre lies. And when we attempt to depict impossible things, impossible people, impossible circumstances, we fail to satisfy the demand for a picture from life. After all, you know, acting and plays are only living pictures.

Even religious plays, she argues, depend for their artistic and dramatic value on the possibility of redemption offered to flawed characters (and human beings): "The peg upon which hangs the success, the permanent, enduring success of every play that depicts the tragedy and sordidness of life—is Hope," she explains. She deplores plays that idealize immorality, insists that *Madame X* does not, claims that good drama provides moral lessons, decides that forgiveness is the sole remedy for Madame X's transgressions, denounces nationalistic assumptions that good can be found only at home and not abroad, and restates her feminine point of view in the conclusion: "Therefore, if our plays are to be convincing; if our theatres are to amuse, entertain and instruct; if they are to take part in making the human race happier—and consequently better—they must have bad women and bad men and good women and good men on the stage."[22] Dorothy invokes *Madame X*, never to toot her horn, but exclusively to illustrate her points. If its readers found this article more intellectual than standard playgoer fare, *Green Book* made it up to them the following month by publishing an eleven-page novelized version of *Madame X*.[23]

The initial negative reviews eventually failed to stop the tide of Chicagoans who flocked to the theatre once the play's success was certain.

Theatregoers braced themselves to be turned away at the door, or, if they were lucky enough to have already snagged a ticket, prepared to shed, in Bradley's words, "ten gallons of tears." Henry C. Bradley, the porter in the play's hotel scene, provided the only comic relief. He decided that the work ought be billed as a nautical drama. *Madame X* merited every teardrop according to Alan Dale:

> But as mere melodrama the Chicago public accepted it, and after a long engagement it came to New York. It made a profound impression. Beginning as mere melodrama, it managed to pass into higher realms. Yet I believe that in our heart of hearts we all have more than a sneaking regard for melodrama. It is so gorgeously improbable. The enemies of melodrama hold that up against it. I hold it up in its favor.[24]

Capitalizing on the play's increasing popularity and the growing public interest in ether, the *Chicago Sunday Tribune* ran a lengthy article, by L. Blake Baldwin, a local physician, on the physical effects of drug addition. The paper illustrated "Ether Drinking Is Europe's Latest Vice" with photographs of Dorothy as Jacqueline in advancing stages of debilitation. The *Tribune* followed it with a second story under a different by-line by the newest authority on drug abuse—Dorothy Donnelly. "I dare say I am quite qualified to write a scientific book upon the subject,"[25] she said, but limited her academic article to three columns. She traces the history of ether from its medical use in hospitals and dentistry to its sociological evolution as the current drug of choice for personal, unsanctioned use. The piece ends on a moral note: "Jacqueline is not a sentimental figure— only a pitiful one—but let us remember our virtues as well as our vices are constitutional and say with John Bunyan: 'There but for the grace of God go I.'"[26]

The play kept Dorothy in Chicago for five full months—an usually long trial run. All this time, her brother Henry lay bedridden. His admiring fans, along with Dorothy, were waiting for news, but when it came in mid-November, it was not good. The *New York Times* announced that he was still critically ill and that his physician was not optimistic. His fondest hope, Henry repeatedly told his wife Kitty during his twenty weeks of illness, was to see Dorothy in the part that since May had been toted by the press as a "plum" and a "prize." His valiant attempt to ward off the ravages of Bright's Disease—marked by traces of albumin in the urine— failed; he died on February 15, 1910. The funeral took place three days later at Our Lady of Lourdes on One-hundred-forty-second Street in New York and the burial at Brookside Cemetery in Englewood, New Jersey, not far from the home he shared with Kitty.

Madame X had opened in Manhattan just two weeks earlier, at the Amsterdam Theatre on Forty-ninth Street. Designed by Herts and Tallant in the art nouveau style, it was large enough to seat 1,700 patrons and to offer a magnificent 100- by 60-foot stage and a 40-foot proscenium. Its beauty and grandeur made this house an appropriate setting for Dorothy's greatest triumph as an actress. In the final hour before the curtain rose, Dorothy found herself once again in the clutches of fear. "I can't do anything more," she whispered to Louise Closser Hale: "I can only do my best."

"And in that sweet humility," added Louise, "she went upon the stage and found her best was glorious."

Dorothy's Madame X was a composite picture, at once cerebral and reflective as well as inspired, created by acute memory in combination with consummate technical skills. To make smoking appear as unnoticeable and effortless as breathing, she held the cigarette in the palm of her hand, hiding it slightly, or let it dangle from her mouth while talking and forced herself to swallow some smoke to provide the audience with unobstructed views of the characters' faces. To convey those deadened facial expressions that speak so eloquently of the addict's utter detachment, Dorothy relaxed her cheeks and let them sag by keeping her mouth slightly open. To demonstrate physical response to drink and drugs, from the second act forward Dorothy continually rubbed her head.

When the curtain rose, the audience saw the addict, not the actress, just as Dorothy intended:

> Now, when I act, I really seem to see Madame X. I have such a vivid picture of her in my mind that I seem to feel how she would act under given circumstances, and unconsciously she seems to suggest to me what to do. *Any amount of rehearsing and study would not produce the same effect.* I give myself up to the part, as it were, and the part plays itself.[27] [Emphasis added]

No one believed her, of course. The critics knew her Madame X was not a miracle of heaven-sent manna but a leavened lump of raw dough that needed pummeling and poking and patting to rise and take shape. Channing Pollock found her interpretation "lined with clinical correctness and unflinching realism," and added, "The performance really is a big achievement." *Theatre Magazine* wrote that Dorothy "gave a faithful, and even terrifying, picture of the effect of hopeless and joyless sin in a woman." The *San Francisco Chronicle* called the play a "leap into prominence for Dorothy Donnelly" and the "most remarkable success in the history of the stage."[28] Klauber of the *New York Times* praised her ability to express mental and physical fatigue. He noted that her performance, rendered with sincerity and emotion, saved the play from becoming "cheap and tawdry": "Sometimes laughter and tears lie perilously close together, but Miss Donnelly safely skirts the one, and brings about the other."[29] Several days later Klauber was moved to write another article that discussed the play. Again he complimented Dorothy, citing her skill in making "the woman's case exceedingly pathetic," and so completely engaging the sympathy of the audience for Madame X that they could not be outraged by her misconduct and dissipation.[30] At long last—did Dorothy think the day would never arrive?—Adolphe Klauber proclaimed himself an admirer.

Another fan was novelist Edna Ferber, who had wanted to become an actress before she turned to writing. "When she attended *Madame X* and saw Dorothy Donnelly drenching a vast audience with her tears and theirs," reports Alexander Woollcott, she "would have given her right arm, her chance of winning the Pulitzer Prize, her future royalties of *So Big*, and whatever money she then had in the bank just to have the ability and the chance to do what that other woman there on the stage was doing."[31] Perhaps her most glowing accolade, however, came from Alan Dale, for some time the *New York American*'s drama critic. He considered all the parts well played but credited the merits of the supporting cast, not to the performers, but to the playwright. Brushing aside Dorothy's past triumphs as Candida, Maia Rubek, Ruth Jordan, and Shirley Rossmore, Dale concluded:

> The role was magnificently played by Miss Dorothy Donnelly. It was a piece of acting that was unforgettable. Had Miss Donnelly come to us as the very latest fad in "crowned head" favorites the song of sycophants would have swelled to the heavens. But she didn't. She came to us merely as a very hard-working actress who, for a dozen years, had been skirmishing in the drama. So while everybody said she was splendid, nobody was astonished. Except perhaps myself. I am always astounded at magnificent acting. It is such an amazing thing. I know it can be, but I am spellbound when I get it. I am an habitual theatregoer, but my enthusiasm for fine acting reaches heights that are absolutely unknown and even incomprehensible to the occasional theatregoer. I shall never forget Dorothy Donnelly in the ether-tippling scene of *Madame X*'s second act, or in the trial scene of the last act, when she sat, a mere figure of indescribable anguish, a battered feminine derelict, with the maternal sense awakening.[32]

Just as *Candida* became the most talked about production of its season, now all attention focused on *Madame X*, noted Burns Mantle in his

Best Plays series. Dorothy moved to an apartment at 121 East Fortieth Street and outfitted it handsomely with Chippendale furniture, Delft china, Asian embroideries, some oil paintings, and American Indian textiles she bought while on the road in Idaho and Montana. She spent hours deciding exactly where to place the newly purchased grand piano. "As it looks as though *Madame X* is going to stay some time in New York, I am doing my best to become settled,"[33] she explained.

Her confidence was not misplaced. *Madame X* enjoyed 125 performances on Broadway prior to its national tour. Eventually more than one million Americans saw the play. A West Virginian drama critic was not one of them, however. Told that *Madame X* was booked to play in town, he replied, "Is that so? By the way, what is she playing this year?" By December of 1910, Eddie Cantor was appearing in *Madame 10*, a travesty of the play, and Sarah Bernhardt was performing the title role for the first time—in French, *naturellement*. Lampooning is one form of flattery; imitation, another.

Dorothy's preparations for the role did not end with the first night. Like Hale's actress, she knew that "'Getting mechanical' ... is nothing more awful than the result of long run, when we have all grown so accustomed to our lines that if we really stopped and thought what we were saying we would probably cease to say it. The inflections remain the same in the voice, we throw the same amount of vigor into our work, faithfully follow the same business, but our sub-conscious is on a trail of thought all its own."[34] To focus on the character, Dorothy would lock the door to her dressing room before every performance, muffle the phone, and deliberately plunge herself into anguish. "Three persons play every part, the one who feels it, the one who does it and the one who watches," Dorothy said, "but the one who felt was always dominant in me."[35] And so the tears Jacqueline shed on stage were real. They prompted "an old and distinguished actress," whose name Dorothy did not disclose, to write: "You are magnificent, my dear. You wrung our hearts. But don't let her wretchedness possess you. Laugh, dear heart. Laugh."[36]

At first this warning seemed meaningless: "As though you ever did anything else," Louise Closser remarked.[37] If Dorothy waged war against high spirits during the play's first season, when the second arrived, she struggled to combat low moods—not "blues" but "blacks," Dorothy called them. To retain her own sense of humor, she wrote limericks and jingles, lively verses to commemorate a birthday or a holiday abroad, little ditties to be used as place cards. On stage she made the audience weep; on paper she made her friends laugh.

Like a nova, whose output flashes intensely and then swiftly fades,

Dorothy's years in the limelight passed too quickly. In August, 1912, the *American Magazine* printed a nine-page article on the ordeal of first nights and illustrated it with photographs of leading players. The cut line beneath Dorothy's identified her as "One of our native players who has been seen in many and various parts, and who has acted all of them well." The timing of the publication could not have been more ironic, since Dorothy had already chucked her solid reputation to appear in another series of inconsequential plays.

Her downfall began the previous winter, when she first met Edward Brewster Sheldon, a prolific and accomplished playwright. Born in 1886 to a wealthy family whose fortune was made in Chicago real estate, Sheldon enrolled at Harvard and signed up for English 47: The Forms of the Drama. The instructor was George Pierce Baker, who believed he could teach play writing just as Fred Williams had known he could teach acting. At the age of 22, Sheldon scored a major hit with *Salvation Nell*, starring Minnie Maddern Fiske and Holbrook Blinn as her leading man. Unaccustomed to meteoric fame, when the audience applauded and yelled, "Author! author!," Sheldon had to be shoved from behind onto the stage, where he grabbed "the proscenium arch for support," bobbed "his cherubic countenance like a startled robin, and then [backed] out of sight."[38] His best known and often most admired plays, like *Salvation Nell*, *The Boss*, *High Road*, and *The Nigger*, effectively confront contemporary social issues, but he also wrote romances. Seventeen of his works met with great success; six failed.

One flop was *Princess Zim Zim*. This play tells the story of Tessie Casey, a Coney Island side-show snake charmer, who falls in love with a millionaire, rejoices when he returns her affection, and despairs when he leaves her with what seems to the modern ear a flimsy excuse: "I'm 24 years old, I'm on the loose, and I'm looking for romance." According to historian Arthur Hobson Quinn, the reply "strikes a responsive chord in our sympathies, [for] he loves her with only part of his nature, and the insistent call of his habits and the love for the woman of his own world take him back at last."[39] Tessie, responding to her professional obligations, wipes away her tears and goes on with the show. *Princess Zim Zim* premiered in Albany, then moved to Boston in December, 1911. Eric Wollencott Barnes, Sheldon's biographer, claims that the young playwright wrote *Princess Zim Zim* especially for Dorothy: "He had been greatly taken not only by her striking gifts as a comedienne but by her winsome, modest personality." Barnes implies that Sheldon fell for that "lilting voice and luminous smile," and she for him, but at the time of their first meeting, Ned was engaged to another actress, Doris Keane.[40]

Dorothy's "striking gifts" could not rescue the play from its trite theme, contrived plot, and jumbled tone. Although *Princess Zim Zim* never made it to Broadway, it determined the future career of Dorothy's costar, John Barrymore, cast as the young millionaire, Peter Milholland. Barrymore had sought to become a painter or commercial illustrator rather than pursue the family trade. Forced by financial necessity to take up acting, he made his mark on Broadway in 1909 with Winchell Smith's *The Fortune Hunter*, a popular though artistically unextraordinary play that ran for 345 performances. A year later, he married a New York socialite, Katherine Harris, the first of his four wives. Yet, he was unwilling to take himself or his unwanted career seriously. Ned Sheldon, on hand during the rehearsals and trial run, dropped into Jack's dressing room one day with the recommendation that he forego comic parts and accept only dramatic roles: "If I were you I should play a part without a bit of comedy in it."[41] Barrymore eventually saw the wisdom of this advice, and with Sheldon's help, landed the lead in John Galsworthy's *Justice*. Directed by Ben Iden Payne in 1916, Barrymore's first significant work met with great success and led to a long, highly acclaimed career on the stage and the screen.

Dorothy could have profited by similar suggestions to expand her repertoire. While *Princess Zim Zim* formed the foundation of her life-long friendship with Ned, it did little to boost her up the professional ladder. Neither did *The Right to Be Happy*. The *New York Times* departed from its time-honored tradition of giving prominent stars only one to two columns of space for a picture and caption and, instead, devoted a full half-page to photographs of Dorothy in scenes from this play. *Theatre Magazine* noted that as Janet Van Roof "Miss Donnelly, acts the heroine with a thorough command of external theatrical aids and a competent and intelligent expression of its psychological necessities." Despite such good publicity and some favorable reviews, this well acted but poorly constructed melodrama folded after 31 performances.

The Right to Be Happy premiered March 25, 1912; three weeks later, its producer was dead. Henry Burkhardt Harris, who had repeatedly cast Dorothy in leading roles, operated the Hudson Theatre and served as director of the Managers Association of Greater New York and also as treasurer of Actor's Fund. Unfortunately, Harris sailed aboard the opulent British ocean liner, *Titanic*, during its maiden voyage from Southampton, England, to the United States. It struck an iceberg in the North Atlantic, off Newfoundland, the night of April 14-15 and sank. Nearly three-fourths of the passengers died, Harris among them.

Dorothy Donnelly enacts the role of Janet Van Roof in The Right to Be Happy. *(Originally published by* Munsey's Magazine *in 1912.)*

In a scene from the 1916 stage production of Justice, *John Barrymore hammers at a barred door and unlocks his career as a gifted tragedian. (Courtesy Michael A. Morrison Collection.)*

When the next drama season opened, it was not Dorothy, but her brother, Thomas, who held center stage. He marched in the Irish Athletic Club's unit during New York City's parade to honor the country's Olympic athletes in September 1912 and spent the next two months on the campaign trail. Near his home on Ninety-second Street stood several major breweries. He palled around with their owners, joined them as a member of the Liederkranz Club, and was gratified when they instructed their workers to vote for him.[42] In November he won the state-wide election for Justice of the New York Supreme Court and was installed the following January by New York's governor, William Sulzer.

Dorothy waited until spring to land another part. She played Domini Enfielden in a road show of *The Garden of Allah*. The play had first opened in 1911, with Mary Mannering in the lead, and surprisingly achieved a record of 241 performances. Though it promised exoticism, it delivered mostly tripe. Cast with Berbers imported from Arabia and set with real dessert sand and live camels, *The Garden of Allah* spent four tedious hours recounting the story of a renegade Trappist monk who falls in love with a young attractive girl.

Dorothy sailed to Europe for the summer to lick her wounds and there, by chance, again encountered Edward Sheldon. His first big box-office success, *Romance*, starring Doris Keane, had opened in February. The play promptly propelled Keane into prominence, and Ned into wealth. He earned $100,000 in royalties from the first production, then assigned all future royalties to her—a generous gift, indeed, since *Romance* kept Keane in the lead for seven consecutive years in both the United States and England. Keane eventually broke off their engagement and shortly thereafter married the actor Basil Sydney.

Dorothy and Ned enjoyed three days together in Paris, sightseeing, dining at the Crillon, and attending a small boulevard theatre.[43] Then Dorothy rushed home to create the title role in an English version of *Maria Rosa*, a Catalan play by Angel Guinera, translated into Spanish by José Echegaray, who shared the Nobel prize for literature in 1904. Once again Dorothy needed to project a wide range of emotion, this time to convince the audience of her love for her murdered husband, and, simultaneously, of her incredible attraction to his killer. A photograph of Dorothy in costume shows a flamenco dancer, her right foot thrust slightly forward, her hand resting provocatively on the hip, her wavy dark hair caught up in a high comb. Over her head she wears a fringed shawl, like a mantilla, and from it, half hidden behind a fold, emerges a flirtatious smile. From her phenomenal memory Dorothy had summoned up and re-created the winsome pose of a young Spanish dancer she had seen in a painting a decade earlier.

Maria Rosa opened January 19, 1914, at the Thirty-ninth Street Theatre and moved three weeks later to the Longacre Theatre. Cast opposite Dorothy was Lou Tellegen, the model for Rodin's sculpture, "Eternal Springtime," and the partner—both on the stage and in bed—of Sarah Bernhardt from 1910 to 1913 during her American "farewell" tour, when he made his New York debut during a four-week engagement with Bernhardt in *La Femme X* at the Globe Theatre, beginning December 5, 1910. Bernhardt's biographer, Cornelia Otis Skinner, describes him as handsome, vain, promiscuous, and utterly devoid of talent without Madame Sarah's coaching.[44] In *Maria Rosa* he gave his first performance in English, but his French accent clashed with the Southern drawl and Broadway speech of the other players. Robbed of authentic local color, the play failed in both houses and closed after 48 performances.

The following season, when Americans sought escape from the tensions raised by war in Europe, they fled from heavy drama and flocked to emotional plays like Sheldon's *The Song of Songs*. Based on an episodic German novel by Hermann Sudermann, the five-act drama tells the story of a naive girl who marries a predatory senator, then plunges into numerous affairs until she discovers true love, as implied by the title's Biblical allusion. This was exactly the type of play Sheldon wrote best, so thought his mother: "Dear Mrs. Sheldon, you could dramatize a muffin!" Dorothy once laughingly accused her.[45]

The play's producer, Albert Woods, sent Dorothy a telegram: "It's eight minutes of acting but it's got to be acting. That's the reason I want you."[46] Calling everyone he met, both male and female, "Sweetheart," Woods used charm and flattery to persuade. Although he handed her a bitter pill, Dorothy swallowed it and accepted a supporting role. "Dorothy Donnelly, one of the most brilliant competent actresses on the American stage," wrote Alexander Woollcott, "is seen in a role that lasts but a few minutes, that serves no purpose whatever and that is in the play only because it was in the book."[47]

The Song of Songs opened on December 22, 1914, at the Eltinge Theatre (named for the renowned female impersonator, Julian Dalton Eltinge). Despite its dramatic flaws—overly long exposition, discontinuity of action, and unnecessary incidental roles, for example—the play enjoyed 191 performances during its five-month run. It was a moneymaker—at least for some. The primary beneficiary was Joe Leblang, a tobacconist who supplemented his meager income by buying unsold theatre tickets and then reselling them. Leblang purchased all the tickets to *The Song of Songs* and agreed to pay Woods $5,000 a week for them. Although the producer retained control of the show, he made no additional money from the play. Dorothy's salary as Anna Markle, by contrast, was large enough to buy the seven and a half-acre Colin Campbell farm on Pine Bridge Road in Croton Lake, northeast of Manhattan on the Hudson River. A beau of Nora's, who was a realtor, found the property in Westchester County for her. It contained a large barn, where Dorothy housed her male guests on weekends, keeping the main building for her female visitors. Thomas Donnelly stayed there only once; after the bustle of New York City, her brother found the countryside too quiet to fall asleep. Nora McCall, however, spent several days there, having come on one occasion to nurse Dorothy through a bad case of poison ivy. Aunt Dolly's grand-nephews, though very young at the time, still recall visits to the country home: "walking through fields, and catching turtles, and returning by train"[48] or "sitting on the chauffeur's lap, and helping him drive the car."[49] Dorothy never mastered the knack of driving, though she owned a car. So, she hired Nora's former window-washer to be her chauffeur.

If the record of her performances these past two years seems a bit meager and less than stellar, Dorothy could consider herself in good company. The box office business slumped dramatically in 1914. Many leading actors played in revivals, such as Barrie's *The Legend of Leonora* and *Peter Pan*, both starring Maude Adams. The most famous actresses of the period, Mrs. Fiske and Sarah Bernhardt, made some appearances, but none on Broadway; instead, they re-enacted their famous scenes and sometimes shared the bill with vaudevillians like W. C. Fields. Shakespeare provided the only jobs for such notables as John Drew, William Crane, Amelia Bingham, William Faversham, E. H. Sothern, and Julia Marlowe. So many actresses were out of work that the Professional [Stage] Woman's League held special benefits to relieve their suffering.

The dry spell ended May 18, 1915, at the Garrick Theatre, when Dorothy re-created Candida, playing opposite her former costar, Arnold Daly. Then she frittered away her talent as Sarah Lusskin, the second wife of a Jewish pawnbroker, in *The Bargain*. Produced by the Shubert brothers, it opened October 6, 1915, at the Comedy Theatre. "Excellent was the work of Dorothy Donnelly, the wife," reported *Theatre Magazine*.[50] Herman Scheffauer's melodrama, billed as "The New Shylock," featured a star-studded cast that included Louis Calvert, whose reputation stemmed from his 1910 Shakespearean performances as Sir Toby Belch in *Twelfth Night* and Sir John Falstaff in *The Merry Wives of Windsor*. However, *The Bargain*'s racial antipathies led to an early demise. With a record of only 13 performances, the play scarcely seems a fitting finale for a long and often illustrious acting career on the stage.

Acting was Dorothy's first real love—an obsession, in fact. If she tallied its personal costs, the list was long. Essentially a very private person, she acceded to requests for interviews, posed for publicity photos, and cast pearls of prattle before the gossip mongers. She pushed herself relentlessly to prepare for each part; swallowed her pride whenever critics wrote unfavorable reviews; traveled all the while resenting road tours and trial runs; and seemingly said yes to every role offered. Once she experienced the joys of having a career and being financially and socially independent, she also renounced any hopes of marriage. No price was too great to pay. Dorothy called acting "the greatest sport in the world"[51] and was not about to give it up without a struggle.

Still in search of parts, she headed for Hollywood—destination for many stage stars like Mary Pickford, George Arliss, John Barrymore and his brother, Lionel. Early on these actors realized that the growing importance of the film industry would curtail their opportunities for stage appearances and inevitably make road shows obsolete. Three times the fledgling film industry tried to capture the magic of her talent on celluloid and, in each instance, failed. Dorothy appeared as Marie Landau in the 1914 production of *The Thief*, costarring opposite Richard Buhler, and the following year as Nahnya Crossfox, the self-sacrificing American Indian, in *Sealed Valley*. In 1916 came *Madame X* with Edwin Fosberg, Ralph Morgan, John Bowers, Robert Fischer, and Charles Bunnell in the supporting cast.

Henry Wilson Savage selected George F. Marion to direct the film. Marion was a competent stage manager and director, but he knew little of technical techniques. According to *Variety*, the camera lingered too long on the scenery in a vain attempt to create atmosphere. Dorothy's make-up was flawed and, by the end of the film, it failed to show the effects that twenty years of addiction and misery produce. Moreover, Marion botched the staging of Laroque's death: he had Edwin Fosberg stand off stage while Dorothy shoots at him through an open door; then his body awkwardly plunges face forward at her feet. Finally, the absence of dialogue was no help; without spoken words the subtleties of characterization and moral debate were lost. The actors moved their lips in silence while short subtitles displayed their lines. The only speech reproduced in full by captions was Raymond's passionate plea to the court. "The young man enacting this role was weak and ineffective, but in spite of him, the speech is so strong that it is bound to touch the most hardened spectator, irrespective of his or her familiarity with the story." After Pathé Gold Rooster released the six-reel motion picture on January 15, 1916, *Variety* correctly predicted that it "will never enjoy anywhere near the same amount of success which the legitimate production did."[52]

Four years later Joan L. Cohen reviewed a new version of the film for the Variety guide to films: "Madame X was a great success in France and then was neglected until a very good actress/writer, Dorothy Donnelly, rediscovered it. She made her own translation and played the title role herself; it became a hit with American audiences. She also made a successful film of the play."[53] Cohen's brief introductory remarks raise interesting, if unimportant, questions. Why, if Dorothy made some suggestions to John Raphael, who translated Bisson's play into English, did she never speak of doing so? Also, is the word "success" more appropriate to her stage performance than to her cinematic portrayal?

Dorothy's appearances in Hollywood made nary a ripple in the filmdom pond. Yet, *Madame X* has continued to create an occasional splash. The film was remade in 1920 with Pauline Frederick, in 1929 with Ruth Chatterton (and Lionel Barrymore as director), in 1937 with Gladys George, and in 1965 with Lana Turner. A Greek film of the play with English subtitles was also presented in New York in October 1960. The sexually liberated woman holds universal and timeless appeal. Even in periods of relaxed morality, she fascinates—and threatens—both men and women. Dorothy's mastery of the role, with its climatic death scene, presented a challenge to many an actress worthy of the name, beginning with Sarah Bernhardt, who first attempted the part at age 65 in New York City's 1910 stage production of *La Femme X*.

CHAPTER 7
Intermission

All the energy that had sustained Dorothy through her years at the Murray Hill Theatre and the ordeal of road shows abated not a whit during her thirties. "To be idle and useless is neither an honor nor a privilege," she said:

> I believe the habit of work is the best of all habits.... It is not only a good disciplinarian, but a good educator of character as well. Application to stage work, complete absorption in its affairs and all the pressure which its duties impose—i.e., rehearsals, studying of parts—are most valuable in training the mind.... The habit of work is as essential for the happiness and well being of woman as of man, even if she follow the stage as a career. For without it she is apt to sink into a state of listless ennui and uselessness, which is always accompanied by illness or an attack of 'nerves'.... I find it absolutely necessary to my health and happiness.... Hard work, steadily and regularly carried on, never hurts anyone. The more useful work one does the more one thinks and feels and the more one really lives.[1]

Dorothy's "complete absorption" in the affairs of the theatre demanded hard work that eventually produced two stunning results: enhancing the respectability of the profession and expanding her own roles within it.

According to Dorothy, "To regard the stage only as a means of obtaining a livelihood or a season's engagement the means of enabling one's self to save enough for a summer's idleness is an utterly wrong view."[2] In her opinion, acting was not only a job or merely a career; but a noble profession. A life member of the Actors' Fund, she participated in its annual drives. One year she hawked stage memorabilia alongside Mary Mannering, Julia Marlowe, Ethel Barrymore, and Nora Bayes. The following spring she helped staff the Twelfth Night Club booth that peddled merchandise donated by manufacturers. During Actors' Fund's 1916 campaign, she took center stage again, wearing a dark dress with a fur collar and a leather-trimmed peaked hat that must have been fashionable but resembled a fancy dunce cap, and demonstrated the latest dance craze, the mannequin glide. When the Stage Society of New York presented a benefit matinee at the Lyceum Theatre on March 30, 1914, she created the title role in *Granny Maumee*. This one-act play by Ridgely Torrance displayed her remarkable versatility. She was cast as a gaunt elderly black woman, proud of her heritage and skilled in the magic of her people, who becomes blind early in life while trying to rescue her son from being burnt alive by white folk. Now in her one-hundredth year, Maumee conjures back her vision to look upon her great-great-grandson, whom she holds lovingly in her arms. One swift glance tells her that the baby has mixed blood. Alexander Woollcott reviewed the 1917 revival of *Granny Maumee* with a different cast and wrote, "This magnificent moment, which should flash to the uttermost corners of the theatre and set a-tingle every spine therein, was superbly realized when Dorothy Donnelly played the part three seasons ago."

Such fund raising and benefit performances were vital in an era that lacked pensions and unemployment compensation. Moreover, they were crucial to the survival of actors and actresses in a period that often denied them access to other forms of charity because of social prejudice. The Actor's Fund, for instance, built the first retirement home—on Staten Island—for elderly performers so that they might live their final days in some degree of comfort and dignity. The many benevolent organizations associated with the stage made small loans or out-right gifts to needy players left stranded on the road when plays unexpectedly folded or who found themselves temporarily out of work. What most theatregoers might merely suspect, an actress definitely realizes: the stage offers more parts for men than for women. A cursory glance at the thousands of pictures spread along more than 350 pages of the pictorial histories of the American theatre edited by Daniel C. Blum visually confirms that fact.[3] A random comment on the filming of *Madame X* offers supporting statistics: "One man drove her to it—one man tempted her—one man degraded her—one man defended her!"[4] The plight of actresses fallen on hard times was miserable indeed.

In 1913 the profession needed reform as well as relief. While the winds of war fanned through Europe, another conflict erupted. The battlefield was Broadway. In one camp stood performers—underpaid, overworked, and often shabbily managed. Several factors convinced them to organize. First, the number of theatres in New York City alone quadrupled between 1900 and 1910, thereby increasing the pool of actors; second, stage actors in London had formed a successful union in 1907; finally, stage hands and musicians had recently voted to become affiliated with the American Federation of Labor. Emboldened by the success of these colleagues, stage actors met at the Pabst Grand Circle Hotel on May 26, 1913. They founded Actors' Equity Association and elected Francis Wilson its president. Their primary hope was to improve working conditions.

Their opposition consisted of a tiny group, most of them members of the Theatrical Trust: Samuel Nixon, Fred Zimmerman, Al Hayman, Charles Frohman, Marc Klaw, and their spokesman, Abraham L. Erlanger. These few men owned most of the theatres from coast to coast and from Boston to the Gulf. "The advantages (of the Syndicate)," according to actress Maude Adams, "were a well-planned, carefully maintained field of operation—the theatres in excellent condition with well-trained constantly employed stage hands; the front of the house well kept; the box office well guarded; the advertisements, the newspapers all attended to; the confusion of independent bookings corrected."[5] This rosy picture lacks an important detail: members of the trust exercised unlimited control. They made exclusive decisions regarding plays to be performed, actors to be cast, changes to be made in the script, and music to be composed or arranged for their productions.

One example suffices to illustrate their stranglehold on the American theatre. As early as the turn of the century, when Dorothy's uncle, Fred Williams, directed *Becky Sharp*, the play was booked at the Fifth Avenue Theatre, one of the few in New York City that did not belong to the syndicate. *Becky Sharp* next moved to the Brooklyn Academy of Music, and, a week later, found itself forced to take to the road, when no other house could be leased to stage the play. Moreover, despite admirable performances by the well-known redhead Minnie Maddern Fiske and Maurice Barrymore, the play failed to draw much critical appreciation, for most reviewers were paid by members of the syndicate, not by their newspaper editors or publishers.

David Belasco finally took legal action. Claiming that the syndicate was drumming himself and other independent producers out of business, he hired attorney Samuel Untermeyer to prosecute the members of the Theatrical Trust under New York State's anti-trust laws. The presiding judge, however, dismissed the indictment, saying that the theatre was not "a business as was contemplated by the Donnelly Act."[6] Whatever juicy comments Dorothy and her brother, Thomas, exchanged regarding that decision were never made public.

When the Jewish, Lithuanian-born brothers Shubert—Samuel, and later Lee and Jacob J.—moved from Syracuse to New York City, their arrival presented a challenge to the tyranny of the syndicate. Although the Shuberts never formally joined the cartel, and often locked horns with the trust, in pursuing their own monopoly they began acquiring one theatre after another. They owned eight theatres in up-state New York and grabbed the lease on Manhattan's Herald Square Theatre and, shortly thereafter, on the Lyric Theatre. Eventually they would own 31 houses in New York City and more than 60 elsewhere, creating the most far-flung, privately-controlled theatrical organization in the world. (J. J.'s surviving heir was Lawrence Shubert Lawrence, Jr., a grand-nephew and eventual controller of the Shubert Organization. By 1988 the Shubert Organization still controlled 17 of New York City's 36 theatres, virtually all debt-free; in 1993 it managed 16 houses.)

The Shuberts tolerated no opposition. For instance, when they invited Florenz Ziegfeld to bring his *Follies* revues into their fold and he refused, the brothers recreated *The Passing Show*, a yearly pastiche of song, dance, and spectacle, to compete with Ziegfeld's success. As late as 1916, they drafted an iron-clad contract for Dorothy to produce and star in *Tiger Lily*, the play's working title:

> You agree to render us your exclusive services to the best of your efforts and ability and to appear and perform the part assigned to you and in general render the services of a star in the play....
>
> You agree to furnish us with the means of acquiring photographs and other data we may need for advertising of all kinds and you give us the right to use your pictures on all advertising at our discretion...
>
> We agree to leave all matters relating to cast and production in your hands provided that you take up all matters relating to cost of the cast and production with us for our approval....[7]

There were other rigid stipulations: she would receive no pay for time spent rehearsing her part; the house itself would dictate the number of her weekly appearances; she must draw the scenery and props from the Shubert warehouse; she could not accept work from anyone else without the Shuberts' consent. The Shuberts agreed to pay her $300 a week as actress and producer and give her 15 percent of the profits—a tidy sum during the year when the average *annual* wage of all workers excluding farmers amounted to $765.[8] Altogether, the contract filled two pages.

This ability of management to dictate virtually every facet of theatrical productions, then, set the stage for the establishment of Actor's Equity Association. Initially brushed off as a social club by the managers, the group lost its preliminary skirmishes with the syndicate and the Shuberts. After admitting women to membership and giving them positions of leadership—Dorothy served on its Executive Committee—the union redoubled its efforts to resolve labor disputes. Their requests seemed moderate: a limit of eight performances a week, Sundays off, extra pay for additional matinees, and some compensation for traveling expenses. Yet, negotiations collapsed. Actor's Equity finally emerged victorious from their war with producers following an unexpected but successful strike in August 1919, when managers recognized it as the bargaining agent for the acting profession.

Although Dorothy banded with her colleagues to support their own, she also generously lent her time and talent to other worthy causes. For example, along with Louise Hale, she appeared in *Disengaged*, based on Henry James' story, "The Solution." The play revolves around the forthcoming marriage of a young man to a compromised girl. Erroneously believing that the wedding stems from his sense of obligation rather than from love, his friends futilely plot to "disengage" the couple. *Theatre Magazine* reported that "the comedy depends for effectiveness largely on skillful shades of speech. In the hands of players less happily selected it would have been painfully flat." Dorothy's cousin, Fritz Williams, staged the matinee performance on March 11, 1909, raising nearly $3,000 for St. Andrew's Convalescent Hospital. Later that same year she re-enacted the trial scene in *Madame X* in a benefit for the victims of the Cherry Mine disaster. By demonstrating concern for and commitment to the less fortunate, Dorothy indirectly proved to the public that actresses, too, could be upright citizens.

To her professional affiliations, she soon added political ones, especially the Women's Democratic Union and the New York Women's Suffrage Association. She believed in equal rights for women but even more strongly in their acting in concert to obtain those rights: "If women would only cease to be false to each other the whole status of woman would be improved," she said.[9] When an actress, by now retired, publicly attacked the extravagance and woeful ignorance of blue-blooded matrons, Dorothy rose to their defense. The actress in question was Mabelle Gilman, a graduate of Mills College for Women in Oakland, California, who had auditioned for Augustin Daly when the impresario was in San Francisco and then moved to New York to accept his offer of a job. She soon left the stage, however, to marry William Ellis Corey. This engineer and self-made capitalist became president of Carnegie Steel and later of United States Steel, and also served on the board of directors for half a dozen other steel companies. Along with a wedding ring, Mabelle

Gilman Corey acquired an imposing home at 71 Broadway in Manhattan, a splendid chateau in the valley of Chevreuse, France, and the authority to speak peremptorily on "art in America and the attitude of our society people toward it." In its March 1909 issue, *Cosmopolitan* magazine published a seven-page article, entitled "Art and American Society," in which Mrs. Corey deplores American ignorance of and lack of respect for the arts. She pleads for "the reconstruction of society on a basis of intellectual gifts and talents being recognized as the open sesame to the finest social life of our land." She longs for an American equivalent of the salons established by the "brilliant" and influential French aristocrats—Madame de Stael, Marguerite de Valois, Madame Récamier, Madame de Lafayette, and others—"imperishable names in the records of art and literature." In her opinion, by contrast, American women of means seem interested only in "the progress of the country's industrial institutions"—a suitable preoccupation for men, not for women, she says. Moreover, she argues, they fail to "take advantage of whatever opportunities of culture there are to be had." In support of this assertion, she cites the example of a young German immigrant woman who gave up the idea of buying furs in the latest fashion to acquire season tickets to the opera. Ironically, *Cosmopolitan* laced the article with photographs of her extensive French estate and of Mrs. Corey in wide-brimmed hats adorned variously with bouquets of flowers or floating white plumes, dressed in the very manner of the women she censures:

> If the great ladies of New York society—hostesses who spend thousands of dollars every year in the most frivolous of entertainments—should devote the energy and money which now go into foolish pastimes to the establishing of a new régime, fashionable affairs would be brilliant and pleasing things, instead of deadly dull gatherings where the ladies yawn behind their fans and the men gather in smoking-rooms bored to death and seeking relief in the soothing narcotic. What a marvelous society could be founded and what a nation this would become![10]

When Dorothy read the article, she grew appalled and then indignant. Despite her "horror of hurting anyone's feelings,"[11] her reaction to this article was terse and direct:

> I have always observed a rule, never to offer criticism upon an utterance of a sister in my profession. The point of view may be so totally different that two people may be absolutely honest and yet disagree diametrically. Still, as Mrs. Corey is no longer a member of my profession and her diatribe has been published far and wide, I think I may be absolved in uttering my views…. My profession has been my life and I have gone very

> little into society, but I have come to know personally women who are
> recognized leaders of society both in America and in Europe, and my
> admiration and respect for them is unbounded.

She called them "philanthropists" and "Samaritans," who often acted
"unostentatiously and without public notice," and spoke approvingly of
Mrs. H. H. Pell's efforts to restore and preserve Fort Ticonderoga, of Mrs.
Clarence Mackey's devotion to educational causes, and of Alva Belmont's
support of women's rights.[12] Following their example of "doing ... God's
great work," as she put it, Dorothy joined the Speedwell Society, established to provide asylum to New York's homeless children. Quietly, she
also saw to the needs of her own family. When her eldest niece was struggling financially as a newlywed, Dorothy bought her an automobile so that
Sally could set up business selling houses as a realtor. Likewise, Dorothy
made certain that her nephew, Ambrose McCall, and his five children were
never in want.[13]

Her political activities assumed a more profound dimension beginning May 7, 1915, that fateful day German U-boats sank the *Lusitania*.
The fast Cunard liner was just ten miles off the southern shore of Ireland, near Kinsale Head, when a German submarine torpedoed the British
steamer. Playwright Charles Klein, producer Charles Frohman, director
Albert Herman Woods, and actor Justus Miles Forman were among the
128 Americans who lost their lives. Another colleague would have perished, too, but when his alarm clock failed to ring, Jerome Kern overslept
and thereby missed the scheduled sailing. On April 6, 1917, the United
States declared war on Germany. After listening to the news, and before
reaching his office, George Michael Cohan had written "Over There," the
song most closely identified with World War I. Nora Bayes' captivating
rendition of the song ensured that sales of sheet music "reached the mil-
lion-and-a-half mark."[14] On Tuesday, April 22, 1917, more than two thousand performers and playwrights assembled at an *ad hoc* meeting of
America's Over-There Theatrical League to hear playwright Winthrop
Ames' impassioned and informative speech as he called for the stage's
support of the war effort. The American Red Cross was entrusted, he
carefully explained, with responsibility for relief; the Young Men's Christian Association (Y.M.C.A.), on the other hand, would have full authority for providing entertainment to American soldiers stationed in Europe.
Vaudevillians and musicians, please apply!

One month later, Dorothy met with Rachel Crothers, Louise Closser
Hale, Josephine Hull, Minnie Dupree, Bessie Tyree, and Louise Drew to
discuss the possibility of forming an organization to provide war relief.

Her favorite handbag dangling, Dorothy Donnelly clutches a bundle of packages, perhaps gifts for convalescing soldiers or homeless children in France. (Courtesy Philip Fahringer Collection.)

Louise Closser Hale (left) and Dorothy Donnelly shared the vice-presidency of the Stage Women's War Relief, founded in 1917. (Originally printed by National Service with the International Military Digest.*)*

Word of the meeting spread quickly throughout the theatre "family." The founders of the Stage Women's War Relief held a massive meeting two weeks later at the Hudson Theatre—"the greatest coming together of the women of the theatre ever known and for the greatest cause," noted Crothers.[15] The playwright Crothers became president and Louise Drew the treasurer, while Dorothy and Louise Closser Hale shared the vice presidency of this independent unit affiliated with the American Red Cross. Wearing a large-brimmed black hat, rakishly tilted to the left, and a cluster of fur pelts draped over a solid gray, straight-skirted dress with three-quarter length sleeves edged in lace, Dorothy stepped to the podium.[16] She explained the activities the group proposed and pleaded for membership. Her speech was heard throughout the nation, and branches of the fledgling organization instantly popped up in Boston, Chicago, Philadelphia, Detroit, San Francisco, and Los Angeles.[17]

Within a single five-month period, from April to August 1917, members of the Stage Women's War Relief sent 60,000 pieces of hospital supplies to the Allies. One afternoon a photographer for *Theatre Magazine* came to 366 Fifth Avenue, where the firm of Acker, Merral and Conduit had lent a workroom to the Stage Women's War Relief. He snapped a picture of Mabel Frenyear, Jessie Bonstelle, Mabelle Adams, Margaret Mayo, Blanche Bates, Margaret Illington, Louise Closser, and Dorothy Donnelly in their relief uniforms. Wearing long white shapeless gowns, hospital caps with a bright red cross stitched to the front brim, and shoulder-length veils that hung straight from crown to nape, the foremost actresses of the day sat serenely, cutting and folding bandages. Because many of their male colleagues enlisted or were drafted, actresses shouldered most of the responsibility on Broadway for the war efforts. They knitted clothing, gathered shoes and garments for children in France, shipped books and magazines to the front, sold ten million dollars' worth of Liberty Bonds, planted vegetable gardens, handed new recruits free tickets to shows, held benefits at the Ritz-Carlton and Biltmore, solicited contributions to support their work (Alf Hayman and the Charles Frohman Company donated the entire proceeds of the three James Barrie plays currently appearing at the Empire Theatre)[18], and walked down the aisles at theatres, holding "dippers" to collect contributions from the audience. At 33 West Forty-Fourth Street they held a "jumble-in," the 1918 name for today's "rummage sale," selling donated "gowns, hats, furs, laces, feathers and frills, house furnishings, odds and ends, old and new, and autographed photographs of stage, opera, and 'movie' stars."[19] Louise and Dorothy rallied the support of the Twelfth Night Club, whose members sent convalescing soldiers raisins, candy, and 4,000 pounds of strawberry jam.

The biggest contribution of stage women to the war effort, however, was more in keeping with their profession—performance. Since the only men with combat experience were those who had served with General John Joseph Pershing in pursuing Pancho Villa across the Mexican border, military training camps speedily sprouted throughout the country. To provide diversions for the raw recruits, the Commission on Training Camp Activities was established with Raymond B. Fosdick as its head. Make-shift stages sprang up overnight on military bases. Entertainment gave the conscripts a welcome break from training and convalescing soldiers relief from the pain of hospitalization. Moreover, the Stage Women's War Relief encouraged actresses to give soldiers "entertainment which will keep them in touch with home and all the things they have given up ... break their isolation and carry them over hard hours of boredom and homesickness."[20] Although theatres were kept dark on Tuesday nights to conserve energy, the rest of the week men in uniform were provided free admission to performances. In New York City, Dorothy quickly organized what became known the "Sunday Shows" and served as its first chairman.

Making bandages, packing supplies, raising money—these were all behind-the-scene jobs, the typical lot for women, just as stimulating to her as peeling onions for the Reverend James Mavor Morrell had been to Candida. So, although she was never a vaudevillian and only a part-time piano playing musician, she enlisted with the American Expeditionary Forces Entertainers. When she donned the gray-blue uniform of the Y.M.C.A., Dorothy became the first American "legitimate" stage actress to serve overseas.[21] She was initially stationed in Chaumont, a village on the Marne River in France, headquarters for the American troops and a rest area for several divisions. After the armistice, however, the A.E.F. assigned her to the Third Army, now headquartered at the intersection of the Moselle and Rhine Rivers in Coblenz, where Dorothy enjoyed the amorous attentions of a general, "a very heavy beau," according to her youngest niece's recollection.[22]

The United States Army faced a tremendous problem with low morale when it began to occupy German territory. Overseas mail delivery arrived at snail-pace. Barrack food filled the stomach but starved the palate. Fraternization with local women was strictly forbidden. Furthermore, troops eager to return home now that the war was over had to wait months for transport; even the fastest ships, the *Great Northern* and the *Northern Pacific*, required nineteen days to make the round-trip crossing; bigger ships, like the *Leviathan* that carried 12,000 passengers, took even longer. The men faced an additional anxiety: the virulent Spanish flu that claimed more than twenty million lives in a single year was rampaging through Germany. Moreover, since few of the Doughboys were professional soldiers, they were unaccustomed to the relative inactivity that followed the cessation of hostilities. Also, much of their work during the occupation was routine and tedious—sorting records and guarding Russian prisoners-of-war, who had been captured by the Germans and were awaiting repatriation. These jobs lacked the stimulation of actual combat. As a result, the need for entertainment grew rather than diminished once peace arrived.

What passed for entertainment, however, was not worth writing home about, as a correspondent for the *New York Times* suggested when describing one production at length. It began with an energetic talk on "counting your blessings," delivered to three hundred homesick boys, many of whom walked out in disgust. Next came a young pianist who professed knowledge of the audience's desire for ragtime, confessed that she didn't know any, and then proved it. Her act was followed by a classical violinist, who played mechanically and badly.[23] The Third Army's entertainment was little improved; it consisted mainly of such bland events as "horse shows, motor shows, track and field events, and aviation shows."[24]

Dorothy was too competent an actress and too experienced with theatre to accept standard Y.M.C.A. fare with complacency. Following the example set by her brother Henry twenty years earlier, she formed a stock company, acquired a business manager, a stage manager and director, two set designers, a carpenter and electrician, and treated 2,000 officers and men to *Seven Keys to Baldpate*, a full-length play about a writer who bets that he can finish a novel within twenty-four hours while staying at the deserted Baldpate Inn. (George M. Cohan dashed off *Seven Keys to Baldpate* in a mere ten days, and Burns Mantle selected it as the best play of 1913.) "It was Miss Donnelly's idea to vary the vaudeville entertainment which forms almost all Y.M.C.A. programs, and the Third Army stock company is the result," wrote the *New York Times* correspondent. He saluted the novelty of her idea, adding she "deserves great credit for her strenuous work in recruiting the personnel and conducting several weeks' rehearsal."[25] It took four trucks to move the show from its trial run in a small town on the Rhine River to Coblenz. By the time it opened there, Dorothy had returned home to appear in *The Golden Fleece* on March 24, 1919, when the Actor's Fund presented a benefit performance with Blanch Bates as Medea at the Broadhurst Theatre. This was Dorothy's final performance as an actress.

General "Black Jack" Pershing later sent Dorothy an inscribed photograph of himself, personally thanking her for all her fine work on behalf of the army through the American Expeditionary Forces Entertainers.[26] President Woodrow Wilson declared December 5, 1919, Actors' National Memorial Day in honor of the profession's contributions to the war effort. Dorothy mentioned just a few of them when she delivered her report to the Stage Women's War Relief: "In the past two years we have played in 58 different camps and training stations, 67 different club and service houses, and on 14 battleships, and during that time we have given 1,430 shows ... of course the shows were free—you all know the phrase, 'Your uniform is your pass'.... I hardly need say that standing room only was the rule at every performance..."[27]

President Wilson's proclamation confirmed what Dorothy had always believed and put into practice: acting was a respectable profession.

CHAPTER 8
In the Wings

D orothy's years of service to her profession and to her country gave her an occasional—and unintended—hiatus from acting. Consequently, they also provided her with time to change, to mature, and to begin creating herself anew: a necessary process, said the French philosopher Henri Bergson; a painful one, too, Dorothy could have told him. As casting calls slowed to a mere trickle, no gong sounded, of course. Yet, it was ringingly clear to Dorothy, swiftly nearing her fortieth birthday, that her career as an actress had reached the turning point.

When he wrote a decade later of Dorothy's dual positions in the theatre as actress and playwright, Alexander Woollcott was still perplexed by her seemingly sudden decision to leave the stage:

> And always all of us are a little surprised when some one who has climbed to loftier heights than the humdrum toilers of the world ever dare to dream about is seen calmly returning to the flat spaces of the world to begin again, stubbornly, indefatigably, the long, long ascent of another hill. Thus I suspect that most of Dorothy Donnelly's neighbors exchanged puzzled glances when she, who had stood so high in the craft into which she was born, who had known what it was to create and play triumphantly throughout the country such great and nourishing roles as Candida and Madame X, walked abruptly out of the stage door for good and all and began humbly her apprenticeship at the trade of putting black words on white paper.[1]

Louise Hale, by contrast, recognized Dorothy's quiet desperation and described her resolve:

> After a while she began writing and accepted her disappointments without a cry…. And went on writing. She grew a little shabby but *never* ever so little sad. She went on writing. She wrote lyrics in small books. She said they were not so hard to write. For her mother had often sent

her rhymed letters when she was a little girl in school. The masters had taught her music. The nuns, languages. She knew the technicalities of the stage. And rhythm was in her Irish heart.

Louise Closser was both a sympathetic friend and a role model, who showed Dorothy how several careers could be combined successfully and simultaneously. Born in Chicago in 1872 to a family of pioneer farmers, she attended public schools in Indianapolis. After making her first appearance on stage, in Detroit at age 23, she set off for the American Academy of Dramatic Arts, determined to become an actress. "It was Fred Williams who had endeavored to teach me Juliet ... and had more than suggested that my Western 'r' was only a consonant to hold together two vowels, and not, as I seemed to feel, the most vital letter in the alphabet. 'No, dear girl, no,' he would protest—and eased me out of the study of Juliet back to Maria and such wenches," she said after a satisfying 30-year career in supporting roles. Louise had met her husband on the set of *Arizona* in 1899 and married him that summer. Although acting first brought Louise and Walter Hale together, it was shared love, common interests, and mutual respect for each other's individual talents that kept them happily married. Separation, Dorothy remained convinced, was simply unworkable: "It is not a good thing for a man to let a woman realize she can get along without him."[2] Louise did not agree, but never persuaded her friend to think otherwise.

After the revival of *Candida* in 1905, when Louise again played Miss Prossy, the Hales drove from Naples through the north of Italy into France and finally to Le Havre. The trip created instant automobile buffs, and from then on they spent every summer motoring. Their adventures also led Louise to write *A Motor Car Divorce* (1906) and Walter to illustrate the book. Subsequent collaborations included *We Discover New England* (1911) and *We Discover the Old Dominion* (1916). Walter retired from the theatre in 1913 to devote himself exclusively to art until his untimely death shortly before Christmas four years later. His lithographs, illustrations, and etchings appeared in books, in the St. Louis Exhibition of 1904, at the Salon of Societe des Beaux Arts in Paris during 1911, and in the San Francisco Exhibition of 1915, better known as the Panama-Pacific Exhibition. He also served as a war correspondent for *Harper's* magazine and authored guide books. Louise, meanwhile, continued to act and to write books, nine in all, both travel guides and novels dealing with theatre life.

The *Delineator* magazine had given playgoers a foretaste of Dorothy's own skills as a writer as early as April 1906, when it published another article in its series, "Shakespeare's Heroines and Their Impersonators."

Dorothy's five-page commentary on Portia in *The Merchant of Venice* begins
with a scholarly examination of the authorship of the plays attributed to
Shakespeare. Dorothy dismisses the notion that any of them could have
been written by Francis Bacon. To anyone with a "practical knowledge of
the stage," she argues, they were obviously "written by an actor to be
acted." She insists that despite the poetry, their literary merit plays second fiddle to their dramatic value. Dorothy also defends playwrights
against charges of writing for a specific performer—was she thinking of
Shaw as well?—by noting, for example, that the role of Shylock was
designed for Burbage. She then describes at length the different costumes
she had worn in her student days when playing Portia to suggest their
impact in revealing yet another facet of Portia's personality. Finally, she
explicates the trial scene section by section to demonstrate Shakespeare's
rising dramatic construction and closes with a final look at characterization: "a sweet, gay, buoyant creature, loving and trustful, full of wit and
resource, with a mind capable of solving a problem that has baffled men;
yet, withal, a woman of women—such is Portia."

Her initial foray into creative writing resulted in a bizarre short story
that appeared in print December 26, 1908. "Christmas Day in Montreal"
opens as an actress enters a cobbler's shop to have her shoes repaired.
From its beginning as autobiography, however, it quickly becomes an
archetypal tale, featuring a monster who imagines himself insulted and
seeks revenge on an innocent child.[3]

When stage managers began lamenting a lack of plays with characters strong enough for her robust ability, "I'll write one," Dorothy
retorted,[4] blithely masking her chagrin. Dorothy's first attempt at play
writing dealt her the fate of most neophytes—oblivion. Her second
attempt, an adaptation of Charlotte Wells' *The Riddle: Woman*, waited
two years for production. She had better luck with her third try, thanks
to John Cort, a major operator of theatre chains in the West. Cort wanted
to produce *Flora Bella*, an operetta in three acts, but this decision was now
risky for two reasons. First, it was based on a book by Felix Doermann,
and American sentiment against Germany was gaining ground. New
York's Metropolitan Opera Company, for example, refused to present German operas and dropped the Wagnerian "Ring" cycle from its schedule
(and Dorothy's brother, Thomas, quietly resigned from the Liederkranz
Club). Moreover, the English version of the operetta by Cosmo Hamilton was too British to appeal to American audiences. So, Dorothy revised
the libretto and produced a "more than adequate book," according to the
New York Times. *Flora Bella*, with lyrics by Percy Waxman, opened September 11, 1916, at the Casino Theatre and later moved to the 44th Street

Theatre. All together it ran for 112 (some records indicate 115) performances—not a bad record for a beginner. One of the first plays to make its way onto hastily erected stages at military training camps, incidentally, was *Flora Bella*—a most unusual and unanticipated road show.

The following spring John Cort produced yet another play she revised. The plot for *Johnny Get Your Gun* came from Edmund Laurence Burke, who left the unfinished script at Dorothy's doorstep when he put on a soldier's uniform and headed for the trenches of France. The play tells the story of a motion picture cowboy stunt man who goes east to rescue his friend's sister from an unfortunate marriage to a fortune hunter and promptly falls in love with her. The farce's humor draws on the comical contrast between the rough ways of the West and the civilized polish of Eastern manners. Louis Bennison, well known to San Francisco audiences as a member of the Alcazar Theatre's stock company, made a successful Broadway debut in the title role. Staged by George Henry Trader, who had directed the Murray Hill Theatre productions, the play achieved eighty performances.

The title of the play, *Johnny Get Your Gun*, may have derived from a song written and composed by Monroe H. Rosenfeld and published by Elcott Shapiro in 1886. "One of those persons with a morbid appetite for analysis says that George Cohan took part of 'Johnny, get your gun, get your gun, get your gun' and a bugle call, and after blending them with a few other strains called the collection 'Over There,'" wrote C. A. Browne.[5] A morbid inclination to speculate would lead to a more likely conclusion: Cohan's first line possibly came from Dorothy's play, which opened at the Criterion Theatre on February 12, 1917, and was still running when Cohan wrote his verses.

Woollcott wrote two reviews of the play before enlisting in the army as a reporter for the *Stars and Stripes*. "If you do not laugh often and loudly at *Johnny Get Your Gun*, you have a curious sense of humor," he began, and then issued a warning regarding Dorothy: "Doubtless she is responsible for a good deal of its fun. She is a fine actress, but she knows a lot, and, if she does not watch out, they will make her into a playdoctor for life. Then we shall see + D. D. on half of the programs."[6]

As an actress, Dorothy had always treated each succeeding role, even the gauche ones, with surgical precision. She dissected the character she would portray, examining her personality, speech, dress, physical appearance, and mannerisms with microscopic accuracy. Then she meticulously sutured each aspect of the part into a unified role. All this training, practice, and experience pointed to the possibility of another career: playdoctor.

Woollcott's term was apt, and his prophecy proved partly true almost immediately. From 1917 until her death, Dorothy read scripts for the Shuberts with an eye to revision or adaptation. In fact, the Shuberts bombarded her with scripts—"Only a Dream," "Inside Out," "Penny-Wise," "Miss Widow," "When Johnny Comes Marching Home," "Hearts Are Trumps," and "Round Love," to name a few. Most of the plays the Shuberts received were unsolicited, submitted by hopeful amateur playwrights. "These 'over-the-transom' scripts apparently received only a cursory review by low-level staff members before they were invariably rejected."[7] Sometimes the reader's comments played better than the script. The following notes, written by William Dunbar serve as an example:

> It took the author the equivalent length of a 600 page novel to tell the above story. And then he told it so badly that it is hardly recognizable. This is not a play—this is a lecture; a lecture on comparative theology, on cosmology, on sociology, on anything down to the relative superiority of milk from Holstein cows. The author told me that he met George Bernard Shaw in person;—it seems to have had a frightful effect on his mind.[8]

The scripts that showed promise with regard to plot or theme as well as potential for commercial appeal were sent to playdoctors along with an accompanying request: "Can you get a good book from it?"[9] The scripts arrived with such speed and frequency that Dorothy felt compelled to write to Lee Shubert:

> I'm awfully sorry that I find it impossible to finish my version of "Lieutenant Gus" at the required time. The pressure of my work has been so heavy that I simply could not get it done. I must ask you to extend the time for its completion for at least four months more, that is three months from December 31st, 1917. Miss Widow [sic] ought to be on by that time, and then I can give my undivided attention to "Lieutenant Gus."[10]

According to a playbill from the 44th Street Theatre in Manhattan, *Lieutenant Gus* had already been performed a year earlier, on November 10, 1916, as an adaptation by Edgar Smith, but, as Dorothy noted, "Some plays need medicine, and tuning, just like a piano needs tuning."[11]

Another way to fine tune a play is to produce it. When the Shuberts commissioned her to produce a play, Dorothy gloated. "I believe there is as much room for a woman in the producing field as there is for men," she said.[12] Meanwhile, the Shuberts' press department boasted:

> Dorothy Donnelly, the well known actress who has been featured in scores of theatricals, including "Madame X" and equally famous

productions, is making her debut as a producer at the Princess Theatre...

For several years Miss Donnelly has longed to enter the producing field. While she has made a great name for herself in leading roles of well known plays, she felt that unless she could produce a play of her own she would be losing much of the glory attached to the theatrical world ... and having accomplished this she has mastered every twist and turn of the most difficult business in the world.

While reluctant to discuss her own success Miss Donnelly is forced to admit that she is the only player-writer-producer since the days of the immortal Shakespeare. There have been players and producers, players and writers, and writers and producers, but Miss Donnelly is the first person to successfully master these three departments.

Yet another press release, written in similar vein, asserted, "There is nothing left for her to conquer."[13]

Attributed to "an earnest young press agent of prodigious build"[14] with an unlikely, but nevertheless appropriate, moniker—A. Toxen Worm—these releases serpentined their way around the truth. They indulged in hyperbole when comparing Dorothy with "the immortal Shakespeare" and erred in fact when conveniently overlooking the careers of David Belasco, Richard Mansfield, Minnie Maddern Fiske, and Rachel Crothers, who also wrote, acted, and produced for the stage. Nevertheless, they validated Bernard Shaw's opinion that "the stage is the only profession in which women are on equal terms with men."[15] For the seasoned, driven, and highly ambitious woman in the theatre during the first quarter of the twentieth century, opportunities abounded.[16] A case in point is the filming of *Madame X*. "Stage Whispers" in the January 1916 issue of *Theatre Magazine* shared this "secret" with its theatregoing readers:

> Experienced actors who go into the "pictures" have a new sensation when they realize the relentless watchfulness of the camera. It seems to them like a mere rehearsal. But it isn't. It is said that when Dorothy Donnelly did her first screen work she could not resist the temptation abruptly to stop acting in the middle of a scene when she felt that some stage business could be improved. She had been accustomed to do it at dress rehearsals, where her suggestions were always respectfully received. But in the movies, when she dropped her hands and stepped forward to say sweetly to the director: "Don't you think, Mr. Blank, it would be better if I did it *this* way?" There was the camera registering it all, and—bang went the film! The picture had to be done all over again. Miss Donnelly has learned her studio lesson now, but they say that at the beginning she inadvertently caused a waste of celluloid which would have made the air blue if she had not been a popular star.

While this aside reveals the pitfalls Dorothy encountered on the film set, it also underscores the willingness of the profession to recognize the competencies of female colleagues.

The Shuberts had assigned Dorothy to produce *Six Months Option*, a lightweight comedy by Ancella Anslee (Ancella Hunter) that deals with mis-mated couples who separate, re-marry, separate again, and ultimately return to their first and true loves. The play or "moralistic farce" to use Alec Woollcott's description, opened in November 1917 "on a day that was otherwise wholly occupied with Thanksgiving."[17] Dorothy had produced a turkey. Notwithstanding all its circus advertisements, *Six Months Option* folded after 28 performances. The Y.M.C.A., not the Shuberts, gave her another opportunity to demonstrate her talents as a producer. Nevertheless, J. J. periodically authorized her to carry out some of the producer's typical obligations such as calling and supervising rehearsals and exercising her opinions at tryouts.

Meanwhile, Dorothy returned to greener pastures. She began collaborating with Edgar Smith on a musical. Written in three acts with a score and lyrics by Augustus Barratt, *Fancy Free* opened at the Astor Theatre on April 11, 1918. The play functioned as a showcase for the intrepid wanderings in Palm Beach of a playboy through a bevy of similarly unattached females. Its main virtue lay in bringing to the stage two competent performers, capably directed by J. C. Huffman: Clifton Crawford and Marilynn Miller. "*Fancy Free* gets up on its toes early in the evening and stays there. The ten best toes belong to Marilynn Miller," wrote Heywood Broun, drama critic for the *Boston Globe*. Miller was a beautiful blonde, with fine porcelain features and a long swan-like neck, whose dancing was graceful, almost "dainty" (the preferred adjective among the critics at the time). When Ziegfeld asked her to appear in his next Follies, the Shuberts threw a fit. This was an unending rivalry, incidentally, for the Shuberts had previously filed charges against Ziegfeld when Nora Bayes defected from their camp. Miller now contacted a lawyer. Extensive legal bickerings ensued. An out-of-court settlement resolved the issue, and Miller worked for both Ziegfeld and the Shuberts, holding center stage unquestionably as one of the most glamourous stars of the 1920s. (She dropped the final "n" from her first name at the recommendation of Florenz Ziegfeld, who later starred her in *Sally*, singing Jerome Kern's hit song, "Look for the Silver Lining.")

The *New York Times* labeled *Fancy Free* "a pleasant musical comedy with a number of very bright moments," found the lines "bright and fresh enough," but bemoaned the lack of humor—a recurring criticism that grated Dorothy like a pebble trapped in a shoe. By contrast,

Theatre Magazine lavished praise: "*Fancy Free* is almost unflaggingly amusing. What more have we been educated to expect from musical comedy?"

The Riddle: Woman, completed two years earlier, finally opened at the Harris Theatre on October 23, 1918. Dorothy based the drama on a popular play by the Danish playwright, C. Jacobi. Or did she? George John Nathan uncovered the truth, but it was Alexander Woollcott who once again let the proverbial cat out of the bag. When he told Dorothy of his plan to write a capsule biography of her, she pleaded with him. "The Irish in her bubbled up and she whispered, in the manner of a lobbyist at Washington, 'Strike the harp gently.'"[18] But Woollcott, tongue-in-cheek, revealed her cleverness first in misleading Arnold Daly about having read *Candida* and then in hoodwinking the public about the birth of *The Riddle: Woman*. "On the eve of her sailing to join the A. E. F. in 1917, she found Bertha Kalich struggling with the manuscript of a German play, and it was the deceitful Miss Donnelly's notion to journey to the Public Library, cram her head with Danish names, towns, titles, and terms, and then adroitly shift the enemy drama to a neutral territory, palming it off as the masterpiece of a young Danish dramatist whom she invented on the spot."[19]

Whatever its cloudy origin, *The Riddle: Woman* takes a page from *Madame X* to explore the plight of Lilla Olrik, who flouts convention by having an affair and then hides her past from her new husband, a prominent merchant (Robert Edeson). Enter Count Helsinger (A. E. Anson), gambler and spendthrift, who compromises young women and subsequently blackmails them. The mystery implied by the title of the three-act play is solved when Lilla reveals that she had been the count's victim prior to her marriage. She tries to save a seventeen-year old girl from a similar fate and half strangles the scoundrel to recover the letters she had written to him. This "striking emotional drama," as the *New York Times* called it, realized 165 performances during its 20-week run. Afterwards it toured the country.

When Dorothy first worked on this play, she intended the role of Lilla Olrik for herself but abandoned the plan:

> I am rather a fatalist about playing. I will never play again unless it is inevitable. Either that I must play to earn my living or a part is offered to me that is so compelling that it demands that I play it. I almost hope that I will never play again. If one is successful she must go with the character she has created in the play she has helped to make successful, on the road. The hardships and discomforts of the actor's life are depressing.[20]

This statement reveals more about Dorothy than any other remarks she ever made to the press. It was a public confession of her initially painful disappointment. She regarded her chances of being offered an irresistible role as mighty slim, even non-existent. How many good parts awaited casting, tantalizing parts like Amanda Winfield, the domineering mother in Tennessee Williams' *The Glass Menagerie*, that would lure Laurette Taylor back to the stage in 1945, 32 years into retirement following the death of her husband? Realistically, Dorothy knew, too, that her crowded schedule as a playwright and playdoctor eliminated monetary concerns for both the present and the future. Though her writing kept her off the stage, it kept her anchored to the theatre. Therefore, she contented herself with directing *The Riddle: Woman* rather than starring in it. Accordingly, the leading role went to Bertha Kalich, who grew up speaking Yiddish but mastered English in five years and moved onto the main stage with superlative diction and admirable skill. Dorothy experienced some anxious moments when Kalich caught a cold during the run and two performances were canceled, but she had no need to worry about having to return to the road herself.

Her next venture, *The Melting of Molly*, had as many writers as leading ladies and plenty of both. Two years in the making, this dramatization by Maria Thompson Davis based on her own novel, began life as straight comedy, but when Irene Franklin was cast in the title role, songs were added. Then the Shuberts bought the rights to the play and revised it for Vivian Wessell. They delegated Sigmund Romberg to compose the score. During its trial run in New Haven, Connecticut, Wessell married and immediately retired. Again the play was rewritten, this time for Alma Tell, but she quit after a tryout in Newark, New Jersey. The Shuberts attempted a fourth production with Florence Nash in the leading role. When this, too, failed, they called the doctor.

"Dear Miss Donnelly, as rehearsals for the 'Melting of Molly' Company are called for 11 o'clock Monday, will you please see that the composers have their music on hand, and oblige." The very next day, April 13, 1918, they sent her a second letter: "Mr. Ralph Herz will accept the part (McTapp) in the 'Melting of Molly' providing you write it up for him."[21] Isabelle Lowe played the title role and Sigmund Romberg composed the music for Dorothy's version of the play. After a tryout in Chicago, it reached Broadway on December 30, 1918. "+D. D." was inexplicably missing from the program. The extent and nature of her contributions to a play determined whether she received recognition for them. Whenever she prescribed extensive treatment by adapting it or transforming the play into a musical, the Shuberts acknowledged her. On the

J. J. (left) and Lee pose beneath a picture of Sam to form a composite photograph of the Shubert brothers, sole owners of the world's largest theatrical empire. (Courtesy Shubert Archive.)

Producer J. J. Shubert (left) and composer Sigmund Romberg, late in their careers, share a rare light-hearted moment at the keyboard. (Courtesy Shubert Archive.)

other hand, whenever she dispensed sample medications like revising some lines, adding a part, or including a song, the Shuberts kept her name off the program. Take *The Charm School*, for example. Based on a story by Alice Duer Miller, it was revised as a play in 1920 starring Minnie Dupree "With a Wee Bit of Music by Jerome Kern," according to the program, and as a musical that opened in Chicago in 1925 with a new title, *June Days*. The musical included a ditty called "Take 'Em to the Door Blues." Dorothy had originally written the lyrics for *Hello, Lola*,[22] but the song was cut from the production during its tryout in Washington, D. C. Robert Milton and Alice Miller received public credit for the script, Cyrus Wood for the musical adaptation, and Donnelly for nothing, although the Shuberts paid her royalties whenever they produced it.

On March 6, 1917, Dorothy signed an agreement with the Shubert Theatrical Company to adapt "Miss Widow." Its terms are typical of the contracts issued at that period. She would receive $250, free and clear, upon signing the contract, one and a half percent of the weekly gross receipts up to $5,000, two percent if the weekly take exceeded that amount, and a quarter percent of the net receipts from stock and motion picture rights. All the moneys would be paid to her representative, Brandt and Kirkpatrick, Inc. As the scripts evolved, so did their names. *Charm School* led to *The School Maid* and eventually to *June Days*. *Miss Widow* underwent similar transformation. The Shuberts directed Dorothy to rename the play *Miss Camouflage*, but never produced it under either title. Whether they ever produced it at all remains questionable. In any case, "+D. D." would not have appeared in the playbill.

Forbidden, Dorothy's only original script and her first without a co-author, was produced by George Mooser at the Manhattan Opera House on December 20, 1919. The play opens with the entry of American troops into the Coblenz Bridgehead, but most of the action takes place thirty miles away, in the hall of the Schloss von der Verde, where the officers are billeted. First Lieutenant John Booth Lawrence (Richard Barbee), known as Boots, falls in love with Countess Hildegarde (Martha Hedman), who returns his affection. They plan to marry until the Countess discovers that Boots was the man responsible for the death of her brother, an enemy sniper who fatally shot the general's son, Boots' best friend. While extenuating circumstances exonerate Boots, the play ends with the separation of the lovers and keeps the audience in suspense regarding their possible reunion. Dorothy seasoned the play with authentic local color and accurately captured the idiom, language, mood, and humor of the American soldiers stationed in Coblenz. Its crap game scene could well have been enacted in any military camp. Alexander Woollcott, who reviewed the play for the *New York Times*, found it both "interesting and often genuinely amusing."[23]

In raising the morale of servicemen with the A.E.F., Dorothy had unwittingly boosted her own. Louise Hale explains:

> To cautious ones that trip looked like the end of what she was finding for herself. Perhaps. But she found a boy at the front playing ragtime for his mates. He has now become a concert pianist. She found a plot over there for her own play, 'Forbidden.' She found cruel cold and discomfort, which in no way depleted her unconquerable soul. She found her soul *was* unconquerable.

Dorothy's tour with the Y.M.C.A. provided her with another happy discovery: "writing is great fun., and added to it one has the delight of producing the play. That to one who loves the stage and lives in it is a delight. I've never gotten away from the stage. Writing and directing keep one in its atmosphere."[24]

Six plays in three years!—an extraordinary record that few can match, an astounding one for an amateur. Her first attempts at play writing knew no limitation and explored a wide range of dramatic form: farce, melodrama, musical, comedy, and romance. Dorothy attributed her success to luck and to providence—"Some One is leading me by the hand," she told Louise Hale—and counted her blessings: "Life is more livable for the playwright. She can keep her home and stay in it. She need not leave friends for a long time. She has hours of quiet when the grind of wheels ceases its torture."[25]

Dorothy, however, spoke too soon.

CHAPTER 9

Behind the Scenes

Whenever the Shuberts grabbed the crank, the wheels ground exceedingly fine. Just as Pershing's troops were about to sail for France, the brothers presented *Maytime,* starring Peggy Wood and William Norris. With a new libretto by Rida Johnson Young in collaboration with Cyrus Wood, a new score by Sigmund Romberg, and a new setting—New York City—this German operetta realized instant popularity. It soon required two casts, playing simultaneously, to meet public demand and achieved a record of 492 performances during its first season on Broadway. Now that the soldiers were home again, the producers tried to lure them back to the theatre with yet another operetta. Their occupation was show business; their emphasis, business. They knew in advance what the statistics for the 1927-1928 drama season would later reveal: straight plays have less than a 25 percent chance of success in recouping their investments or showing a profit, revues enjoy a rate of 50 percent, and musical comedies top them all at 63 percent.[1]

Lee Shubert asked Dorothy to call on him. "Will you please do so at your earliest convenience as he has two or three plays that he would like to talk to you about," wrote his personal executive secretary, Mr. Jack Morris, to Dorothy.[2] She received another telephone call the morning of March 24, 1920. A letter followed.

> With reference to our 'phone conversation of this morning, will you please start working immediately on *Dreimaedlerhaus.* I am sending the score under separate cover to-day. Mr. Shubert will agree to give you $250 now and $250 upon delivery of the completed manuscript. The matter of royalties, he will take up with you later.[3]

Initially it was Edgar Smith, not Dorothy, the Shuberts considered for the job. J. J. Shubert had seen *Das Dreimaedlerhaus (The House of the*

Three Girls) on one of his European scouting trips.[4] The operetta premiered January 15, 1916, in Vienna but captured international interest only after the war, when enmities dissolved. In a letter to Gustave Schimer, who held the rights to foreign shows imported to the United States, Jake mentioned his interest in having Edgar Smith translate the play and write a libretto.[5] Smith had begun working for the Shuberts as early as 1909 and already written 21 libretti for them. What motivated them to deliver the commission to Dorothy instead? Perhaps they recognized theatrical competency in her revisions of *Fancy Free* or the *The Melting of Molly*. Maybe they respected her fluency in German, learned at school and honed during her stay in Coblenz. It's also possible—since speculations sprout as swiftly as mushrooms on the thick damp carpet of the forest—that they were merely scraping the bottom of the barrel. "A good book is essential," insists Gerald Bordman: "It contributes 50 percent of the success of the operetta."[6] The problem was that no one cared to write it, says William Green:

> In the first place, the composer could not do the job himself. He needed the cooperation of the librettist. But this was not an era of talented librettists. Besides, there was little to attract an author to libretto writing. Producers and composers tended to regard song, dance, and spectacle as individual entities, with no need to establish relationships among them and with no concern for encasing all in a tight plot with well constructed characters. Furthermore, as Carl Wilmore pointed out in an article in the *Dramatic Mirror* of March 10, 1917, most American authors regarded libretto writing with scorn. Therefore, they kept away from the musical stage entirely or made no attempt to master the special problems it presented.[7]

Historically, the book primarily served as an excuse to visit exotic locales or as a vehicle to provide a bony frame for dialect comedians or offer a skimpy skeleton for song and dance. Most musical shows depended on the personal magnetism of their stars, who didn't hesitate to introduce their own material and songs into the production without any regard for the plot, much less the script. Rarely did the book progress from a beginning through a middle to the end, using dialogue to advance the plot and develop defined characters. "Interpolations were business as usual," says Ethan Mordden. "Musicals weren't supposed to be integrated or authoritative; they were supposed to be entertaining, and who cared how they got that way!"[8] Another historian of the musical theatre, Martin Gottfried, acknowledges the importance of the book in making a unified whole of the musical. Since most libretti are assigned or commissioned, he adds, they are not "written with the personal dedication given to a play, and the professional librettist tends to think of his work as less an art than a craft." He also notes that "because its practitioners have been slighted and its importance ignored, book writing, then, is the least developed of the musical theatre's disciplines."[9] Whatever prompted the assignment—and heedless of these retrospective *caveats*—on April 21, Dorothy signed the contract engaging "services of the Author to revise and adapt the book and lyrics of said play."[10]

Where many men feared to tread, a few women bravely strode to fill the void. Like Dorothy, these pioneers had seen some of their earlier plays produced before they attempted to write libretti and lyrics. In 1906 Anne Caldwell teamed up with her husband, James O'Dea, to write *The Social Whirl*. Caldwell also wrote the book and lyrics for *The Top of the World* (1907), *Chin-Chin* (1915), *Pom-Pom* (1916), *The Lady in Red* (1919), and, *She's a Good Fellow* (1919). The librettist and lyricist, Rida Johnson Young, has a long string of credits and successes. Although *Maytime* became her greatest box-office hit, she wrote *Naughty Marietta* with composer Victor Herbert (1910), *The Red Petticoat* (1912), *Her Soldier Boy* (1916), *Sometime* (1918), and *Little Simplicity* (1918). All but *The Red Petticoat* surpassed the record of 100 performances. Catherine Chisholm Cushing contributed *Glorianna* to the musical stage. Rudolf Friml composed the score, and John Cort produced the play in 1918. Earlier she had also written *Sari* and a musical version of *Uncle Tom's Cabin*. None of Dorothy's precursors attained the commercial success that she would achieve, however, nor made the lasting impact on the theatre that began with *Blossom Time*, her adaptation of *Das Dreimaedlerhaus*.

The play's plot was loosely based on the work and life of the composer, Franz Schubert, whose biography virtually called for fictionalizing. Born January 31, 1797, outside Vienna, Schubert was one of 14 children. The family was so desperately poor that nine of his siblings died in infancy. The local choir master, Michael Holzer, befriended the boy and taught him music.[11] Without any formal study of composition, he wrote hundreds of songs and three important symphonies. Symphony No. 8 in B minor, familiarly known as the "Unfinished" symphony, arguably remains incomplete rather than unfinished. "There are but two movements instead of the usual four.... But in a larger sense, it is utterly perfect in finish. It leaves nothing unsaid."[12] When he died in 1828 at the age of 31 from typhus fever, still unrecognized, Schubert left behind an estate of ten dollars and a treasury of music that ranks him among the greatest musicians of all time.[13]

A. M. Willner and Hans Reichert based *Das Dreimaedlerhaus* on two earlier works, the novel, *Schwammerl* (*Little Toadstool*), by Rudolf Hans Bartsch and the operetta, *Franz Schubert*, composed by Franz von Suppe in 1864. The librettists invited composer Heinrich Berte to build the score for their musical around a single tune, Schubert's "Impatient" song, but the results disappointed. Consequently, Berte was directed to rewrite the music, this time using only Schubert's melodies.[14] Eventually translated into more than 20 languages, the plot would remain fairly constant, although the names of the sisters changed from Hederl, Haiderl, and Hannerl in the original German to Tili, Lili, and Wili in England (*Lilac Time*); Annette, Jeannette, and Nanette in France (*Chanson d'Amour*); Edi, Hedi, and Medi in Bucharest; and Mitzi, Kitzi, and Fritzi in Dorothy's *Blossom Time*.

Dorothy worked around Berte's arrangement to create the libretto. *Blossom Time* was already in rehearsal when the Shuberts called in Sigmund Romberg, their in-house composer, to rescore it. Born July 29, 1887, in the Hungarian village of Nagykanisiza, Sigmund Romberg was named for his paternal grandfather, a practicing physician. His father, Adam Romberg, a chemical engineer by trade and a pianist by avocation, was fluent in six languages; his mother, Clara Berg Romberg, wrote poetry and short stories. Romberg showed early promise as a musician: he had already mastered the violin and organ during in his teens and soon taught himself to play the trumpet and drums as well. Even while in elementary school, he composed a short piece, "The Red Cross March," dedicated to the Grand Duchess, head of the local Red Cross.[15] His practical parents, however, decided that he should have a dependable career and sent him to the Politechnische Hochschule in Vienna to study civil engineering. Tossing aside his slide rule as often as prudence permitted, he reached for a cello or drum sticks while continuing to practice and perform. After graduation he worked at the Theatre-an-der-Wien variously as assistant manager, coach, and accompanist. When his parents renewed their objections to a career in music, he entered the military and became attached to the Nineteenth Hungarian Infantry Regiment, stationed in Vienna. After his service, to dissuade him further, his parents encouraged him to travel. Romberg went to London first and then came to the United States in 1909, arriving with only 300 dollars in his pocket.

He found employment at the Eagle Pencil Company that paid him seven dollars a week. To augment his income, Romberg played the piano in New York City restaurants and night clubs. At Bustanoby, an upscale restaurant, he conducted a small orchestra and, long before it became standard practice, played music for dancing. In 1913 Joseph Stern published three of Romberg's songs: "Some Smoke," "Leg of Mutton," and "La

As depicted on the cover of the souvenir program for Blossom Time, *Austrian composer Franz Schubert appears successful and content, but he died dogged by poverty and obscurity. (Courtesy Center for the American Musical, Canada College.)*

Sheet music for the duet "Song of Love," sung by the leads for Mitzi and Schubert, accompanied the Broadway opening of Blossom Time *in 1921. (Courtesy Center for the American Musical, Canada College.)*

Poeme."[16] Louis Hirsch, the house composer for the Shuberts, tendered his resignation in December, and J. J. offered Romberg the position. Hoping that he could support himself and still send some money abroad to his parents, Romberg signed a contract with the Shubert Theatrical Corporation. Beginning with *The Whirl of the World*, he composed hundreds of songs, seemingly effortlessly. In just three years, for example, from 1914 to 1917, often writing from midnight to dawn, he composed 175 songs for 17 musicals. He wrote the music for *The Passing Show*, annually presented at the Winter Garden Theatre, where "a dress not cut to the waist line at the back is a curiosity—an impudent attempt at welcome modesty."[17] So read the house's handout. Romberg was infinitely prouder of his score for *Blue Paradise*, which introduced the memorable song, "Auf Wedersehn," and for *Over the Top*, which introduced a sensational pair of young dancers, Fred Astaire and his sister, Adele. Following a brief stint with the United States Army, he teamed up with Max Wilner to form a short-lived company that produced only two musicals before dissolving: *The Magic Melody* in 1919, whose appearance unfortunately coincided with the actors' strike, and *Love Birds* in 1921.[18]

The Shuberts selected wisely. Romberg doted on the Viennese melodies that he had written for earlier operettas, *Blue Paradise* (1915) and *Maytime* (1917). He knew Franz Schubert's music and liked it. Money was another incentive: his brief attempt to break away from the Shuberts and mount his own productions ended in financial disaster. So, with mixed feelings, he accepted the assignment and formally signed a contract with the Shuberts on April 30, 1921. Since the agreement between the Shuberts and Actors' Equity called for five weeks of rehearsal for *Blossom Time* and the schedule could not be extended, barely four weeks remained to revise the score. According to Alan Jay Lerner, whenever Romberg thought of a melody, he would jot down on a card a few bars of music, often not more than four, and add some marginal notes like "good baritone solo."[19] The cards could then be drawn in succession as needed: tenor solo, then a soprano song, followed by a duet. This system enabled him to write with speed. To construct "Song of Love," the duet first sung by Shoeber and Mitzi, Romberg borrowed the cello melody from first movement of Schubert's B Minor "Unfinished Symphony," interwove it with bars from yet another Schubert composition, and added a connecting theme of his own. He based "My Springtime Thou Art" on Schubert's Waltz, opus 9, number 2. "Three Little Maids," "Lonely Heart," and "Tell Me, Daisy," other hit songs, now mainly forgotten, were similarly adapted; only Schubert's "Serenade" and "Ave Maria" remained unchanged.

The race to meet the deadline for the Broadway opening continued unabated. Dorothy hurriedly dashed off lyrics for the new songs and revised the libretto as needed to provide some context for each of them. The reviewer for the *New York Tribune* recognized her efforts: "Melodies are introduced with an appreciation of the dramatic relation to the action on the stage."[20]

Act I of *Blossom Time* takes place during May, 1826, outdoors at the Prater Restaurant in Vienna. The ensemble sing their paean to spring, "Hail, Let Us Greet the Spring," and thereby establish the mood. "Three Little Maids" introduces the sisters, who have gathered for lunch. Kitzi and Fritzi are there to meet their fiancés in secret. Mitzi, serving as chaperone, will help them hide news of their engagement from their father, the court jeweler, by pretending to arrange for music lessons. Franz Schubert, a retiring, relatively unknown, but musically talented youth, sits near by with four of his artistic friends—painter, opera singer, draughtsman, and poet. He falls in love with Mitzi, but like Cyrano de Bergerac, he is too shy to address the object of his affections directly. Instead, he reaches for the restaurant's menu, turns it over, scribbles notes on the back, and has his friend Baron Franz Shoeber woo Mitzi with "Serenade" while accompanying him on the piano. Perhaps confused by the similarity of their names, and decidedly swept away by the music, Mitzi rushes into Shoeber's arms and confesses her love. Although she eventually becomes aware of her error and joins Schubert in singing the duet, "Song of Love," it's too late; Schubert realizes that he will never win the girl. Meanwhile, the arrival of Kranz, the father, provides a comic touch, for he proceeds to drink excessively, agrees to a double wedding, then falls asleep at the table.

The setting for Act II is the drawing room of the Kranz home. As Mitzi and Shoeber sing another duet, "Thou Art My Love," they are overheard by Bellabruna, one of the wedding guests. She, too, has succumbed to Shoeber's charms and warns Mitzi against her lover's heartlessness. Bellabruna's husband, Count Sharntoff, aware of his wife's dalliance, challenges Shoeber to a duel. It never takes place, however, for in Act III, Schubert affirms the character and sincerity of his friend. Heartbroken, he finds some satisfaction in having brought the two lovers together and greater consolation in his music. He begins his masterpiece, leaves it unfinished (Dorothy provided a plausible explanation by having him declare that he lost his inspiration when he lost his love), falls ill, summons up enough strength to compose his "Ave Maria," then dies.[21]

Blossom Time first appeared at the Globe Theatre in Atlantic City, New Jersey, on March 21, 1921, then moved to Poli's Theatre in Washington, D. C. on March 27, traveled to the Auditorium in Baltimore a week later, and returned to the Globe on September 21. Since negative reviews of Broadway openings can doom a show, most plays open out of town. While major overhaul of any play generally takes place during rehearsals, tryouts, by contrast, provide the tune-up that keeps a play running smoothly. The reaction of audiences, the response of critics, and the attitudes of those involved in the production, all allow for minor changes to costumes, dialogue, music, lyrics, and so forth. Furthermore, the trial run gives the cast an opportunity to grow into their roles and to coalesce ensemble performances.

It also provokes panic attacks. J. J. Shubert, who was personally supervising the operetta, interrupted one performance to bark at Romberg as he was conducting the orchestra: "So, why is the God-damned orchestra playing so loud I can't hear the words?" When Romberg explained that only the fiddles were playing, J. J. directed him to use a single string: "I want to hear the words!"[22]—Dorothy's words. Even years later, the operetta remained "a never-ending source of tears for Jake. He would walk into remote theaters, sit in an empty seat in the back row, and cry bountifully whenever 'Song of Love' or 'Ave Maria' were performed."[23]

The publicity advertisements in Philadelphia read "Music from Melodies of Franz Schubert and H. Berte, adapted by Sigmund Romberg, under the direction of J. J. Shubert."[24] The reference to Berte must have chafed Romberg. Still bitter about having been asked to rearrange the music rather than compose his own, Romberg brooded. Dorothy, buoyed by the success of the trial runs, assured him the show would live for years. Since Schubert's music had already lasted for a century, he tartly replied, surely it was destined to survive another 20 years.[25]

Blossom Time first hit Broadway on September 29, 1921, with a cast of trained vocalists: Olga Cook as Mitzi; Bertram Peacock as Franz Schubert; and Howard Marsh as Baron Franz Shoeber. Ralph Herz, for whom Dorothy had written a part in *The Melting of Molly*, played Kranz, the father. Dorothy sent a letter to Mr. Morris, asking him to reserve several seats in the orchestra for her family and friends and two in the balcony for herself and her nephew, John Ambrose McCall. "I want to sit upstairs as I get so fidgetty [sic] at an opening," she confided.[26]

The *New York Times* review began with a startling benediction: "After jazz, what? They tried a new answer on Broadway last evening…." Alexander Woollcott added that "Dorothy Donnelly and Sigmund Romberg have adapted it adroitly to American uses and the Shuberts have produced it without stint." While admiring the "quiet tempo of the talk" and Dorothy's "deft adaptation," he panned the acting, especially of William Danforth (whose first big hit came in the 1910 production of Gilbert and Sullivan's

The Mikado) and Bertram Peacock, whose "neat presence" and tenor voice he nevertheless appreciated. He noted that Howard Marsh, cast as Shoeber, "sang—alas! shouted too."

The audience did not agree, however. They warmed to the excellent singing and requested encores of several songs, especially "Serenade," silkily delivered by Marsh. Critic Charles Darnton praised the music: "Tell it not in Tin Pan Alley, but Broadway has discovered Schubert. Accordingly, there is surcease from jazz and like assaults upon the ear ... 'Blossom Time' last night proved to be a veritable bouquet of songs."[27] Ludwig Lewison, writing for *The Nation*, began his review by apparently denouncing the show:

> Professional devotees of music—and devotees of music are apt to be a little professional—will not be pleased with the whole scheme of "Blossom Time." They may merely disdain the act of building a play around the life of Franz Schubert. But to trick out that play with Schubert's songs, to ring all the possible changes on the everlasting Standchen, to use the great melody from the Unfinished Symphony quite as the leitmotif and enveloping tune is used in the cheapest musical shows! Yes, it is barbarous. And the American production added new atrocities to the old. The tempo of the loveliest of the Wiener Walzer was shamelessly accelerated—"jazzed up" is the better expression.[28]

Although he continues in this vein a little longer, he soon finds himself concurring with critics Woollcott and Darnton regarding the quality of the music:

> But when, on leaving the theater, we heard the usher call out: "All the hits of the show at forty cents a piece!" and saw the honest bourgeois with still glowing faces crowd forward to buy "the hits of the show," we felt certain that the American producers of the "Drei Madelhaus" had done a good deed—vital, beautiful, beneficent.... Yes, we insist now, if not before, the Messrs. Shubert have shown themselves public benefactors and have wiped out a multitude of their quite unquestionable sins.[29]

In a season that produced such popular tunes as "I'm Just Wild about Harry," "Oh Me! Oh My!," "My Mammy," "Ma, He's Making Eyes at Me," "Ain't We Got Fun," "I'm Nobody's Baby," "The Sheik of Araby," and "Careless Love," *Blossom Time* pleased not only by what it included— waltzes, marches, and the famed "Ave Maria"—but also by what it omitted—jazz and rag-time.

The operetta proudly set a record of 592 performances during its first season. In January 1922 attendance figures received an unexpected boost from the Schubert Memorial Committee, formed to celebrate the one hundred and twenty-fifth birthday of the composer Franz Schubert. Was it mere coincidence that led the committee to adopt as its headquarters the Ambassador Theatre, where *Blossom Time* was currently playing? One of the committee's press releases gave the following report:

> Early in a Broadway season that has had more than its share of plays advertised by outraged enemies, a noted New York divine declared from his pulpit: "The jazz dance and song of modern musical comedy are responsible for the bad manners and low morals of the recent flappers."
>
> Broadway received the indictment in the casual silence with which it hears all criticism, and a few days later revealed a quiet answer to the charge of decadence with "Blossom Time," a musical effort for which the great master of melody, Franz Schubert, furnishes not only the music but the play theme.... From [Schubert's Eighth Symphony] the beautiful "Song of Love" has been made, to express the sentiment of lovers of all time, and the greatest romance in musical history has become an involuntary witness for the defense in the case of critics versus the morality of modern musical plays.[30]

Blossom Time reopened in August 1922 for 626 performances, and, beginning May 21, 1923, played simultaneously at two theatres—Forty-Fourth Street and the Shubert, both on the same block! Sound showmen, the Shuberts distributed ballots during an intermission so that the audience could elect the cast that would take the show to London. They then took the play to Philadelphia, the first leg of a long journey. Dorothy considered herself fortunate to remain at home.

Working together on *Blossom Time* drew Dorothy and Romberg together not only as future collaborators but also as friends. In 1922, when Romberg called on his parents in the Croatian border town of Belisce and returned from his annual visit despondent by their ill health, Dorothy tried to bolster his spirits. She impulsively wrote to Clara and Adam Romberg, telling them that they need not worry about their son and could look forward to seeing him again next summer.[31] She also took Romberg with her on one of her frequent visits to Ned Sheldon.

About seven years earlier, sometime in 1915, Sheldon had begun complaining about stiffness in his knees. Years of hospitalization and laboratory testing made the diagnosis indisputable: crippling, progressive arthritis. When every movement became painful, he drew on his royalties and installed himself in a comfortable penthouse, 14 stories above Madison Avenue, at 35 East Eighty-fourth Street. Although invalid and eventually blind, Ned never became idle. He remained a powerful force in the theatre; few actors took important steps without consulting him. He also wrote more plays. Another 12 of them were produced following the first signs of illness. He "received an endless flow of visitors in the beautiful Italianate drawing room, its walls paneled in blue brocade, of his New York apartment," said actress Helen Hayes, who married on August 17, 1928, Sheldon's sister's brother-in-law, Charles MacArthur, a former writer for the *Hearst International Magazine* and co-author with Ben Hecht of the successful play, *The Front Page*.[32] (Dorothy's nephew, Ambrose McCall, coincidentally, obtained MacArthur's divorce, making this remarriage possible.[33]) Hayes often dined with Ned on her opening nights:

> He steadied me, gave me inner strength and balance. He knew every play I did and was always ready to discuss it with me. If this or that scene worried me, he would suggest the right way to handle it. He never intruded, but if I needed his help, he was always there to offer advise [sic] and encouragement.[34]

Sheldon worked patiently with other playwrights, suggesting ways of mastering a tricky scene and bolstering their confidence. He sent telegrams to essayist Anne Morrow Lindbergh (who wrote of him in the *Reader's Digest* series, "Most Unforgettable Character I've Ever Met") and to Alec Woollcott during their brief hospitalizations. In Lionel Barrymore's words, "brilliant as Sheldon was in his own works, his great bountiful gift was human kindness.... He was the theatre's acolyte and its people's priest."[35] His brother, John, however, rarely came by.

John Barrymore's debts to Sheldon were many. In addition to suggesting that Barrymore give up comic roles, Ned groomed him for *Richard III* and *Hamlet*. John's biographer, Gene Fowler, also claims that Ned rewrote "speeches, scenes, or even entire plays for him."[36] Sheldon used an Italian work by Sem Benelli to write *The Jest*, a play that opened in 1919, featured both Barrymore brothers, and appealed 13 times to the stage-struck, teenaged Tallulah Bankhead. (Besotted by affection for John Barrymore, the future screen actress stopped at 13 only because that was her lucky number.[37]) By this time, however, John had substituted the screen—and alcohol—[38] for the stage. Nightly performances and long runs bored him; drink and chorus girls or anyone remotely attractive held greater fascination. Nevertheless, "The presence of John Barrymore haunted the American theater long after he had deserted it," writes Lloyd Morris, adding that his acting set a standard as well as a challenge for aspiring actors.[39] "'I love that son of a bitch,' John Barrymore said of Ned. 'But he's my conscience and I can't face him.'"[40]

According to Eric Barnes, Edward Sheldon's biographer, "no one had done more to keep Sheldon close to the world of theatre than Dorothy Donnelly."[41] With Romberg at the piano playing melodies from *Blossom Time*, Dorothy retold its story to the bedridden playwright.[42] On an earlier occasion, Dorothy also brought her youngest niece to visit with Sheldon; Dolly describes him as well-to-do, "a handsome man, a knock-out and a charmer," and remembers being flattered when Ned asked her how she was doing in school. ("*He* gets A+s," Dolly later whispered to her aunt.[43])

To her concerns about Romberg's depression and Sheldon's immobility was added yet another worry—her brother's ill health. Thomas had been faring poorly for almost a year. On his good days, the judge returned to the bench, but he was frequently confined to bed. Dorothy knew only one solution for pain. "Writing is a dreadful labour," Thomas Carlyle once wrote, "yet not so dreadful as idleness."[44] Dorothy plunged into work. She finished her revisions for *Poppy*, continued collaborating on *The Student Prince* with Romberg, and met with Ned Sheldon as she was writing *The Proud Princess*.

With *Poppy*, Dorothy ploughed new territory—new for her, anyway. Revues like Ziegfeld's *Follies* and the Shuberts' *Passing Show*, and the more risqué *Artists and Models*, made annual appearances and profits. Gaudy and brash and sometimes genuinely funny, the revues jumbled dances routines with comedy and interspersed these with songs written by composers and lyricists with a cash register at their side, hungrily anticipating the sale of sheet music. When Dorothy decided to cook up a pastiche of her own, she peppered it with preposterous names like Amos Sniffen and Princess Vronski Mameluke Pasha Tubbs, larded it lavishly with songs, sprinkled it with a score by Stephen Jones and Arthur Samuel, and glued the concoction together with a simple story.

In the opening scene the audience learns that Poppy's mother, a runaway, has died after giving birth. Another circus drifter, Professor Eustace McGargle, adopts the orphan and teaches Poppy to become a fortune teller. Delighted by her success and tempted by greed, he takes her with him to Connecticut to claim an inheritance. Poppy, however, refuses to take part in the swindle. In the best tradition of melodrama, Poppy becomes acknowledged as the rightful heir, and the play ends happily when she marries a decent, and wealthy, city boy whom she's met on the circus grounds.

Dorothy made little attempt to integrate the songs with either the plot or the characters. These were show tunes designed to unearth an audience of their own as singles. She penned the lyrics for 12 of *Poppy*'s songs, including "Two Make a Home" and "On Our Honeymoon," which became instant hits along with two interpolations: Stephen Jones wrote the music and Irving Caesar the lyrics for "Whaddye Do Sundays, Mary" while Arthur Swartz wrote the music and Howard Dietz the lyrics for "Alibi Baby."

The play first opened at the Apollo Theatre on September 3, 1923, to a mixed reception. On one hand, Ludwig Lewisohn of *The Nation* magazine found it neither musical nor comic; on the other, he concluded that "out of juggling and slap-stick material and burlesque make-up [*Poppy*] builds up a character worthy of Mark Twain at his best." John Corbin declared that "*Poppy* emerges as an exceptional musical comedy." Heywood Broun of New York *World* wrote, "In the musical comedy field *Poppy* is the best we know." The *New York Times* insisted "it can never be claimed that Dorothy Donnelly's book is funny per se," but declared its assets plentiful and its shortcomings unimportant and then concluded, "it was just a good show." It had 328 performances and was still running as late as June 15, 1924.

If the book lacked humor, Dorothy made up for it through superlative casting and direction. *Poppy* introduced dramatic comedienne Madge Kennedy as a singing star in the title role; the 19-year-old's energetic liveliness was considered perfect for the part. Pantomime artist and silent juggler, W. C. Fields (William Claude Dukenfield), played the unconventional professor. His stocky build, bushy mustache, and bulbous, rosy nose lent themselves remarkably well to the character. His costume—top hat, walking cane, cigar, and boldly checkered black and white pants held up by wide suspenders—rivaled the outlandishness of Petruchio's wedding garb so humorously described in Shakespeare's *Taming of the Shrew*. Of Fields' performance, critic Heywood Broun noted that he couldn't "remember anyone who ever made us laugh more."

Within days of *Poppy*'s opening, on September 27, 1923, in fact, Dorothy was elected to the American Society of Composers, Authors, and Publishers. When the American inventor Lee De Forest developed a three-electrode vacuum tube amplifier that broadcast the golden tones of operatic tenor Enrico Caruso in 1910, and when Wanamaker's relayed phonograph music from its department store in New York to its branch in Philadelphia, composer Victor Herbert did not dawdle. Quickly and accurately assessing the potential of this new invention to change radically the world of music, Herbert founded ASCAP in 1914. With radio readily available, audiences no longer had to purchase theatre tickets to hear the latest tunes; now hit songs floated freely through the air into their homes. Composers and lyricists earned royalties from the sale of sheet music through copyright laws, but, until the advent of ASCAP, received not a penny for their songs whenever these were performed outside the theatre. ASCAP never attempted to govern dramatic or stage rights, but it protected the performing rights of musical compositions by selling licenses to hotels, restaurants, radio stations, dance halls, cabarets, motion picture films, any establishment or industry that had previously "borrowed" songs for free. At the end of each year, according to a complex formula, ASCAP distributed its revenue from these licenses among its members.

How ironic that between the original production of *Poppy* and its revival a year later Dorothy wrote her first major flop—*The Proud Princess,* a modern fairy tale in four acts.[45] Mystery surrounds its origin. Perhaps her triumph as Madame X and her partial success with *The Riddle: Woman* bound her, as inevitably as a drone to his queen bee, to a plot constructed around blackmail and an ambitious woman. Perhaps *The Proud Princess* was based on an earlier play by Dorothy, entitled *Circus Dame* or *The Lady of the Circus* and commissioned by the Shuberts or—since speculation runs rampant—was a reworking of her very first attempt at play writing. As late as 1918, *Theatre Magazine* referred to her first script written with a collaborator identified solely as a "distinguished litterateur":

> Each still possesses a copy of it. Each believes it has worth. Both, knowing that Broadway conditions are as changeful as the sea set about writing other plays. Both, though not together, have attained the happy state of production.[46]

Now, in 1923, *Theatre Magazine* reported that "Dorothy Donnelly and Edward Sheldon are still in the throes of making ready the play they have concocted together."[47]

If *The Proud Princess* was indeed the play destined for oblivion, there it should have remained. The protagonist, Minnie Johnson, persuades her parents to move to New York City from their native Oklahoma, after they struck oil and woke up one morning unexpectedly wealthy. She consents to blackmail in hopes of breaking into high society, but remains socially rebuffed until escorted by a prince. Her hero is Guiseppe Ciccolini, an impoverished organ grinder. As the audience quickly and correctly guesses, he is indeed a prince, seeking to be loved for himself and not his rank—foreshadowing *The Student Prince?* The imposter carries Minnie, now grandly calling herself Mimosa, off to his tenement in New York's Little Italy. The drama critic for the *Baltimore Evening Sun* concludes his review of the play in scarcely glowing terms: "[The prince] finally gets what he wants, Ma and Pa Johnson get rid of the troublesome Minnie, and every one is satisfied."[48] *The Proud Princess* began its tryout tour in Baltimore but never reached Broadway.

No one missed it. Both *Blossom Time* and *Poppy* were playing in revivals and *The Student Prince* was about to open. In the meantime, on Friday, October 31, 1924, Dorothy's brother suffered a relapse. Thomas Frederick Donnelly died the following afternoon at four o'clock. Many flocked to his funeral: justices of the New York Supreme Court, judges, magistrates, members of the state and city bar associations, and delegates from the New York Athletic Club, such Irish social societies as the Friendly Sons of St. Patrick and the Irish Athletic Club, and Democratic party organizations to which the judge had belonged. He left his estate to his sisters.[49] Nora McCall, alone once more, sought consolation in her children; Dorothy, in her plays.

The contract for *The Student Prince* arrived in August, 1922. "My dear Miss Donnelly," it read:

> Confirming our conversation, it is understood that you are to write for us a musical libretto of the play, "OLD HEIDELBERG." You are to write all the lyrics that shall be necessary from time to time and make such revisions in the manuscript so that it can be used as a play with music. In consideration of the same, we are to pay you the sum of Two Hundred fifty ($250.00) Dollars on the signing of this agreement and a further sum of Two Hundred fifty dollars on the delivery of the completed manuscript embodying the lyrics and the changes necessary for a musical play...[50]

The Shuberts had long been fascinated by the play. Their brother, Sam, had first produced it as *Heidelberg* with Aubrey Boucicault on December 15, 1902. "He was every inch a prince in appearance, and acted the part with great romantic delicacy and comprehension," wrote Lee Shubert.[51] Nevertheless, the play closed without fanfare after 32 performances. Certain of its merits, Sam Shubert chose to revive it a year later with Richard Mansfield in the lead to show off the newly built Lyric Theatre, planned by the multi-talented Reginald De Koven, a composer and playwright, and designed by the architectural firm of Hert and Tallant. "The opening night was a fourfold triumph: for the distinguished actor, for the play, for the new theatre (which was the handsomest in New York at the time), and for my brother whose judgment and zeal had made the occasion possible," noted Lee Shubert.[52]

Although Mansfield was too old for the part—at least 50 by 1903— the *New York Times* thought his "character study as convincing as it is charming" and praised his "exceptional facility as an actor."[53] Mansfield believed that as an actor he should strive to be true; if he sought to be original, he thought, he'd miss both marks. "The actor lives for his art," he said; "the world may see the picture he paints, the lessons he inculcates; he breathes life into them for a moment; they fade away and die; he leaves nothing behind him but a memory."[54] An unwitting but most fitting epitaph, for Dorothy had seen the 1903 production, and her memory of Mansfield as Prince Karl remained vivid and fresh for another twenty years. With a script on hand and Mansfield's performance in mind, she easily met the deadline—November 14, 1922—set by the Shuberts.

Romberg had seen *Alt Heidelberg* during one of his visits to his parents and expressed his interest in the play to his friend and agent Isidore Witmark.[55] Although Romberg waited until July 11, 1924, to receive a contract from the Shuberts, manuscripts of the score indicate that he began working on it at an earlier date.[56] He kept "Gaudeamus Igitur" unchanged but scrapped all other songs. The new ones, all 29 of them, retained the distinctive sound and style of Viennese music. Only slightly Americanized, they included waltzes, reprises, marches, fox-trots, tunes that called for "counter harmonies and extensive ranges in the duets, the demanding solos, and the lusty male choral numbers."[57]

In the prologue that begins the play, young Prince Karl Franz prepares to leave for the University of Heidelberg with his tutor, Dr. Engel, who sings "Golden Days" as he remembers his own student days there. Act I, set in 1860, finds them at the Inn of the Three Golden Apples. Students arrive, singing "To the Inn We're Marching." Beer steins in hand, they launch into the robust "Drinking Song" and express their appreciation for Kathie, the compliant waitress, who cheerfully responds, "I'm Coming to Your Call," and encourages their high spirits in "Come Boys, Let's All Be Gay, Boys." They happily comply in "Gaudeamus Igitur." Enchanted with heretofore unknown freedom, charmed by the gaiety of student life, and attracted to a pretty girl, the prince woos the lowly barmaid with "Serenade." They express their love in a moving waltz duet, "Deep in My Heart."

Act II begins with a tune extolling student life. Then comes word that the prince's grandfather lies ill and longs to see Karl formally betrothed to Princess Margaret. The prince persuades Kathie to join him in escaping from Heidelberg. At first they sing "We're off to Paris," but, when reality confronts fantasy, they convey their sorrow in "Farewell, Dear." The Prince promises Kathie he will return. Act III takes place two years later at the court. Margaret, too, has postponed the engagement, for she, likewise, has fallen in love. The princess and Captain Tarnitz proclaim their affections in "Just We Two" but agree to part. In Act IV Prince Karl, faithful to his word, returns to Heidelberg in "The Magic of Springtime" for a brief farewell to Kathie. The "Golden Days" have passed; the garden at the inn stands deserted; the prince's former old friends receive him glacially. Karl sorrowfully resigns himself to his fate as heir to the throne. Most of the music consists of reprises that recall happier times for the prince, the princess, and the waitress. Satisfied that the future Queen genuinely loves the prince, Kathie announces that she will marry a former suitor. They bid each other goodbye, but "Deep in My Heart," they promise to "remember forever" their love.[58]

Since most musicals are written in two acts, sometimes three, Dorothy chose an unusual form for the libretto: four acts preceded by a prologue. "I have read the Prologue and first and second act of 'Alt Heidelberg,'" began J. J. Shubert in a letter he sent Dorothy on August 21, 1922. "While I think it is charming, I think a great many improvements can be made in the way of the prologue." He suggested having the prince meet Margaret before dashing off to the university, making him "stiff and pompous" and she "very cold," and creating a longer lapse of time between the prologue and the second act. "Bringing the Princess back in the second act is a very good idea," he noted. "I am sorry you did not consult me before getting so far," J. J. continued, "as we could have gotten together on a great many things which might have improved it a whole lot. However, I am waiting for the third act, and it might change my entire idea of the play." He closed with encouraging words: "I want this play to take the place of Blossom Time [sic], and I am sure you are on the right track. It is very well written, and I know you are very enthusiastic, otherwise you could not have put so much in the play."[59]

This letter was but the first of many objections. When Lee Shubert discovered that Dorothy had added a bittersweet conclusion to *Alt Heidelberg*, he complained. "People don't like sad endings," came the protest: "People pay money for tickets so they can walk out of the theatre satisfied."[60] J. J. also balked: "In a musical, people expect the hero and the soprano will be kissing for the final curtain—or, anyway, dancing." On this point the brothers agreed. On most other issues they quarreled, sometimes vociferously, often without speaking to one another without resorting to intermediaries.. While many of their advertisements and programs read "Messrs. Shubert Present," Lee generally handled the "straight" plays, while J. J. mainly supervised the musicals. They shared a financial office but maintained separate quarters, shabbily furnished, across the street from one another in facing buildings.[61]

Meanwhile, Romberg was developing his own theory concerning the ingredients for a successful operetta. The first of these necessary elements was the libretto, said Romberg. "If I do not get a real thrill from the book, I cannot write the score," he said: "On the other hand, if I feel the book, I immediately mark the spots where the songs are to be inserted, sometimes eliminating part of the dialogue, sometimes inserting a dance number, and orchestral number, or a chorus."[62] The second component is a competent lyricist. "I never read more than the first two or three lines of a lyric. After I write the music for what I think the song should be, the lyricist has to write the words," he explained.[63] The third essential is time for rehearsals:

> It might be discovered that the range of the soprano's voice cannot comfortably take the high note, or that the song arranged for the tenor is not as important in effect as it had been hoped. Then again, the solo might be lacking a great climax. Perhaps there is too great a lull in the second act between the first and second songs. Perhaps some patter, or a bit of the chorus humming, might improve that.
>
> Sometimes I have worked for hours on a certain scene, and ... I realize that it should be eliminated. With the sagacity and confidence of the surgeon, I cut it out. Only the novice has heart-pangs over such an operation; the experienced one realizes that it will be for the great result.[64]

Romberg's formula makes no mention of happy endings. There is another, more glaringly obvious omission—great music. Never short of self-confidence regarding his musical talents, Romberg didn't bother to include it.

When the operetta began its trial run as *In Heidelberg* in Atlantic City and received only a lukewarm reception, J. J. as well as J. C. Huffman, the director, were sufficiently provoked to exert their authority. They expressed disappointment with "Serenade" ("Overhead the Moon Is Beaming"); its operatic quality, in their opinion, would not appeal to Broadway. They continued to plead for a happy ending. Other grounds for contention involved the large orchestra, the cast of excellent singers, the huge chorus: all these entailed enormous expenses. Moreover, Romberg proposed a *male* chorus whereas the Shuberts long preferred a line-up of leggy and female beauties[65] that gave their annual *Passing Show* (1912-1922) and *Artists and Models* both notoriety and commercial attraction. "Forty men singing that crap? Who needs it?" said Lee, possibly miffed because Romberg had accepted a commission from a rival, Florenz Ziegfeld. He put his foot—and check book—down: "Twenty men is enough, and that's final."[66]

During a tryout in Newark tempers flared. J. J. Shubert tried to change the ending, or at least disguise the fact that it was unhappy, with recommendations for brightening up the score. Romberg resisted: "I will not have my music perverted." Jake exploded: "Throw this man out of my theatre.... Throw him out before I kill him. And take his name off the marquee too!"[67]

Dorothy and Romberg still refused to capitulate. This time it was *their* judgment that ultimately mattered—not the producers', not the critics', nor even the audience's. To be sure, theirs was an informed opinion, backed by knowledge of the theatre, a string of past successes, and sheer confidence. Romberg most succinctly expressed his belief in the moving power of heart-rending songs when he discussed, two years later, the enormous popularity of *The Desert Song*:

> Casting no reflection, you will notice today that there are types of musical comedies which "flop," in the parlance of the theatre. On the other hand, you will find one here and there that plays for a seemingly endless time to capacity houses. The latter, if you will observe, is usually the musical comedy which leans toward the operatic rather than the jazz type.[68]

The collaborators must have spoken very persuasively and Romberg's attorney, Howard Reinheimer, very convincingly,[69] for the operetta next moved unchanged to Philadelphia, where it was scheduled for a second, short trial run. Because of its popularity, however, it remained there several additional weeks.

Minor changes were made to the music. Two songs—"May I Come to See You, Dear" and "For You"—were discarded (but published as sheet music by Harms in 1925 and 1928 respectively).[70] Also, the Shuberts renamed the play. At the turn of the century, the producers had purchased the rights for stage performances of Wilhelm Meyer-Foester's *Alt Heidelberg* from Schimer and Sons. Now they needed permission to adapt the play as a musical. They sent an agent to Berlin, home of the author and his representative, and entered into protracted negotiations that would not be fully resolved until the week before the Broadway opening. Fearing legal repercussions for clinging to the name "Old Heidelberg," they dubbed the operetta *The Student Prince in Heidelberg*.

Despite their differences in aesthetics, Dorothy and the Shuberts established a cordial working relationship. They occasionally exchanged greetings and gifts. When J. J. sent her a plant for Christmas, Dorothy reciprocated with a present for his son. "I am sending this little Chinese game 'Mah Jongg' to your son as I'm sure you'd rather have it that way than anything I could think of for yourself. Young folks are fond of novelties and I think he will like it as I know from my own experience that it is very good fun. And to yourself," she added, "I send you my warmest good wishes and my very real regard."[71]

Romberg, by contrast, never forgot the contre-temps:

> Often it is not only the critics who condemn the production, but the producers themselves. You might be surprised to know *The Student Prince*, which has proven one of the biggest financial hits, was damned by the producers before it opened here. They objected to the large male chorus, and were certain the public would take exception to the German tale. But when we opened in Philadelphia the audience applauded so enthusiastically that the producers realized that they had a success.[72]

For a composer of his caliber, he thought, it was demeaning to be writing for the yearly revues staged at the Winter Garden Theatre; galling to have his more operatic music treated with contempt; maddening to face threats.

Its title not yet shortened, *The Student Prince* finally opened on Broadway, December 2, 1924, at the Jolson Theatre. The modern 1,400-seat house had excellent acoustics, a pit big enough for the expanded orchestra, and a stage that amply accommodated a male chorus of 36 or so (different versions of the number exist and range as high as 60). Max Sheck choreographed the dance numbers, and Oscar Bradley served as music director. The operetta showcased superb singers. Ilse Marvenga made her American debut as Kathie. The tenor Howard Marsh, subsequently cast as the lead in *Show Boat*, starred as Prince Karl and hit the high "C" effortlessly. They were ably supported by other well trained vocalists: Greek Evans as Dr. Engel, John Coast as Tarnitz, and Roberta Beatty as Princess Margaret. At the last moment it was decided to scrap the intermission between and third and fourth acts. The cut tightened the action, increased the tension, and decreased the running time of the operetta, already three hours long. In its stead, Romberg himself conducted the "Serenade Intermezzo" to great applause.[73] During the two remaining intermissions, however, Dorothy's uniformed chauffeur pranced down the aisles. He gave instructions and greeted everyone in the audience—he practically knew them all—"as if he had written the play" himself.[74]

The Student Prince received instant recognition from audiences that snapped up tickets at $4.40, a bargain reported Abel Green, editor of *Variety*.[75] They did not consider it too highbrow despite the Shuberts' early fears. Although set in mid-eighteenth century Germany and Austria, the musical had its contemporary moments. Playgoers of the Roaring Twenties could readily identify with its university setting. After all, this was the period of rah-rah and raccoon coats and caps, the heyday of college life, when, within the decade, the number of bachelor degrees conferred increased nearly three-fold. "Come, Sir, Will You Join," the invitation sung by members of the Saxon Corps, reflected the growing popularity of fraternities on campus. Then as now, entry into a fraternity requires an initiation. In the case of German universities and of *The Student Prince,* this consisted of the Salamander Toast, repeated three times. The "pledge" and his future brothers stand at attention on either side of a table. At a signal they rub the bottom of their beer steins in a synchronous circular motion on the table, producing an awesome percussive sound; at the cry, "Drink!" they hoist their steins and sip. Audiences also delighted in "Drinking Song," for it held particular appeal to those suffering through the days of prohibition. Furthermore, operetta buffs appreciated the quality of singing unheard in more conventional musicals and admired the well-drilled male chorus. The Shuberts did not fail to notice and quickly reintroduced the choral work in future productions, namely *My Maryland, Princess Flavia,* and *Rose-Marie.* Nor did they hesitate to advertise the play with a banner headline that read "Most Sweeping Triumph in History of the Theatre."

The reviewers raved, too. George S. Kaufman, writing for the *New York Times,* called it "a romantic operetta of the old school" and "a perfect example of its kind" that "is richly scored and magnificently sung, and merited even the cheers that were sent across the footlights by a friendly audience." Then he tossed in a gratuitous aside: "Not even the comparative absence of the comic element is of importance in 'The Student Prince'; the piece concentrates so successfully upon its prime ingredients that nothing more is needed."[76] Arthur Hornblow of *Theatre Magazine* found it "of transcendent worth," beautifully acted, costumed, sung, and staged.

Most historians of the theatre consider *The Student Prince* Romberg's finest achievement. "Musically it is one of the strongest compositions of its kind, both in the intrinsic merit of the songs themselves and in the highly professional handling of the solo voices and the ubiquitous chorus of male students."[77] Although Romberg still receives most of the credit for its success, Dorothy deserves her rightful share. The book served the music remarkably well. To intensify the age-old conflict between royal obligation and personal desire, Dorothy created a subplot: she had Margaret fall in love with Captain Tarnitz, sing of her longing for a relationship with him in "Just We Two," then, in an act of self-renunciation, give

The barmaid, Kathie, hoists a glass of beer on the program cover for The Student Prince in Hei-delberg. *With music by Sigmund Romberg and lyrics by Dorothy Donnelly, the play has been revived annually since its opening on Broadway in December 1924. (Courtesy Shubert Archive.)*

him up when bowing to a higher call—duty. In the third act's reprise of "The Magic of Springtime," which introduces the final rendition of "Deep in My Heart, Dear," she has the prince interrupt Kathie. He mournfully begs her, "Oh, Kathie, Oh, Kathie, don't go away," thereby increasing the

In this early photograph Edward Sheldon, serious and intense, reveals his keen sense of the theatre, which he generously gave to plays and performers alike. (Courtesy Michael Morrison Collection.)

dramatic tension. Donnelly made yet other changes to the script that kept the story from being wholly traditional, according to Gerald Bordman:

> The saddened but essentially unrebellious lovers accept the social dictates of their world. The heroine is not discovered to have royal blood, nor is there any hint that future generations will resolve their woes. There is, instead, a touch of fatalism rare in pieces of the period.[78]

She also determined the action that takes place on stage during the musical numbers. Furthermore, while most of the lyrics adhere to the monosyllabic convention of operetta, Dorothy deliberately altered the pace. In "Drinking Song", for instance, she used the alliterative lines, "Here's a hope that those bright eyes will shine lovingly, longingly soon into mine" and "Here's a hope that those soft arms will twine lovingly, longingly soon around mine."[79] The lyrics reveal not only an understanding but also a feeling for the music. As the *New York Times* noted, "she hase [sic] done a first-rate job for the purpose at hand." The effectiveness of the libretto and lyrics can best be gauged by a fascinating anomaly: in September 1927 Metro-Goldwyn-Meyer released a silent film of *The Student Prince* with Ramon Navarro, Jean Hersholt, and Norma Shearer in the leads and a new score by David Mendoza and William Axt.

Even before the end of the Broadway run, the Shubert brothers profitably engaged nine to fourteen traveling companies to meet the enormous demand for *The Student Prince*. The show's original run achieved 608 performances, an outstanding record for the decade, and filled the houses to capacity during its first two years. It premiered in London a year later at His Majesty's Theatre with Marvenga and a new prince, Allan Prior. The elaborateness of the costumes, some created by the acclaimed designer Erté, could not rescue the play from Prior's bad acting and worse singing. It closed after 96 performances, but traveled successfully that same year throughout England with an all-British cast, starring Harry Welchman and Rose Hignell.

Romberg's imaginative biographer, Elliott Arnold, tells of one unrecorded performance of *The Student Prince*. Apparently, one Sunday evening Dorothy and Romberg assembled the stars of the show, trouped into Ned Sheldon's apartment, and, with Romberg at the piano, performed the entire operetta for him.

CHAPTER 10
Final Curtain

Despite recurring bouts of kidney problems, Dorothy maintained a high level of productivity during the final years of her life. Ever since the Shuberts first engaged her as a playdoctor, there had been no respite from the barrage of commissions. The ink on the libretto for *The Student Prince* had barely dried when J. J. Shubert sent her *Love Mask* along with a note. "I wish you would read this play immediately with a view of adapting it," he wrote. "I think this is one of the best propositions I have read in a long time."[1] Early in 1923 the Shuberts handed her *The Master of Montmartre* but recalled it that April; she scarcely had time to finish her revisions to this script, a fictionalized biography of French composer Jacques Offenbach, which eventually opened as *The Love Song* at the Century Theatre on January 13, 1925.

While Dorothy was scribbling script and lyrics for *Poppy* and dashing off the short-lived *The Proud Princess*, Sigmund Romberg composed songs for 14 more musical comedies and revues. His output continued as prolific as his love life was initially turbulent His first marriage disintegrated, although the final decree of divorce did not arrive until June 1923. Two years earlier, he had worked at a resort in the mountains of upstate New York with Harold Atteridge and Buddy G. DeSylva to create *Bombo*. The 1921 musical starred Al Jolson and introduced the perennially popular songs later interpolated into the script, "Toot, Toot, Tootsie" and "California, Here I Come." It also provided Romberg a chance encounter with Lillian Harris, who was vacationing at the retreat with her mother. Distance and parental objections made their courtship an on-again, off-again affair, for Lillian continued to live with her mother in Washington, D. C., and Mrs. Harris repeatedly voiced her disapproval of Romberg's profession. Dorothy finally brought the pair together for good. She had recently moved to 145 East Thirty-fifth Street—still remaining in the shadow of Broadway's lights and within walking distance of the cluster of theatres—and developed a friendly relationship with Lillian. Dorothy planned a quiet dinner at her new home for the young lovers.[2] A few months later Romberg and Lillian eloped to Paterson, New Jersey, where they were married in the city hall by Mayor Colin McLean on March 28, 1925. Hugo Romberg served as his brother's best man and Dorothy as maid of honor.

She waved an affectionate goodbye as the newlyweds left for their three-week honeymoon in the South. Then Dorothy dragged herself back home, haggard, worn out, and sick. Like her brother Henry, she apparently suffered from Bright's Disease, an outmoded term lacking specificity that has been replaced by "glomerulonephritis." This condition results from the inflammation of the filtering structures within the kidneys that allows proteinuria, minuscule traces of proteins or blood cells, to escape along with waste products. Typically, the disease leads to swelling and eventual kidney failure.

To Louise Hale, it was clear that Dorothy was now paying "physical toll for mental effort." She recalled one particular hot summer night, when Dorothy returned from a "blaring musical rehearsal":

> The sweat of exhaustion was pouring from her finger tips. She sat upon my little sofa, stooped over, arms lax. "Why do you go on with it?" I argued. "You have enough. You can be comfortable. Why go on with this musical show?" She lifted her drawn face. "Oh, but it's so gay!" she bleated. Then we both laughed.

Laughter was an acceptable response to a friend who required few explanations, and "comfortable," a conventionally polite, understated term for characterizing Dorothy's wealth. In fact, "she made money hand over fist," says Dolly McCall, speaking more bluntly of her aunt.[3] Louise Hale, however, shared Dorothy's belief in the value of work to provide, not only the discipline and habit that Dorothy esteemed—or the financial independence both self-supporting women required—but also the satisfaction and happiness that comes from feeling useful and productive. As a working actress, she recognized, moreover, Dorothy's attraction to the stage, to the challenge of a new role, to the exhilaration of ovations. Although Dorothy held no illusions about the drawbacks of an acting career, she recognized its innate joys and gloried in them. The adulation of her peers and the admiration of her fans, Dorothy also prized:

> All the friends she has ever had, and an eventful and successful career has brought her many, are sending their sisters and their cousins and their nieces to her for counsel. They come in droves seeking

> encouragement and find anything but that. If the damper doesn't work,
> however, and the young thing still clings to her dream of a Dusean
> future, ... the hopeful is folded into the arms of the counselor who pro-
> nounces a happy benediction.[4]

Dorothy deliberately, vividly painted the stage in horrid colors: "I do all
that because if a girl is not determined with all the soul that is in her to
become an actress she doesn't belong on the stage. There are so many
hardships and disappointments and delays that only the stage-struck
belong."[5] But her ploy to dissuade the young failed:

> It is hard to understand how this woman can discourage any one, for
> what weight can arguments of misery and pain carry when all the time
> the girl is looking at a person who has no indications of hardship about
> her? How can a cheerful, mellow and professionally enthusiastic person
> like Miss Donnelly draw a convincing picture of the terrors of the stage?
> It just wouldn't work.[6]

And when the ruse fizzled, she sent the aspiring actress off to a stock
company.

    As an author, whose most recent novels, *Home Talent* and *The Canal
Boat Fracas*, would both be published in 1926, Louise also understood
how Dorothy could celebrate the merits of acting even while praising the
advantages of playdoctoring. So, she was not in the least surprised to hear
Dorothy explain:

> I'm not away from the theatrical life, you see, and it's nice to be so sort
> of free and easy with life. I wouldn't go back. I don't blame anyone for
> wanting to go on the stage, for, with all the rough spots, it's a great life.
> And now I'm out of it, yet still in it; and it's wonderful.[7]

    In spite of her fatigue and illness, Dorothy packed her bags and sailed
for Europe in May 1925 "to walk again the French fields and roads she had
last traveled in the gray-blue uniform of the Y.M.C.A," wrote Alexander
Woollcott. "As she settled back in her steamer-chair and let the puttering
deck-steward tuck the thick rugs around her," he added, "it must have been
pleasant to reflect upon the fact that, with the single exception of the Miss
Nichols, who wrote the prodigious *Abie's Irish Rose*, no other woman writing for the theatre anywhere in the world could so well afford the vacation
of which the lazy weeks stretched invitingly ahead." At this very moment
three companies of *Blossom Time* and *The Student Prince* "were speaking her
lines and warbling her lyrics in America, and ... two companies of her
Poppy were disporting themselves in various parts of England."[8]

Although it "sounded so damned dull" to her, she determined to follow her doctor's advice "to take the cure."[9] Some patients equate recovery with inactivity. Not Dorothy. "No inroads upon her body could deprive her of her spirit," said Louise. Indeed, the change of scene drew forth new energy. She wandered through the shops of Paris, hunting for presents to take back to the family: books to delight her sister Nora's large horde of grandchildren and silk dresses for one of them, Sally Ann Conway—Sarah McCall Conway's daughter and Dorothy's six-year old grand-niece.[10] She also brought her namesake and youngest niece along with her to France, giving young Dolly her first glimpses of Europe and memories that lasted a lifetime.

Even while in her nineties, with hearty chuckles interrupted by gleeful refrains of "Can you imagine that!" Dolly still recounted stories of this trip with Dorothy. She recalled that her aunt had sent her off to attend along with two friends—Margaret Murphy, a school chum, and Virginia Vaughn—the canonization of Madame Madeleine Sophie Barat, foundress of the religious order known internationally as the Society of the Sacred Heart. Dolly reminisced about Dorothy's generous gift of $500 "spending money," about nearly losing it all when she unknowingly dropped her pocketbook during the canonization ceremony, and about her incredible good fortune when the orchestra's conductor noticed the happenstance and stopped the music to retrieve the purse for her. After their return from the papal summer home at Castle Gondolfo to Paris, Dolly remembered, Dorothy treated the three girls to lunch "at the Bois." Nor could Dolly forget that glorious moment, two years later, while present at the reception for Charles Lindbergh, when "Lucky Lindy" received a $10,000 prize for completing the first solo transatlantic flight and when she proudly wore the custom-made suit and matching hat that Dorothy had ordered for her in Paris.[11]

Always at work, Dorothy also scoured the continent for new plays and detected a promising one in *The Call of Life* (*Der Ruf des Leben*). It's inviting to compare her dual careers and to suggest that just as she chose to be cast in emotional roles, so, too, did she agree to be typecast as a playwright of operettas and musical comedies. Such a tidy parallel would fail to do her full justice, however. She also showed some interest in play-doctoring more cerebral plays. While in the midst of adapting Booth Tarkington's *Seventeen* as a musical, Dorothy joined Actors' Theatre, and with George Arliss, Ethel Barrymore, Elsie Ferguson, Alfred Lunt, and Florence Reed formed its board of directors.[12]

Actors' Theatre was one of the independent houses that sprang up during the decade following the formation of Actor's Equity in 1913.

Groups of actors banded together in cooperatives as a revolt "against the growing commercialism and the spiritual emptiness of the theatre."[13] They tried to pattern themselves after the national theatres of Europe by encouraging native writers, reviving the classics, developing local talent, and presenting "New Drama," the name given by Ben Iden Payne to plays of intellectual import. Although Lee Shubert, who idolized the director and producer David Belasco,[14] was also attracted to "first-class" plays and occasionally produced a few works by Shaw, Maeterlinck, and Pirandello, these were not box-office successes. "We know that people like youth and beauty," he said, explaining his policy on producing:

> We know that they will go down in their pockets and pay gladly, if you give them something that will make them laugh. They like to see a play that holds their attention, keeps it from straying off to their worries and troubles. Probably that is the reason they are so keen about something new. People want a play to have plenty of action. A few persons will go to a "talky" play and be interested, if the talk is clever and brilliant. But those persons form a very small group.[15]

Such cliques produce an occasional "plonk" of the cash register. By contrast, larger audiences supply more frequent "pings," music to the ears of a producer in search, and need, of a profit.

The small independent houses, however, considered commercial theatre a mortal enemy. They sought to bypass control of major producers, just as, years later, public television and national public radio would come into being as a protest against mass-media entertainment provided by "for profit" television and radio. The best known among them included Provincetown Players (pioneers of Eugene O'Neill's plays), Washington Square Players that became the Theatre Guild (the crucible for refining ensemble playing), Neighborhood Playhouse, Stagers, and Equity Players Group of New York—an offshoot of Actor's Equity, renamed Actors' Theatre in 1922. With season subscribers, and wealthy guarantors like Ralph Pulitzer and John D. Rockerfeller, Jr., to provide committed patronage and financial backing, Actors' Theatre began by reintroducing American audiences to European plays. They successively produced *The Wild Duck* and *Hedda Gabler* with Blanche Yurka in the principal roles, *She Stoops to Conquer*, *Candida* (in 1924), and Dorothy's translation of *The Call of Life* (in 1925).

The Call of Life was written by Arthur Schnitzler, a Viennese physician who abandoned his practice to write novels, short stories, essays, and literally dozens of plays. Familiar with the latest theories in psychology and psychoanalysis, he gradually adopted the view that a serious playwright must interpret people and the events in their lives as symbols. "We all play parts," he said; "happy he who knows it."[16] This perspective he embodied in *The Call of Life*, completed in 1905. Two elements combined to make the play distinctly avant-garde for its time: the psychological analysis of a woman required to make a decision and the thematic insistence that love between man and woman can provide relief from prevailing melancholy.

Dorothy's translation of the play retained the symbolism and philosophical lyricism of the dialogue in the original. Actors' Theatre chose a capable director in the leading Irish actor, Dudley Digges, and selected a cast of remarkable quality: Derek Glynn, Eva La Gallienne, Thomas Chalmers, and Egon Brecher. John Brown Mason, writing for *Theatre Arts*, called the first act of *The Call of Life* "as devastating a piece of writing as the present season is likely to offer." Whether the impact of the second and third acts, good but less memorable, could be attributed to the acting or the drama itself, especially its deathbed sentimentality, remains uncertain. Regarding the plot, the *New York Times* wrote, "the play has been ingeniously constructed with a vagueness and softness well suited to the theme."[17] George Jean Nathan tackled Schnitzler's philosophy, summing it up as "it is better to be alive than dead," and objected "to staying up until eleven o'clock at night to hear him say it."[18] Ashley Dukes, on the other hand, praised the dialogue, declaring it "woven without waste into the tapestry" of the theme.

Paradoxically, *The Call of Life* may have precipitated the death of Actors' Theatre. The president, Francis Wilson, a playwright himself, protested the company's emphasis on foreign drama. Furthermore, internal squabbling pivoted around the high cost of lavish productions with all-star casts. "First of all, one can't succeed by ideals alone," explained Digges: "The reason why most art movements break up before they have achieved anything is because they have been unable to overcome the basic hard facts of real estate and the difficulties of raising the curtain; and until those problems are resolved good efforts will usually be short-lived."[19] Eventually, in 1927, Actors' Theatre fused under the leadership of Kenneth Macgowan with the Greenwich Village Players, itself a successor to the Provincetown Players.

When Dorothy returned to the Shubert fold the last few months of 1925, she discarded the theatre of ideas in favor of the mundane, transplanted herself from Europe to America, eschewed poetry for colloquialism, and substituted adolescent infatuation for adult love. In short, she wrote *Hello, Lola*. A play based on Booth Tarkington's comic novel, *Seventeen*, had premiered December 2, 1918, attaining moderate success with

225 performances. She borrowed its script, written by Hugh Stanislaus Strange and Stannard Mears, to transform the book into a musical. William B. Kernell composed the score, while Seymour Felix staged the ensembles. The novel, more successfully than the play or the musical, served as a humorous precursor of the "coming-of-age" story. Writing for the *New York Times*, J. Brooks Atkinson, provided a succinct outline of the plot: "the growing pains of a youth [named Willie Baxter] beset by a blabbing sister, the flamboyant wiles of the embryo coquette, the campaign for a dress-suit becoming man's estate, the nice social problems of a youth who owes allegiance to boyhood but aspires to the unreasonable prerogatives of maturity." But the critic lambasted the casting, the songs, and the score. Of the 26 musical numbers in *Hello, Lola*, Atkinson wrote, "none of them is distinguished in melody or lyric."[20] Historian Gerald Bordman took on the librettist as well: "Dorothy Donnelly's book was competent but not good enough to overcome [the] flaccid score."[21]

Although *Hello, Lola* bombed, its failure did not tarnish Dorothy's reputation as a competent playdoctor. Consider the case of *Show Boat* as evidence. Florenz Ziegfeld, who had labored long and hard to obtain Edna Ferber's reluctant consent for converting her novel into a musical, initially invited Oscar Hammerstein II to write the script. According to Ziegfeld's biographer, the producer "was pleased with Kern's score as it came in, but he was disappointed by Hammerstein's sprawling book."[22] Believing that Hammerstein II's first attempts were only half-hearted, Ziegfeld fired off a telegram to composer Jerome Kern. Long, direct, and lacking the usual stops, the wire read in part, "I HAVE STOPPED PRODUCING FOR CRITICS AND EMPTY HOUSES I DON'T WANT ... ANYONE ELSE IF HAMMERSTEIN CAN AND WILL DO THE WORK IF NOT THEN FOR ALL CONCERNED WE SHOULD HAVE SOMEONE HELP HOW ABOUT DOROTHY DONNELLY OR ANYONE YOU SUGGEST OR HAMMERSTEIN SUGGESTS."[23] Kern made no telephone calls, however. Hammerstein finally succeeded in producing a book that eliminated some minor characters, reunited major ones at the play's end, and tried to confront miscegenation and black-white relations realistically, winning himself credit for accomplishing a major breakthrough in the history of the American musical.

Dorothy couldn't possibly have undertaken another assignment in any case. Her struggles with intermittent kidney problems increasingly became more frequent and more severe.[24] She decided to take a cruise and chose an Italian ship, the *Colombo*, based on the recommendation of friends. While on board the liner, she wrote a letter to her nephew, John A. McCall, who had given her some cigarettes as a *bon voyage* gift. Long, undated, and packed with minute details, this letter shows a dramatist's flair for listening closing and watching carefully.

> I have just started on my second box of cigarettes, so you see I have a constant reminder of you, though I don't need one by a long sight.
> So far the trip has been very uneventful, with dreary cold weather, but today we are getting near the Azores. The sea is blue and covered with dazzling white foam, and the sun is brilliant. I am feeling wonderfully well and sleeping almost all of the time, the only occasion on which I rouse myself from my slumbers being meal time. The food is good but as I don't eat spaghetti or veal or fritto misto I have to skin through on vegetables [,] cheese and salad with an occasional dash of soup.

Her next remarks concern the head steward, who hovered over her at mealtimes, she noted, "always imploring me to order 'something special'." He paid her particular attention and, unknowingly, drew it to himself. "I am now an authority on his birth place, career, various places of interest that he has seen, the ages and sex of his children; in fact, if any one want any information pertaining to his life, let them come to me." She established a routine aboard the ship, and, although she had always enjoyed the special cocktails her brother Tom delighted in making for both his sisters,[25] became a temporary teetotaler.

> The passenger list is made up almost exclusively of unmarried ladies of all ages, sizes, and shapes, and we all sit around solemnly after dinner and hear the band (three pieces) play Madame Butterfly, Aida, and other Italian classics, which they applaud with enthusiasm. Then I bolt to my room and bed and read thousands of books....
> We are due to get to Casa Blanca on Friday, which to my surprise, turns out to be in Africa, quite a way down on the coast. There are two excursions ashore, one of them quite a long ride fifty miles each way. So I shall content myself with just a visit to the city as I'm afraid the longer one would exhaust me, and I'm in such good shape that I want to keep that way.
> Just think I haven't had a cocktail since I started which shows what rest can do.

Dorothy finished her chatty letter by asking her nephew about his job (John McCall currently worked as banquet manager for the Commodore Hotel in New York City). "Give my love to all the family," she said in closing, then signed her handwritten note, "Lots of love from your devoted Aunt Dolly."[26]

Dorothy's leisurely voyage at sea ended too quickly. She returned home to juggle two scripts at the same time. The first of these was *My Maryland*. Its rocky beginning probably made her long for additional rest and one more sip of Scotch, which had been her brother Tom's favorite drink. When she and Sigmund Romberg sat down with J. J. Shubert to plan *My Maryland*, the two collaborators had recently joined a new trade organization. The Dramatists Guild, an offshoot of the Authors League of America, was formed in March 1926 to protect the rights of play-wrights, authors, and composers. Although dramatists received some legal protection as early as 1856, when the first copyright law passed, releasing a flood of plays by new writers, playwrights continued believing them-selves unjustly treated. In their judgment, producers were still paying very little for play scripts. Second, dramatists remained convinced that they received insufficient royalties for revivals. The latest and most devastat-ing affront, in their opinion, involved the film industry. With the emer-gence of sound in motion pictures and its swift evolution during the 1920s, stage producers quickly sold production rights to film companies, often in exchange for financial backing, without compensating the writers or composers.

While most major stage producers had signed contracts with the Dramatists Guild by April 1927, the Shuberts continued to hold out. Dorothy's several letters to them—generally directed to James Morris, Lee Shubert's secretary—provide an amusing example of their tight-fisted-ness. Whenever ordering tickets to a performance, she always enclosed a self-addressed stamped envelope, mailed a "cheque" for the number of seats requested, and pleaded, "Please, please send me good ones."[27] Although the Shuberts kept a close rein on her income, they spent her talents freely. The brothers revived *Blossom Time* for a third season, on March 8, 1926, with Beulah Berson as Mitzi and Knight MacGregor as Franz Schubert. Meanwhile, *The Student Prince* was playing in Chicago, Los Angeles, and San Francisco, with Ilse Marvenga as Kathie and De Wolf Hopper as Karl. The obvious success of these shows, incidentally, may have prompted the numerous revivals of *Madame X* throughout the rest of the decade in the role Dorothy had created.[28] It certainly moti-vated the Shuberts to sell the rights to film *The Student Prince* in 1927.

Neither Dorothy nor Romberg was economically stupid when it came to understanding the value of royalties. Dorothy had already appointed her attorney and nephew, Ambrose Victor McCall, to oversee her rights as lyricist, librettist, and playwright. Just in time, too, for the sale of sheet music from *The Student Prince* remained vigorous for two solid years and, coincidentally, wiped out Romberg's debt to Isadore Witmark, the music publisher. The partners asked for higher fees or, at least, for a larger

"*Everybody is talking about it*"

" 'MY MARYLAND' bids fair to be one of the most popular and most successful of all the recent operettas."
—*Public Ledger*

"The music moves with a rhythmic vigor in keeping with the subject . . . 'MY MARYLAND' must be voted a success."
—*Inquirer*

" 'MY MARYLAND' is operetta at best . . . . No musical production presented in recent years has won the hearts of a Philadelphia audience so speedily as 'MY MARYLAND'."
—*Evening Ledger*

"A musical romance with every element essential to popular success . . . . . The music has a patriotic stir."
—*Philadelphia Ledger*

LYRIC THEATRE
PHILADELPHIA
NOW PLAYING
Matinees: Wednesday & Saturday

Dana T. Bennett Co., New York

The 1927 advertisement for My Maryland *in Philadelphia reprints snippets of raves published by local newspapers and features Evelyn Herbert in costume as Barbara Fritchie. (Courtesy Shubert Archive.)*

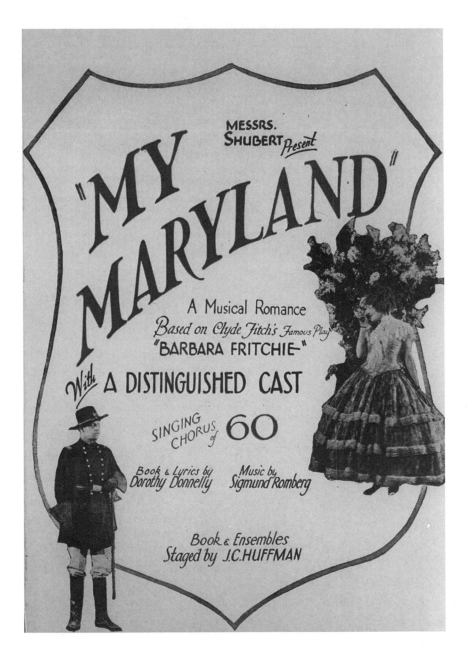

The promotional flyer for My Maryland *lists all the ingredients the Shubert brothers hoped would guarantee its success: an acclaimed source, cast, writer, composer, director and large singing chorus. (Courtesy Shubert Archive.)*

percentage of the profits, but the Shuberts turned them down, perhaps miffed by Romberg's temporary desertion of their camp. (He left them in 1926 to write *The Desert Song* with lyrics by Oscar Hammerstein II and Otto Harbach.) Disappointed, the two collaborators nevertheless agreed to honor their prior commitment to *My Maryland*. Before the show opened, however, although it rubbed against the grain, the Shuberts finally and without fanfare recognized the Dramatists Guild as a legitimate bargaining agent for writers and composers—an unacknowledged tribute to Dorothy's persistence in securing economic justice for her colleagues in the profession.

The sources for *My Maryland* included both a poem and a play. "Barbara Frietchie," written by John Greenleaf Whittier and published by the *Atlantic Monthly* in 1863, became the most successful ballad of the Civil War with its famous call to patriotism: "Shoot, if you must, this old gray head / But spare your country's flag." Clyde Fitch had used that same title, *Barbara Frietchie*, for his play, selected by Burns Mantle as the best play of 1898.

Dorothy changed the outcome of Fitch's drama, this time capitulating to Daniel Frohman's observation that audiences like clean theatres and happy endings. Her heroine, transformed from a gray-haired woman into a young girl, is saved from certain death. Like *The Student Prince*, this musical is another account of the conflict between love and duty. Set in the Civil War, amid strains of "Dixie," it tells the story of a Southern belle from Maryland (Evelyn Herbert, a gifted soprano, played the lead) courted by two enemies, the Confederate Jack Negly (Warren Hull) and the Yankee Captain Trumbull (Nathaniel Wagner). When the Union officer is wounded in battle, Barbara bravely smuggles him upstairs and tenderly pleads for his safety in "Mother." She disappoints her parents by preferring a Northern wooer, and outrages her compatriots by dangling the American flag from her window. Just as she is about to be shot by her rejected suitor's father, Colonel Negly (Louis Casavant), Stonewall Jackson (James Ellis)[29] arrives in the nick of time. Admiring her courage, he leaves her home unscathed and puts the young lovers under his protection.

Staged by J. C. Huffman and supervised by J. J. Shubert, *My Maryland* began its scheduled tryout in Atlantic City, then moved to Philadelphia for a stint of two or three weeks. The public would not let it go, however, and it remained there for an unprecedented 40-week trial period.[30] The Shuberts capitalized on rave reviews to promote the play. "'MY MARYLAND' is operetta at its best," proclaimed the *Evening Ledger*, adding "No musical production in recent years has won the hearts of a

Philadelphia audience so speedily as 'MY MARYLAND'." The *Philadelphia Ledger*, meanwhile, called it "a musical romance with every element to popular success."

It opened on Broadway at the Jolson Theatre on September 12, 1927, one of the 51 (according to Burns Mantle) or 53 (according to *Variety*) musicals—a record high, never duplicated—during a single New York season.[31] *My Maryland* achieved 312 performances, attaining popular if not critical acclaim. It found itself in Atlanta, Georgia, the following January. Most of the compliments went to Romberg for successfully weaving American tunes into the texture of European operetta. The marching song of the Connecticut regiment, for example, begins as a typical French march and concludes with a reworking of "John Brown's Body." "Your Land and My Land" ends with a snatch of the "Battle Hymn of the Republic." Other songs given special mention by reviewers included "Won't You Marry Me?" "Silver Moon," and "Mother." "The very fact that *My Maryland* has been held over in Atlanta for a second week," according to drama critic Ruth Hinman, "shows that people are enjoying this wholesome musical romance and that the two principal songs have rather haunting melodies is demonstrated by the audience for many of them leave the theatre humming 'My Land and Your Land' and 'The Same Old Silver Moon,' a sure test of popularity."[32]

Memories of the war years, of the hours spent with Louise Closser Hale shipping preserves overseas, Dorothy crowded into the words of the song, "Strawberry Jam." A surprising tribute to her talents as a lyricist came from New York's Representative Emanuel Celler, who proposed a congressional bill to have "Your Land and My Land" replace "The Star-Spangled banner" as the national anthem.[33] Regarding the libretto, *New York Times* critic J. Brooks Atkinson wrote that it "serves the music as a sufficient vehicle" and shows "theatrical competence." Yet, he regretted the paucity of humor and singled out for special praise the only two comic figures in the play, the Colonel and Zeke Bramble (George Rosener). "The librettist's task," said Atkinson, "involved not only writing the lyrics, but injecting comedy." His review of *My Maryland* continued:

> In the present case … it is quite fair to say that the lyrics are better than the comedy. However, there is an old rascal—played with native favor and spirit by George Rosener—who gets to be unmistakably funny after a while—just in time to pull a bit of sentiment and put it over—and the stock comic Southern Colonel … is also funny—after you get used to him.[34]

If Dorothy could brush aside petty complaints, she could no longer ignore her illness. In the fall of 1927, while working on *My Princess*, she collapsed. Whenever sickness raised its threatening head, as it had done periodically for the previous five years, Dorothy had successfully distracted herself by writing. No more. Romberg had already completed the score, and Dorothy had finished the lyrics for the show when Edward Sheldon was asked to put the finishing touches on the libretto—an easy task, as the play was a musical adaptation of *The Proud Princess*. Since Dorothy could no longer visit Ned, they talked with each other daily by phone. She hoped he would come see her, but as he was virtually paralyzed, Sheldon's doctors thought the risk too great. According to his biographer, Eric Barnes, Ned "felt this disaster with real poignancy, for it marked the final chapter in one of his oldest and deepest friendships in the theatre."[35] Barnes also says that, at the time, Ned even contemplated suicide.[36]

My Princess, the first of Dorothy's musical plays set in an American locale during contemporary times, premiered successfully in New Haven. During this tryout, seven songs were cut, thereby advancing the action and curtailing the distractions of superfluous specialty songs. Then it enjoyed a brief run in Boston, where it was temporarily called *My Golden Girl*, with all references to royalty removed, perhaps to suggest the universality of the theme. Finally, *My Princess* opened on Broadway, at the Shubert Theatre on October 6, 1927, while Dorothy was still hospitalized. The lone exception among the Donnelly-Romberg operettas, *My Princess* showed some progression of character. By the end of this play the two principals, the oil heiress and her organ-grinder, cease fantasizing and begin to explore their identities and their real relationship to each other. Accordingly, the play closes with a new finale that deliberately eliminates reprises of earlier tunes.[37]

Alexander Woollcott praised the play: "The prolific partnership between Dorothy Donnelly and Sigmund Romberg was never happier in its product, I think, than in the case of 'My Princess,' a pleasant operetta full of cleanly [sic] romance and sweet, caressing music."[38] This time most of the kudos went to Dorothy. The *Boston Globe* reported that "to an extent rare in musical comedy, the situations and characters are drawn from typical American life. There is a well knit plot, sufficient to make a play without the music."[39] Writing for the *New Yorker*, Charles Brackett called *My Princess* "the best of the Donnelly books."[40] Although admiring the score and the dancing, J. Brooks Atkinson remained less captivated by the plot:

> The story of "My Princess" comes from a play entitled either "The Proud Princess" or "Princess Zim Zim" (for the sidewalk oracles did not agree last evening), which was written by Edward Sheldon and

> Dorothy Donnelly, but never produced in "this great big city of New
> York." It recounts the amazing adventures of an innocent parvenue who
> tries to break into high society by flaunting a spurious Italian prince
> as her fiancé....&c., &c."[41]

Opinion regarding the star of the show, Hope Hampton, was mixed.
Woollcott noted in New York's *The World* that "She has a sweet, true voice
of some power..."; *Variety* thought the play established her as a prima
donna; J. Brooks Atkinson felt she lacked "the fullness desirable for music
of such force and versatility"; and Gerald Bordman concluded that she
overacted, "resorting to that school of emoting that expresses grief by
pressing a fist against the forehead."[42] Nearly every critic condemned the
production itself. When *My Princess* folded after 20 performances in New
York City, Dorothy's career as a playwright, like her years on center stage,
fizzled to a close.

Although her physicians turned away business colleagues, Romberg
included, they admitted Louise Closser Hale and Dorothy's family.
"We always laughed, even on our last night together, when I fed her
grouse with a spoon," Louise wrote, recalling Dorothy's enduring hos-
pitality:

> "A spoon and the sporty grouse!" she gasped. She was concerned over
> my welfare. "Where is Mrs. Hale's dessert?" she asked the nurse, her eyes
> half sightless. They scurried together the semblance of a sweet for me.
> "And a napkin—embroidered," she reproved. Ah! The great lady!

Nora came with her children and grandchildren to pay their respects.
Dorothy's nieces and nephews had grown up in awe of the actress who
brought joy and glamour to their childhood and gifts galore, including
trips to Europe. As adults, they admired the playwright whose musicals
were still making the front page of the drama section. Ambrose Victor
McCall, for instance, sat through 300 performances of *The Student Prince*,
says his son, Thomas McCall, who himself remembers timidly approach-
ing "the lady in bed."[43] Meanwhile, Dorothy's grandniece, Sally Ann Conway, still recalls how Aunt Dolly "put on wonderful magic acts for me that
would produce play tea sets and dolls much to my wonder!!"[44]

If the young ones failed to realize the end was near, Dorothy herself
held no such illusions. One night a substitute nurse was hastily summoned
to Dorothy's bedside. She was an elderly woman, who lost her struggle
to remain awake, dreamed as she slept, and recounted her dream to
Dorothy the next morning. "It had been a dream," wrote Louise, but
Dorothy wisely interpreted it as a message:

Dorothy's mother had appeared in the old woman's dream, dressed in the style of wrapper she had always affected and looking (from the description) as her child remembered her. "Tell our daughter," said the mother, "that her father says she can play with her friends in the afternoon. But she must come home to us in the evening."

The dream all too soon proved prophetic.

CHAPTER 11

Curtain Call

"Dorothy Donnelly, Dramatist, Dies" announced the *New York Times* on January 4, 1928. At ten minutes past one o'clock that morning at home, Dorothy succumbed to nephritis-pneumonia. Calling her "a well-known actress who in recent years had won renown as a musical comedy librettist," the article proceeded to review her early experiences in the theatre, her career as an actress, and her successes as a playwright and director.

Her funeral took place at ten o'clock Saturday morning, January 7, just three weeks shy of her forty-eighth birthday. Her sister, Nora, the last survivor of the Donnelly children, followed the cortege from St. Agnes Church to the grave site at the Gate of Heaven in Westchester, New York. Dorothy was buried in the spot she had chosen many years before as the Donnelly plot. Her grave sits high upon a hill, surrounded by a circular bench.

She died as she had lived, quietly and privately. Although she had enjoyed male friendship and companionship, she never married. Maybe the Irish penchant for late marriages, or her incredibly active career, or even Sheldon's unfortunate illness at a very young age, served to keep her single. Perhaps these reasons and one other—her lifelong practice of the Roman Catholic faith—conspired to keep her, to all appearances, celibate. She kept a scrapbook of clippings, but personal journals and most pieces of private correspondence have not surfaced. What they might have revealed to keep her newsworthy remains secret. And, without children to maintain and bolster her reputation long after her death, it died too quickly. The press routinely reviewed her performances, interviewed her at length, discussed the merits of her plays, kept track of her comings and goings. They were never privy to her feelings, however. As an actress, she needed publicity; offstage she shunned the spotlight. No sordid scandals, no sensational headlines, no troubled personal history, nor even a hint of impropriety (except for the occasional "white" lie) ever shattered her relative anonymity as a very private public figure.

Dorothy's will, filed for probate a week later, named her eldest niece as primary beneficiary. Sally McCall Conway received lifetime interest from the sum of $50,000[1], the principal to be divided upon her death, among her three children, Thomas Conway, Henry Conway, and Sally Ann Conway Ryan. She also inherited a formal portrait of Dorothy, who had commissioned the painting to commemorate her success in *Madame X*.[2] Most of her personal possessions, however, Dorothy bequeathed to her namesake and youngest niece, who had undertaken minor roles in a few plays such as Rachel Crothers' *Everyday*, starring the young Tallulah Bankhead, before turning to social service work. These included a triptych of photographs featuring Henry Donnelly in various roles, a painting of the Virgin Mother and Child, a *prie-dieu* that an interior decorator had purchased for Dorothy, both copies of *Candida* inscribed by Shaw, and, wrapped in plastic covering, the very script Dorothy had used for the play.[3] Edward Sheldon's mother, incidentally, asked for—and the family, chagrined, returned to her—a star sapphire ring that Ned had given to Dorothy many years earlier.[4]

The balance of the estate—about $100,000—was equally divided among Dorothy's sister and Nora's other five children: Madam Nora Donnelly McCall, Ambrose Victor McCall, Kathleen O'Neil Regan, John A. McCall, Dorothy Donnelly Fahringer. Since Dorothy's estate consisted mainly of "copyrights, manuscripts, and other literary, dramatic and lyrical compositions and rights therein and contracts thereto,"[5] her death did not sever her relationship with the Shuberts.

Her nephew served as executor. A graduate of Fordham University, Ambrose Victor McCall had become a prominent attorney and an expert in estate and trust law. While Assistant State Attorney General of New York, he successfully prosecuted stock manipulators and effected the indictment of Richard Whitney, president of the New York Stock Exchange, on charges of taking securities from the New York Yacht Club. His work eventually led to the formation of the Securities Exchange Commission. As the overseer of Dorothy's estate, Ambrose McCall was clearly a formidable match for the Shuberts' longtime attorney, William Klein. As late as 1938, Klein wrote to J. J.: "I have not concluded the agreement with Mr. Ambrose V. McCall, with respect to the Dorothy Donnelly rights, because I have not been able to get as good a contract as I had hoped for."[6] What tipped the scales for Dorothy's family was McCall's insistence that the Shuberts open their *personal* books as well as their business records. The wangling between the parties was protracted and acrimonious. McCall "surely would have had J. J. Shubert in a death hold on many an occasion, but denied himself only because he believed in a future life and a day of judgment," reports his son, Thomas McCall. "The Shuberts and A. V. McCall were on opposite sides of everything," he adds, "and any mention of the name meant that we were to respond with a chorus of 'boos.'"[7] An out-of-court settlement resolved questions regarding the ownership and size of royalties. For "the limited sum of $2500" McCall agreed to sell the royalties (but not the rights) for future stage productions of *Blossom Time*, *The Student Prince*, *My Maryland*, *The Charm School*, and *Hello, Lola*. He also retained all film and broadcasting rights and royalties from the sale of sheet music. The royalties from subsequent productions of Dorothy's plays and the income from ASCAP as well sales of sheet music, incidentally, provided significant financial support for the Society of the Sacred Heart, the religious order which her niece, Nora McCall, joined in 1909 and eventually headed.

To her friends and acquaintances, Dorothy left delightful memories. Reporters who interviewed her spoke unfailingly of her keen sense of humor. "She is natural and frank in her manner, and her way of expressing even commonplace facts shows a fund of humor and wit which she probably inherited from her Irish ancestors," said one.[8] Hosts of anecdotes reveal her remarkable thoughtfulness. When Robinson Locke wrote her a congratulatory letter, she replied, "I am so glad you liked my work and that you took the trouble to tell me so."[9] She continued to thank him for sending her clippings of reviews and for his encouraging words. She bought tickets for the premiere of *Rose of Stamboul* because Romberg had composed its score. "Tell us what you said to the man on the ship," she once encouraged Louise Hale. "And since I had forgotten what I said," wrote Louise, "she would tell the story herself, making the most of the incident, as she was in no ways hampered by the truth." When J. J. Shubert left on yet another of his frequent cruises to Europe, Dorothy had a gift delivered to his stateroom on the steamer *Olympic*. A gracious hostess, "she had a trick of bringing out our little contributions which would make a dinner party flash into color," Louise explains:

> We would get up from the table, each one of us feeling he was the individual success of the evening. It was a long time before I realized that she was the success, with her intense will back of us, her desire to make us shine. I was a longer time learning that this form of power at least is for all of us who care to share the spangles of life.

What remains to be said of Dorothy's legacy to American theatre? Throughout her acting career, drama critics offered a litany of praise:

"Her face is wonderfully mobile and expressive"; "Her soul lives in her eyes"; "superb characterization;" "infectious laughter;" "excellent interpretation." Competent, intelligent, and versatile—these were the adjectives most frequently used to describe her performances. Whatever tributes her acting reaped, however, permanent name recognition was not one of them. Her complicity in becoming typecast as an emotional rather than a dramatic actress restricted her to a limited repertoire. So did her attachment to Edward Sheldon—especially to his escapist plays. Nevertheless, she deserves to be remembered for creating acclaimed title roles, especially in *Candida* and *Madame X*. Moreover, she set a standard for performing Bernard Shaw, "making the Irish wit and epigrammatist the most popular playwright of the day"—a popularity that "owed much of its force, if not its inception, to the intellectual interpretation of the complex character of the parson's wife by Miss Donnelly."[10] Her portrayals of Candida and the Strange Lady, along with her subsequent proselytizing on behalf of Bernard Shaw, created an enduring home for the Irish playwright in the repertoire of the American theatre.

She considered acting not only as a career, but as a profession. She belonged to all the trade organizations of her time and often held leadership roles in many of them. For instance, she served on the Executive Committee of Actor's Equity during its formative years, in a period when fewer than one in fifteen wage-earning women was a union member and less than seven percent of all women were organized workers.[11] She occasionally presided at dinners hosted by the Authors' League of America, which acknowledged her many contributions to the organization through a notice that accompanied her obituary: "The Author's League of America mourns the loss of an active and loyal member." The notice was signed by the League's president, Owen Davis. Moreover, since she had only three female predecessors as a librettist—Anne Caldwell, Catherine Crisholm Cushing, and Rida Johnson Young—and few successors as a lyricist—Dorothy Fields and Betty Comden, to name two—Dorothy remains one of the small number of women members of ASCAP. In the Popular Music Collection, housed in the Pullen Library at Georgia State University, for instance, only 45 women composers and songwriters are represented—another indication of their limited number. Among them are lyricists Dorothy Donnelly and Dorothy Fields. As a pioneer in positions of leadership and avenues of the theatre generally restricted to her male counterparts, she merits mention in women's studies.

Dorothy's response as a professional entertainer to the war efforts endures. It created a precedent for future artists like Bob Hope, who spent every Christmas with troops during both times of war and peace. It also encouraged men to join the Stage Women's War Relief. In 1920, for example, they formed their own committee to offer help to the civilian population suffering from the effects of the war. In addition, Dorothy's efforts for World War I helped lead to the establishment of permanent support groups for American armed forces, especially the creation of the United Service Organizations during the second great war. Following the air raids on England, the Stage Women's War Relief became a branch of the British War Relief Society. After the bombing of Pearl Harbor, however, the organization turned its attention to needs at home. More than 50 distinct units evolved to meet diverse goals from entertaining wounded men in Navy and Marine hospitals, to offering specialized recreation in neuro-psychiatric units, and to writing short plays which dramatized and deliberately encouraged discussion of specific problems that confronted families dealing with separation and the subsequent homecoming of returning veterans. As she stood along the banks of the Moselle River, watching her fledgling stock company rehearse *Seven Keys to Baldpate*, little did Dorothy dream that one day the Stage Women's War Relief would validate her instincts and prophetic vision of what constituted appropriate entertainment for military bases.

Renamed the American Theatre Wing in 1940, incidentally, the organization produced a movie, *Stage Door Canteen,* and donated the proceeds—$75,000—to the USO to "inaugurate" legitimate theatre for armed forces personnel overseas. Their first offering was *The Barretts of Wimpole Street*, starring Katherine Cornell. The Wing also established the Tony awards in honor of Antoinette Perry, who headed the American Theatre Wing during World War II. A rival to the Oscars annually presented by the Motion Picture Academy of Arts and Sciences, the Tony awards recognize Broadway's outstanding plays, performers, directors, scenic designers, and the like.

As a woman writing for the theatre, Dorothy was not a novelty. By 1925, according to an estimate by Burns Mantle, more than one in eight plays produced during the drama season were written by women.[12] Other figures give an even higher ratio for the decade.[13] "I was really forced into it," Dorothy said of her career as a writer:

> I had made a couple of suggestions about a musical show, and the author didn't have time to make the alterations. So they asked me if I would. The play was in rehearsal at the time, and I had just ten days to do it. But I dug in, and everything seemed to go as it should. It was a miracle....[14]

A miracle, maybe; hard work, more likely. As a result, Dorothy realized the success that evades most playwrights: her works survived her.

Pathé released a six-reel black and white silent film of *The Riddle: Woman* in 1920, and the Thomas Wilkes Stock Company in Los Angeles revived the play in April 1923. The star of *Johnny Get Your Gun*, Louis Bennison, appropriated it in 1927, revising it as a comedy in prologue and three acts. Nor did *Fancy Free* disappear after 116 performances on Broadway. Instead, it reemerged as a short ballet, choreographed by Jerome Robbins to music by Leonard Bernstein, and in 1944 as *On the Town*, with a fresh score, more modern dance numbers, and lyrics by Betty Comden and Adolph Green, who also wrote lyrics for *Wonderful Town*. This play, too, retells *Fancy Free*, changing genders and presenting two girls coming from Ohio to New York to seek their fame, fortune, and fun as a writer and an actress.

Despite their limited survival, Dorothy's early plays—the straight ones, not the musicals—lack artistic quality and fail to meet the standards set by many of her female contemporaries. One of them, Zona Gale, captured the 1921 Pulitzer Prize in drama for *Miss Lulu Bett*, just four years after the award was instituted to recognize an American play, preferably original and dealing with American life. Susan Glaspell would win the Pulitzer Prize in 1931 for *Alison's House*. Burns Mantle's *Best Plays* series serves as another reliable measure of excellence. Mantle routinely chose a work by a female dramatist to represent the best play of the year. Dramatic merit, not sexism, determined the selection. *Good Gracious Annabelle* by Clare Kummer, *Nice People* and *Mary the Third* by Rachel Crothers and *Déclassée* by Zoe Akins received this distinction during Dorothy's lifetime. Hers did not. Her play writing made an impact on American theatre, not on American drama. It is a truth universally acknowledged among historians of the theatre that, no matter how deft or comprehensive, a libretto will never rank with the classics of dramatic literature. Thus, Dorothy will never be entitled to an altar of her own in the pantheon of women playwrights. As a librettist and lyricist, however, she deserves at least a niche for setting precedents in musical comedy and operetta that would shape the dramatic output of the future American stage and screen.

Poppy immediately took on a life of its own. David Wark Griffith, whose 12-reel, three-hour long epic, *Birth of a Nation*, dates from 1914 and still remains a cinematic triumph, made a silent film version of *Poppy* in 1925. Griffith cast W. C. Fields in the lead, renamed the play *Sally of the Sawdust*, and brought it up-to-date with bootleggers, car chases, and even an airplane. Fields recreated the role again in a talking motion picture of *Poppy* in 1936. His mistress for 14 years, Carlotta Monti, recalled that when required to deliver the line, "I will now play the 'Moonlight Sonata,'"

Fields burst forth with an ad-lib: "I will now render the allegro movement from the Duggi Jig Schreckensnack opera of Gilka Kimmel, an opus Pepitone." The script girl inhaled long and deeply, gamely asked how to spell it, and the director kept the improvisation.[15] In 1938 Lux Radio Theatre broadcast *Poppy* and subsequently released recordings of it.

The play helped launch the careers of comedienne Madge Kennedy, W. C. Fields, lyricist Howard Dietz, and composer Arthur Swartz by giving them their first entrée to musical theatre. Following the success of "Alibi Baby," Swartz and Dietz teamed up again and again, writing such memorable songs as "You and the Night and the Music," "Something to Remember You By," "The Moment I Saw You," and "Dancing in the Dark." No one owes *Poppy* more credit than W. C. Fields, who was 44 when he first played McGargle. On June 2, 1924, with Madge Kennedy on vacation and Victoria White as her replacement, W. C. Fields received top billing and a 20-minute standing ovation during intermission. In the audience were two comedians whose applause mattered: Sam Hardy and Will Rogers. The role of the "con" man, slightly shady and dissolute, often outlandishly garbed, became Field's future trademark. The looseness of the plot allowed him to introduce a poker game, a routine that eventually became another permanent part of his repertoire, and occasionally to improvise, as he explains:

> In *Poppy*, I was a small-time confidence man whose philosophy, you may remember, was "never give a sucker an even break." In one scene I was alone in a dark library, hunting on tiptoe for cards that I intended to mark, so that later I could cheat in a poker game. One night, as I was stealing around the stage, being careful not to wake up anybody in the house, somebody, off-stage, accidentally knocked over a pile of boxes with a crash that shook the theatre. My scene was ruined for the moment.
>
> I had an inspiration. I stole down to the footlights and whispered to the audience, "Mice!"
>
> We kept that in the act, too.[16]

Poppy also launched lingering curiosities. Dietz was new to Broadway and to its convention of limiting program credits. For instance, the programs for *Hearts Are Trumps* and *June Days* omit "+D. D." even though the Shuberts' press releases boast about Dorothy as an author of *Hearts Are Trumps* and the song, "Take 'Em to the Door Blues," cut from the *Hello, Lola*'s tryout in Washington, D. C., was interpolated into *June Days*. Once *Poppy*'s popularity was certain, Howard Dietz appealed to its producer, claiming that he had written the role for Fields. At least one compilation, *American Song: the Complete Companion to Musical Theatre*, identifies him as co-librettist. Stanley Green also mentions that Donnelly kept Dietz's name off the program and the sheet music.[17] Nevertheless, none of the publications at the time of *Poppy*'s opening and few since accord him credit for more than his lyrics to a single song. To appease Dietz, *Poppy*'s producer, Philip Goodman, sent him a pipe along with the assurance that this gift was rare and valuable. As late as 1974, when he published his autobiography, *Dancing in the Dark*, Dietz still faults Dorothy for denying him credits and the producer for refusing a share of the royalties, although he expresses satisfaction with the pipe.[18] Dorothy's family tell a different story, however. She apparently completed *Poppy* before Fields was even considered for the male lead, and her nephew, Ambrose McCall, recalled how the family sat around the table, discussed the play, and laughed as Dorothy made repeated attempts to come up with a good ending until she struck gold with the oft-repeated line (later the title of a film, starring Fields): "Never give a sucker an even break."[19]

The Shuberts revived *Blossom Time* again and again. Why not? The show was cheap to produce with period settings, ample costumes that completely covered every size and shape, consisting of pantaloons with tiers of ruffled lace, dresses with full skirts, and broad-brimmed bonnets, and its "bargain-basement casting."[20] Historian Ethan Mordden observes that "no cast was too lurid, no production too cheesy to discourage the regional public."[21] At some point there were as many as 14 national touring companies of this operetta. Musical theatre historian Gerald Bordman says that a "road company of *Blossom Time*" eventually became a phrase used in the trade to express contempt,[22] and Steven Suskin mentions that "a standing joke well into the 1950's was that there was a lost company of *Blossom Time* still out on the road. Somewhere."[23] The continuing popularity of the show was not lost on other composers, librettists, and lyricists. Almost immediately *Blossom Time* spawned imitations as fast as a pregnant herring. *Kismet* (Borodin) and *Carmen Jones* (Bizet) also rely on a single musical theme by a composer. Other stage operettas that fictionalize the lives of composers and adapted their music on stage include *The Love Song* (Offenbach), *White Lilacs* (Chopin), and *Song of Norway* (Grieg). *Amadeus* (Mozart) and *Immortal Beloved* (Beethoven) show the popularity of the form transferred to the screen.

According to Brooks McNamara, even *My Maryland* remained in the repertoire of summer stock companies until 1976, since amateur productions were welcome to borrow both sets and costumes from the Shuberts' Century Library.[24] According to *The Playmakers*, "The late Jack Small, general manager for the Shuberts, was once asked if a chair in his office was from The Student Prince, and he replied, 'We ran out of Student Prince furniture last year.'"[25] The Shuberts, who considered the theatre as "a machine that makes dollars,"[26] dragged out tired sets and bedraggled costumes year after year or lent them from their library. Regrettably, this practice cheapened the revivals and prevented them from appearing fresh in the eyes of reviewers.

The Student Prince has passed the ultimate test of quality: time. Despite its sentimentality, it has demonstrated universal appeal. In 1926 Heidelberg University adopted its hero to create a mascot that still remains an armored prince astride a regal horse. Seventy years later, a Cantonese movie company borrowed its theme to make Xuesheng Wangzi, a movie presented during the 1996 Hong Kong International Film Festival. Scores of companies have mooched its name for a variety of products: a beer from the Heidelberg Brewery in Covington, Kentucky; a hotel near Sydney, Australia; a guitar with a mahogany body, rosewood fingerboard, and adjustable bridge; a two-star restaurant in Springfield, Massachusetts. In all probability none of these manufacturers know how or why "the student prince" has become a familiar logo. Even a wrestler in Las Vegas calls himself "The Student Prince," and it's highly unlikely that he's ever heard of Sigmund Romberg or, indeed, Dorothy Donnelly. "Deep in My Heart," incidentally, lent its title to two biographies of Romberg. One was the fictionalized book by Elliott Arnold, published in 1949 and based on the author's lengthy interview with Romberg in 1947. The other was a 1954 film based only partly on Arnold's book and released three years after the death of Romberg. The motion picture starred José Ferrer as Romberg and Merle Oberon as Dorothy and featured an incongruously interpolated song, "Mr. and Mrs." (Fresh from his *tour de force* as Toulouse Lautrec in the film, *Moulin Rouge*, Ferrer sang it with his wife, Rosemary Clooney, who was expecting their second child and wore a special costume to disguise her pregnancy.)

The Student Prince survives on discs, in film, and on the stage. "Although the original production made stars out of Howard Marsh and Ilse Marvenga, neither ever recorded any of its songs," writes Dwight Bowers, performing arts historian at the Smithsonian's National Museum of American History. The Smithsonian collection, however, includes a British recording of "Deep in My Heart," originally sung by Harry Welchman and Rose Hignell in the first English production of the operetta. Kathie and Karl's dialogue introduces the song in this rendition, which, according to Bowers, meticulously preserves "both the song and its dramatic context."[27] Several American recordings of the operetta have been subsequently made, however: one with Nelson Eddy and Rise Stevens, a

In the finale (detail) of My Maryland, *Barbara Fritchie hugs her wounded Confederate soldier while prominently displaying the American flag, a courageous act that prompts Stonewall Jackson to save the young lovers and safeguard the home. (Courtesy Shubert Archive.)*

second featuring Lauritz Melchior, and yet another with opera stars Jan Peerce, Roberta Peters, and Georgio Tozzi. In 1927 Pathé filmed *The Student Prince* as a black and white silent, directed by German-born Ernst Lubitsch, with a new score—a subtle compliment to Dorothy's libretto. In 1954 Metro-Goldwyn-Meyer released a new version that retained only the most popular songs from the original: "To the Inn We're Marching," "Serenade," "The Drinking Song," "Gaudeamus," "Deep in My Heart," and "Golden Days." It added new songs with new lyrics and cast the mellifluous Ann Blyth as the workaday barmaid; tall, dark, and handsome aristocratic Edmund Purdom as Karl; and, off-screen, Mario Lanza, who sang the male lead's songs. "It's not a farce and it's not drama. Just a pretty love story of peaches and cream," noted the reviewer for *Variety*.[28]

Although burdened by illness and the pressure of work, Dorothy Donnelly maintains her typically erect posture and presents her right profile, seldom seen in photographs because she thought her nose too large. (Courtesy Philip Fahringer Collection.)

By contrast, *Magill's Survey* of the cinema described it as a "ruthless social commentary about the emptiness of life that exists only for duty and without love."[29] Mario Lanza later released a "greatest hits" record with the main songs from *The Student Prince*. By 1945, the musical began playing annually in Chicago and already had racked up 93 weeks of performances there. The New York City Opera revived the operetta four times during the 1980s and twice more in the 1990s. It also traveled with *The Student Prince* to Taiwan in 1988. The Ohio Light Opera company presented the operetta during its 1982 festival; it came to life on the stage of the Rugby Theatre in Warwickshire, England, in 1996; and Opera Delaware performed it in 1997. In February, 1997, slightly revised, it was performed at the San Gabriel Auditorium in Southern California; in the audience sat 97-year-old Violet Carlson, who played Gretchen, one of the barmaids, in the original Broadway cast.

Dorothy's lyrics have provided generations of aspiring tenors with fodder for their résumés. One need only to "surf" the Internet for a few moments to judge how many singers have cut their teeth on songs from *The Student Prince*, especially "Golden Days," "Beloved," and "Serenade," and boast about it. The radio show, *Railroad Hour*, aired excerpts from *The Student Prince* on October 25, 1948, *Blossom Time* on January 1, 1949, and *My Maryland* on May 26, 1952. *Musical Jubilee* featured "Serenade" from *The Student Prince* in a montage of musical theatre songs that opened November 13, 1975, and ran for 92 performances. As recently as 1994 the San Francisco Opera included songs from *The Student Prince* in its series of summer recitals. Their continuing popularity surely entitles Dorothy to a belated induction into the Songwriters Hall of Fame.

A further word must be said about comedy—or lack of it—in Dorothy's musicals. Drama critics of the period tended to view these musicals as commercial theatre pieces, much like *Poppy*, whose principal objective is to provide an audience with predominately light-hearted content. During the 1920s the terms "musical comedy," "operetta," "comic" or "light opera," and "musical theatre" were interchangeable, in both reviews and concepts. Today, on the other hand, purists define them *ad nauseum*. Many contemporary historians of the musical form, notably Gerald Bordman, Abe Laufe, Ethan C. Mordden, and Richard Traubner, concede that operetta or "little opera" is frequently juxtaposed to its more sober sister, opera. "Critics have resisted operettas that attempt to be serious, or thoroughgoingly romantic, rather than trivial," notes Traubner,[30] accurately characterizing the predilection of Stark Young and Brooks Atkinson and other critics of the period for taking their aisle seats to watch a musical with the predetermined objective of uncovering its humor. If opera is thoughtful and tragic, then operetta must conversely be entertaining and comic. "The problem is symmetry," adds Mordden: "how to equalize the straight parts with the buffoonery, how to satisfy the public's demand for entertainment and yet come up with an elegant libretto."[31]

Dorothy's solution to this problem was two-fold. She introduced a requisite comical character in her operettas: Kranz in *Blossom Time*, the valet, Lutz, in *The Student Prince*, and the Confederate Colonel Negly in *My Maryland*, for instance. However, she primarily used lyrics to provide the humor. Here, for example, is a verse of the fox-trot "Etiquette" from *My Princess*:

> When you are dining with a lady you shouldn't let her pay the bill.
> Don't keep your hat on in the parlor unless you do it with great skill.
> If at the seashore you have met her and take her rowing in a boat,
> It isn't courteous to upset her till you're sure that she can float.[32]

Songs like "Ker-choo!," which describes sneezing, or "Old John Barleycorn," which elucidates the effects of imbibing, both from *My Maryland*, are what William Arlie Everett identifies as "specialty" songs. Their existence, he says, demonstrates the influence of the revue on these operettas—a contention supported by the notation in Romberg's own hand on the first page of "When You're in Mexico": "à la Wintergarden (not too fast)."[33] Generally written merely to entertain, these songs seldom advance the plot or offer further characterization.[34] Wherever they were superimposed on the operettas, rather than integral to them, they ruptured the dramatic integrity of the musical.

Dorothy must plead guilty to yet another charge: writing schmalz. "It cannot be denied that these works are tuneful and entertaining," says William Green, "but their plots are sentimental and romantic and their settings unreal."[35] Robert Sherman, a critic of classical music, concurs:

> I must confess that various stage revivals ... have not tempted me into attendance. I find something terribly dated about the plots, the lines, the whole heart-on-sleeve romantic atmosphere, and I much prefer to hear the lovely scores on disc, unencumbered by all the extramusical trappings.[36]

So does musical theatre historian Alfred Simon:

> During the last generation or so it has become fashionable to be contemptuous of anything as sentimental as operettas.... There is no doubt that indifference or disdain for operetta music is completely genuine in many instances; with that I do not quarrel. But far too many people find

it necessary to apologize for really liking the songs from *The Student Prince, Rose Marie*, or [Victor Herbert's] *The Red Mill*.[37]

There are grounds for such arguments. Donnelly's operettas make no intellectual demands on the theatregoers. The themes, even when well defined and meaningful, are simple and, for modern audiences, not particularly vital. The settings are often remote either in place or time or social milieu. The characters usually remain static. In *The Student Prince*, for example, they are drawn from both ends of the social spectrum, royal and common; they are blessed with sterling qualities, personally, morally, and socially; their dialogue is simplistic and high blown, lyrical rather than realistic. Furthermore, with the exception of *My Princess*, Dorothy made no attempt to develop them as the situation unfolds.

Nevertheless, Dorothy's romantic libretti for *Blossom Time* and *The Student Prince* led to a revival of traditional European operetta for the rest of the decade. They provided the audience in the 1920s for *The Desert Song* and *The New Moon* by Oscar Hammerstein II and Romberg and *The Vagabond King* and *The Three Musketeers* by composer Rudolf Friml. The "touch of fatalism" that Dorothy injected into *Blossom Time* and *The Student Prince*—and almost guaranteed the latter would not graduate from script to production—paved the way for other operettas that would explore the darker side of human nature. *Show Boat* and *Porgy and Bess*, both of which demonstrate the cruel effects of slavery and racism, immediately come to mind. Once Dorothy established a precedent for confounding those who looked for comedy or "light" in light opera, the stage was set for *Pal Joey, Oklahoma*, and *Carousel*. Even more modern works like *Les Misérables, Into the Woods, Sweeney Todd, Assassins*, and *Miss Saigon*, says William Everett, can trace their lineage to *Blossom Time* and *The Student Prince*. The heartbreak and death of Schubert and the selfless renunciation of Kathie and Prince Karl were not six-lane highways but hand-lettered signposts on a country road that meanders across cow paths and unmarked dusty lanes until it arrives at the serious treatment of the unpleasant.

Ranked like plankton on the bottom of the food chain, the musical nevertheless sustains the life of the theatre. It remains the dominant genre of Broadway offerings. With today's ticket priced at $60 or more, what does "a night out on the town" represent to the businessman, tired by Friday evening, or to the visitor from out-of-state, entranced with his first glimpse of New York City? Contemporary theatregoers are reluctant to gamble on new plays, especially provocative ones that may require them to think. They are, instead, attracted to spectacles, like the crashing of the glass chandelier in *The Phantom of the Opera* or the rotating blades of the helicopter in *Miss Saigon*.

Veterans in the business of providing entertainment search for that elusive balance between the light and the heavy. According to *Current Biography 1945*, "Acting on his theory that people were a little tired of hearing jazz or serious music at concerts, [Sigmund Romberg] contracted to conduct six concerts in Eastern cities, a program called *An Evening with Sigmund Romberg*." Midway through one evening of selections from his operettas, he addressed the audience:

> I have been told that the music I have lived with for many years now belongs to the past…They tell me today is the day of radio, telephone, the airplane, fast cars, and that life has speeded up so fast that no one can slow down to a waltz. Perhaps this is so. If so, they are right and I am wrong. But if some of the lovely music you have listened to this evening and will listen to again when I've finished this rambling talk, if this music has touched you and made you remember that life was livable once and that it will be again, then I am right, and they are wrong.

He was right. By January 1944, the six originally scheduled concerts stretched to 277, the number of cities expanded to 128, and the box-office took in more than $700,000. "Louisville, for example, heard the program five times."[38] The program included mostly Romberg's compositions and occasionally other popular pieces by George Gershwin, Jerome Kern, and Franz Lehar.

In terms both of years and number of performances, *Blossom Time* and *The Student Prince* outlasted *Show Boat*, which most historians claim to be the masterpiece of American operetta, heralding it as the first seamless fusion of plot with score and the introduction of realistic, or at least, plausible characters. *The Student Prince* endures. Any hints of eventual interment seem premature.

Although "the dialogue is wooden and the wit remote to modern ears," as Bernard Holland notes, "all of this is moot when *The Student Prince* sings at its best. "Overhead the Moon Is Beaming' and 'Golden Days" are irresistible; and while they are in progress, critical faculties, doubts and questions quite correctly melt away."[39] According to performing arts historian Dwight Bowers, "*The Student Prince* may well be the ultimate American operetta; at least it is the most wildly and widely successful of its unashamedly romantic genre."[40] The very lack of complexity in *The Student Prince* and its lyrical emphasis on fantasy hold the key to its remarkable survival. The operetta permits the theatregoer to escape the strain of reality and the daily drudgery of the commonplace.

Transported to another time and place, audiences continue to enjoy the great achievement that Dorothy and Romberg attained—a unified romanticism of libretto, lyrics, and score. "For its songs, but more specifically for purely sentimental story reasons," says Traubner, "*The Student Prince* has remained a favorite."[41] And it remains a permanent monument to Dorothy Donnelly, the first person, perhaps the only one, male or female, to serve the stage in every capacity—as actor, director, producer, playwright, lyricist, librettist, and benefactor to the profession. Hard working, happily independent, occasionally magnificent on stage, eager to accept new challenges and persevering in defeat, Dorothy deserves her monument.

Notes

Introduction

1. Herbert G. Goldman, *Fanny Brice: The Original Funny Girl* (New York: Oxford University Press, 1992), p. 23.
2. Richard Mansfield, quoted in Toby Cole and Helen Krich Chinoy, *Actors on Acting* (New York: Crown, 1970), p. 371.
3. Ward Morehouse, *Matinee Tomorrow: Fifty Years of Our Theater* (New York: McGraw-Hill, 1949), p. 106.
4. Humphrey Bogart, quoted in Susan Goodman, "She Lost It at the Movies," *Modern Maturity* March-April 1998, p. 52.
5. Alan Hewitt, "Repertory to Residuals," *The American Theatre: A Sum of Its Parts* (New York: Samuel French 1971), p. 84.
6. Alexander Woollcott, *New York Times*, 20 January 1914, p. 9.
7. Amy Henderson and Dwight Bowers, *Red, Hot & Blue* (Washington, D.C.: Smithsonian Institution Press, 1996), p. 53.
8. Don B. Wilmeth and Tice L. Miller, eds., *Cambridge Guide to the American Theatre* (New York: Cambridge University Press, 1993), p. 450.
9. Helen Krich Chinoy and Linda Walsh Jenkins, *Women in American Theatre* (New York: Theatre Communications Group, 1987), p. 333.
10. Hyman Howard Taubman, *The Making of the American Theatre* (New York: Coward McCann, 1965), p. 193.
11. Hollis Alpert, *Broadway! 125 Years of Musical Theatre* (New York: Museum of the City of New York, Arcade, 1991), p. 84–85.
12. Martin Gottfried, *Broadway Musicals* (New York: Harry N. Abrams, 1979), p. 9.
13. Arthur Laurents, quoted in Otis L. Guernsey, Jr., ed., *Broadway Song and Story* (New York: Dodd Mead, 1985), p. 384.
14. Gottfried, *Broadway Musicals*, p. 53.
15. *Ibid.*, p. 391.

Chapter 1: Beginnings

1. Louise Closser Hale, "Dorothy Donnelly," *The World*, 9 January 1928. Following the death of Donnelly on January 4, 1928, Alexander Woollcott invited

her closest friend to write her eulogy and added a preface to the column: "To-day this platform is given over to a memorial service for the first Candida. It seems fitting that the first Prossy should be the one summoned to say some of the words that lie close to so many hearts in the American theatre.—A. W." All future references to Hale pertain to this eulogy unless otherwise cited.

2. Kerby A. Miller, *Emigrants and Exiles* (New York: Oxford University Press, 1985), p. 41.

3. Carl Wittke, *We Who Built America* (New York: Prentice-Hall, 1939), p. 130.

4. Francis Wyse, quoted in Miller, *Emigrants and Exiles*, p. 203.

5. George Potter, *To the Golden Door* (Boston: Little Brown, 1960), p. 21.

6. Wittke, *We Who Built America*, p. 137.

7. It closed on June 2, 1903, prior to its demolition, with a final speech delivered by the stage manager, Dexter Smith Seymour, who recited from a Shake-spearean play, Hamlet's plea, "I beseech you, remember."

8. Wittke, *We Who Built America*, p. 378.

9. *Ibid.*, pp. 378–379.

10. James Grant Wilson and John Fiske, eds., *Appleton's Cyclopedia of American Biography* (New York: Appleton, 1888), vol. 2, p. 485.

11. Dorothy McCall Fahringer, taped reminiscences of Dorothy's youngest niece.

12. Marvin Felheim, *The Theatre of Augustin Daly* (Cambridge: Harvard University Press, 1956), p. 148.

13. *Ibid.*

14. John Gassner, *Best Plays of the Early American Theatre* (New York: Crown, 1967), p. xxii.

15. Cole and Chinoy, *Actors on Acting*, p. 538.

16. Edward B. Marks, *They All Had Glamour* (New York: Julian Messner, 1944), p. 432.

17. *Ibid.*, p. xx.

18. Lloyd Morris, *Curtain Time* (New York: Random House, 1953), p. 222.

19. Helen Ormsbee, *Backstage with Actors* (New York: Thomas Y. Crowell, 1938), p. 175.

20. Gassner, *Best Plays of the Early American Theatre*, p. xix.

21. *Robinson Locke Collection of Dramatic Scrapbooks* (hereafter cited as Locke), Billy Rose Theatre Collection of the New York City Public Library, vol. 160, p. 13. Many of the clippings have been truncated and therefore lack one of the following: the name of the writer or of the newspaper or the date of publication.

22. Eileen O'Connor, "From Mme. X to Musical Comedy," *Theatre Magazine*, August 1918, p. 84.

23. Fahringer, taped reminiscences.

24. Catholic Cemeteries, Roman Catholic Diocese of Brooklyn, letter to Mr. Thomas Conway, 5 November 1984, a photocopy of which was sent to the author. Mr. Thomas Conway is the great-nephew of Dorothy Donnelly. Christina Donnelly's date of death is listed as 17 September 1880. She shares the grave in St. Mark's section, range K, plot 31/32, with Dorothy's parents.

25. Arthur Hobson Quinn, *History of the American Drama* (New York: Harper and Brothers, 1927), vol. 1, p. 379.

26. Dorothy Donnelly, 1 April 1906, Locke, p. 13.

27. George Clinton Densmore Odell, *Annals of the New York Stage* (New York: AMS Press, 1970), vol. 14, p. 50.

28. Alexander Woollcott, "The Actress Who Became a Playwright," *Pictorial Review* September 1925, p. 113.

29. Fahringer, taped reminiscences.

30. *Ibid.*

31. *Ibid.*

32. *Ibid.* Both the letter from Sara Donnelly and the painting are in possession of Reuben Philip Fahringer, Dorothy's grandnephew and son of Dorothy Donnelly Fahringer—Dorothy's niece.

33. *Ibid.*

34. Odell, *Annals of the New York Stage*, p. 470ff.

35. O'Connor, "From Mme. X to Musical Comedy," p. 84.

36. Marie Louise Padberg, RSCJ, letter to author, 27 April 1988. Sister Padberg reports recorded payments of tuition "for the account of Miss D. Donnelly."

37. Mary Ranncy, RSCJ, letter to author, 15 March 1988.

38. Louise Callan, *Society of the Sacred Heart in North America* (New York: Longmans, Green, 1937), p. 766.

39. Gustav Kobbe, *Famous Actresses and Their Homes* (Boston: Little, Brown, 1905), p. 240.

40. *Ibid.*, pp. 240–241.

41. *Ibid.*, p. 241.

42. O'Connor, "From Mme. X to Musical Comedy," p. 84.

Chapter 2: On Stage

1. Morris, *Curtain Time*, p. 192.

2. Morehouse, *Matinee Tomorrow*, p. 4.

3. Cole and Chinoy, *Actors on Acting*, p. 539.

4. Howard Siegman, "On Stage," *Selected Theatre Reviews from the New York Times*, edited by Bernard Beckerman and Howard Siegman (New York: Arno Press, 1973), p. xiv. The tradition of stock companies survived in major cities like New York, Philadelphia, Boston, and San Francisco, says Morris, *Curtain Time*, p. 192.

5. Kenneth Macgowan, *Footlights Across America* (New York: Harcourt, Brace, 1929), p. 61.

6. "Henry V. Donnelly Dead," *The New York Dramatic Mirror*, 16 February 1910, p. 5.

7. Ada Patterson, "Morning's Chat with Candida," *Theatre Magazine*, 1904, p. 171.

8. Locke, p. 13.

9. *Ibid.*

10. Some references to reviews printed in the *New York Times* or *Theatre Magazine* have been omitted since they are available in indexes to those publications.

11. *New York Times*, 26 September 1899, p. 7, col. 1.

12. Morehouse, *Matinee Tomorrow*, p. 26.

13. Gladys Malvern, *Curtain Going Up* (New York: Julian Messner, 1943), p. 64.

14. Ward Morehouse, *George M. Cohan: Prince of the American Theatre* (Westport, Connecticut: Greenwood, 1943), p. 46.

15. Locke, p. 13.

16. Jane Gordon, "In 29 Weeks of Memorizing," *The World*, 9 May 1901, in Locke, p. 3.

17. Woollcott, "The Actress Who Became a Playwright," p. 113.

18. Sally Donnelly Conway Ryan, letter to author, 25 March 1988.

19. Ada Patterson, "Martyrs to the Stage," *Theatre Magazine*, July-December 1909, p. 182.

20. Hewitt, "Repertory to Residuals," p. 112. Laura Hope Crews, incidentally, played the fainthearted Aunt PittyPat Hamilton in the original, 1939, film production of *Gone with the Wind*.

21. Patterson, "Morning's Chat with Candida," p. 172.

22. *New York Times*, 31 October 1900, p. 6, col. 6.

23. Unidentified newspaper, 10 April 1901, in Locke, p. 2.

24. *New York Times*, 28 November 1899, p. 5, col. 1.

25. Locke, p. 3.

26. Thomas McCall, S. J., telephone conversation with author, 6 May 1988.

27. Locke, p. 3.

28. "Miss Donnelly Effects a Rescue," *Bohemian*, January 1907, in Locke, p. 56.

29. Patterson, "Morning's Chat with Candida," p. 171.

30. Locke, p. 3.

31. Patterson, "Morning's Chat with Candida," p. 172.

32. Patterson, "Martyrs to the Stage," p. 182.

33. Cornelia Otis Skinner, *Madame Sarah* (Boston: Houghton Mifflin, 1967), p. 215.

34. *Ibid.*

35. *Ibid.*, p. xi.

36. Locke, p. 3.

37. Kobbe, *Famous Actresses*, p. 201ff.

38. Nancy Fahringer, (daughter-in-law of Dorothy McCall, Dorothy's youngest niece and goddaughter), in telephone conversation with author, 9 June 1988.

39. Fahringer, taped reminiscences.

40. James Kotsilibos-Davis, *Great Times, Good Times: The Odyssey of Maurice Barrymore* (Garden City, New York: Doubleday, 1977), pp. 428–429.

41. Madge Robertson Kendal, quoted in *New York Times*, 28 March 1900, sec. 6, p. 6.

42. Mollie Morris, "Girl at the Matinee: An Actress with Intellect," *Chicago News*, 3 October 1906, in Locke, p. 76.

Chapter 3: Breakthrough

1. Gerald Langford, *The Richard Harding Davis Years* (New York: Holt, Rinehart and Winston, 1961), p. 168. Davis received $5,000 from *Scribner's* for the book.

2. Morehouse, *Matinee Tomorrow*, p. 24.

3. *Ibid.*, 190ff.

4. Fahringer, taped reminiscences.

5. Locke, p. 7.

6. Fahringer, taped reminiscences.

7. *Ibid.*

8. Kobbe, *Famous Actresses*, p. 242.

9. *Ibid.*

10. George Bernard Shaw, quoted in Margot Peters, *Bernard Shaw and the Actresses* (Garden City, New York: Doubleday, 1980), p. 146.

11. Richard Mansfield, quoted in Archibald Henderson, *George Bernard Shaw: His Life and Works* (Cincinnati: Stewart & Kidd, 1911), p. 438.

12. Richard Mansfield, quoted in St. John Greer Ervine, *Bernard Shaw: His Life, Work, and Friends* (New York: William Morrow, 1956), p. 340.

13. Richard Mansfield, quoted in William Winter, *Life and Art of Richard Mansfield* (New York: Moffat, Yard, 1910), vol. II, p. 230.

14. *Ibid.*, p. 158.

15. George Bernard Shaw, "Author's Note," *The Playgoer*, official program of the Curran Theatre, San Francisco, 27 September 1938, p. 14.

16. Henderson, *George Bernard Shaw: His Life and Works*, p. 444.

17. Helen Ormsbee, *Backstage with Actors*, p. 209.

18. *Ibid.*, p. 208.

19. Dorothy Donnelly, 1 April 1904, quoted in Locke, p. 13.

20. Archibald Henderson, *George Bernard Shaw: Man of the Century* (New York: Appleton-Century-Crofts, 1959), p. 407. See also Ormsbee, *Backstage with Actors*, p. 314. Ormsbee reports that the actor, "William Gillette lent [the money] to Daly and Smith, though this fact was not known at the time." Gillette, also a playwright as well as an actor, was an uncle of Winchell Smith.

21. Morris, *Curtain Time*, p. 303. *Theatre Magazine* also recounted the anecdote.

22. Woollcott, "The Actress Who Became a Playwright," pp. 113–114.

23. Morris, *Curtain Time*, p. 303.

24. Henderson, *Man of the Century*, p. 443.

25. George Bernard Shaw, quoted in Hesketh Pearson, *G.B.S.: A Full Length Portrait* (New York: Harper & Brothers, 1942), p. 170.

26. Fahringer, taped reminiscences.

27. Kobbe, *Famous Actresses*, p. 236.

28. Locke, p. 13.

29. Arnold Daly, quoted in Archibald Henderson, *Bernard Shaw: Playboy and Prophet* (New York: D. Appleton, 1932), p. 408.

30. *Ibid.*

31. Arnold Daly, quoted in Adolphe Klauber, *New York Times*, 8 May 1904, sec. 4, p. 6.

32. Dorothy Donnelly, quoted in Patterson, "Morning's Chat with Candida," p. 172.

33. Forrest Arden, "A Talk with Miss Donnelly," *Chicago Sunday American*, 30 October 1904, in Locke, pp. 19–20.

34. *Ibid.*

35. *Ibid.*

36. *Ibid.*

37. Patterson, "Morning's Chat with Candida," p. 171.

38. Pearson, *G.B.S.: A Full Length Portrait*, p. 203. Shaw dated the letter "21st & 22nd Dec. 1903."

39. *The [New York] Commercial Advertiser*, 31 December 1903, p. 1.

40. The theatres and dates selected for subsequent productions of *Candida* are taken from Burns Mantle's best plays series. Henderson, however, writes that the play "crowded the house for weeks," referring to the Madison Square Theatre.

41. Adolphe Klauber, *New York Times*, 5 January 1904, sec. 5, p. 3.

42. Henderson, *Playboy and Prophet*, p. 408.

43. Patterson, "Morning's Chat with Candida," p. 172.

44. *Ibid.*

45. *Ibid.*

46. Locke, p. 9.

47. Kobbe, *Famous Actresses*, pp. 236–237.

48. Henderson, *Playboy and Prophet*, p. 409.

49. Henderson, *Man of the Century*, p. 477.

50. Arden, "A Talk with Miss Donnelly," in Locke, p. 20.

51. Henderson, *Playboy and Prophet*, p. 408. Henderson gives the number of New York performances as 150.

52. Kobbe, *Famous Actresses*, p. 242.

53. Peter Robertson, "Of Shaw's 'Candida,'" *San Francisco Chronicle*, 30 September 1904, sec. E, p. 1.

54. Locke, p. 9.

55. Allan Chappelow, *Shaw, the Villager and Human Being* (New York: The MacMillan Company, 1962), p. 201.

56. Locke, p. 45.

57. Olivia Coolidge, *George Bernard Shaw* (Boston: Houghton Mifflin, 1968), p. 106.

58. "Dorothy Donnelly: At Close Range," *Des Moines Register*, 6 December 1908, in Locke, p. 80.

59. The inscribed copy, owned by Philip Fahringer, was displayed at a performance of *Candida*, presented in 1996 by the Arizona Theatre Company in Tucson.

Chapter 4: Beyond the Footlights

1. *"Friquet,* The Tree Sparrow, Moults at Its First Performance," *The Evening Sun*, 1 February 1905, in Locke, p. 21.

2. *New York Times*, 8 March 1905, sec. 9, p. 1. The play's title was listed as *When We Dead Awake* in all reviews at the period.

3. *Ibid.*

4. *The New York Evening Mail*, 25 April 1905, in Locke, p. 24.

5. "Proud Laird's Canny Comedy," *The New York Sun*, 25 April 1905, in Locke, p. 24.

6. *New York Times*, 25 April 1905, sec. 7, p. 1.

7. Hassard Short eventually left acting to become a director, principally for the Shubert brothers.

8. Unidentified newspaper, 9 May 1905, in Locke, p. 25. Several reviews, often truncated, of *Mrs. Battle's Bath* in local papers appear here and on the following pages.

9. Unidentified newspaper, 10 May 1905, in Locke, p. 26.

10. *New York Times*, 4 February 1906, sec. 7, p. 4.

11. *Ibid.*

12. *Ibid.*

13. *Ibid.*

14. Alice Rohe, "All Women Feline, Few Real Cats," *New York World*, 13 February 1906, in Locke, p. 35.

15. Dorothy Donnelly, letter to Robinson Locke, 5 Jan. 1906, in Locke, p. 32.

16. Locke, p.34.

17. *Vanity Fair*, 16 February 1906, in Locke, p. 36.

18. *Vanity Fair*, n.d., in Locke, p. 31.

19. Alan Dale, *New York American*, 26 January 1906, in Locke, p. 30.

20. Locke, p. 38.

21. Acton Davies, *The Evening Sun*, 26 January 1906, in Locke, p. 29.

22. Locke, p. 31.

23. *Ibid.*

24. *New York Times*, 30 September 1907, sec. 7, p. 5.

25. *New York Times*, 8 May 1904, sec. 7, p. 4.
The drama critic for this period of time has not been identified by the *New York Times*. There is no byline, and searches through histories of the paper and inquiries directed to the paper have not borne fruit.

26. Acton Davies, *The Evening Sun*, 26 January 1906, in Locke, p. 29.

27. *New York Telegram*, 12 September 1907, in Locke, p. 63.

28. Patterson, "Morning's Chat with Candida," p. 172.

29. *New York Times*, 30 September 1907, sec. 7, p. 5.

30. "Playhouse Gossip," *Theatre Magazine*, 4 February 1906.

31. Arden, "A Talk with Miss Donnelly," in Locke, p. 19.

32. Quinn, *History of the American Drama*, vol. 2, pp. 100–101.

33. Percy N. Stone, *Herald Tribune*, 7 March 1925. One clipping in the Locke scrapbook indicates that she played with the Bellow Stock Company in Denver the following spring.

34. "Henry V. Donnelly Dead," *The New York Dramatic Mirror*, 16 February 1910, p. 5.

35. *Best Plays of 1894–1899* (New York: Dodd, Mead, 1899), p. 233.

36. *New York Telegraph*, 9 November 1906, in Locke, p. 49.

37. Frederic Edward McKay, "Daughters of Men' Bombastic and Boresome," *Evening Mail*, 22 November 1906, in Locke, p. 51.

38. *New York Times*, 20 November 1906, p. 9, col. 3.

39. Locke, p. 45.

40. "Want Dorothy Donnelly to Replace Gorky in Russia," *Toledo Blade*, 15 December 1906, in Locke, p. 55.

41. George Bernard Shaw, quoted in Peters, *Bernard Shaw and the Actresses*, p. 187.

42. *Des Moines Register*, 6 December 1908, in Locke, p. 80.

43. *Spokane Review*, 7 April 1906, in Locke, p. 43.

44. Fahringer, taped reminiscences.

45. *Baltimore Star*, 11 November 1908, in Locke, p. 79.

46. Daniel Frohman, *Memoirs of a Manager* (New York: Doubleday, Page, 1911), p. 198.

47. "Mac's Gossip of the Stage," *Theatre Magazine*, 8 May 1909, in Locke, p. 86.

48. Locke, p. 13.

49. Locke, p. 67.

50. Willard Holcombe, "Clara Morris," *Famous American Actors of To-day*, Frederic Edward McKay and Charles E. L. Wingate, eds. (New York: Thomas Y. Crowell, 1986), p. 88.

51. Fahringer, taped reminiscences.

52. *New York Telegram*, 12 September 1907, in Locke, p. 67.

53. Arden, "A Talk with Miss Donnelly," in Locke, p. 19.

Chapter 5: On the Road

1. *New York Times*, 13 February 1910, sec. 10, p. 8.

2. Goldman, *Fanny Brice*, p. 59.

3. *Chicago American*, 24 October 1908, in Locke, p. 78.

4. Skinner, *Madame Sarah*, pp. 287–289.

5. *New York Times*, 13 February 1910, sec. 10, p. 8.

6. Locke, p. 83.

7. Colgate Baker, "'Lion and the Mouse' Scores Once More," *San Francisco Chronicle*, 4 February 1907, p. 24, col 2.

8. Skinner, *Madame Sarah*, pp. 190–191. A similar anecdote, placing the incident outside New Orleans, is recounted in Morris, *Curtain Time*, pp. 249–250.

9. Morehouse, *Matinee Tomorrow*, p. 36.

10. *Ibid.*, pp. 38–39.

11. "Mac's Gossip of the Stage," *Theatre Magazine*, 20 April 1906, in Locke, p. 44.

12. 12 April 1906, in Locke p. 42.

13. 11 May 1906, in Locke, p. 44.

14. Goldman, *Fanny Brice*, p. 70.

15. *Chicago Tribune*, 13 December 1908, in Locke, p. 80.

16. *Charleston News*, 2 February 1908, in Locke, p. 75.

17. *Los Angeles Times*, 26 November 1907, in Locke, p. 72. In the Robinson Locke scrapbook the name of the newspaper is mistakenly identified as the *Los Angeles Examiner*.

18. Lillian Russell, "Is the Stage a Perilous Place for the Young Girl?" *Theatre*, January 1916, p. 22.

19. Louise Closser Hale, *The Actress* (New York: Harpers, 1909), p. 74.

20. Stuart W. Little and Arthur Cantor, *The Playmakers* (New York: W. W. Norton, 1970), pp. 279–303.

21. Ryan, letter to author, 25 March 1988.

22. *Toledo Blade*, 13 March 1907, in Locke, p. 61.

23. *Fort Wayne Record*, 7 February 1909, in Locke, p. 64.

24. *Chicago Tribune*, 23 September 1908, in Locke, p. 76.

25. Morris, *Curtain Time*, p. 198.

26. "Mac's Gossip of the Stage," in Locke, p. 86.

27. *Ibid.*

28. *Green Book*, October 1909, in Locke, p. 94.

29. Arden, "A Talk with Miss Donnelly," in Locke, p. 19.

30. Glenn Loney, *20th Century Theatre* (New York: Facts on File, 1983), vol. 1, p. 51.

31. *New York Times*, 6 October 1907, part 6, sec. 2, p. 1, and 17 November 1907, part 5, sec. 9, p. 4.

32. Experiments in the photography of movement took place both in Europe and America during the 1880s.

33. Walter Prichard Eaton, "The Theatre: The First Night Ordeal," *American Magazine*, August 1912, p. 490.

34. Hale, *The Actress*, p. 2.

35. *Ibid.*, p. 97.

36. "Mac's Gossip of the Stage," 8 May 1909, in Locke, p. 86.

37. Hale, *The Actress*, p. 162.

38. *Ibid.*, p. 185

39. "Mac's Gossip of the Stage," 8 May 1909, in Locke, p. 86.

40. Hale, *The Actress*, p. 123.

41. *Ibid.*, p. 8.

42. *Ibid.*, p. 127.

43. *Ibid.*, p. 6.

44. Skinner, *Madame Sarah*, p. 185.

45. Hale, *The Actress*, p. 129.

46. Woollcott, "The Actress Who Became a Playwright," p. 26 and p. 113.

47. Arden, "A Talk with Miss Donnelly," in Locke, p. 20.

48. *New York American*, 26 January 1906, in Locke, p 30.

49. *Toledo Blade*, 29 December 1905, in Locke, p. 27.

50. *New York Times*, 13 February 1910, sec. 10, p. 8.

Chapter 6: The Limelight

1. Edward Morgan Forster, "Our Diversions: The Game of Life" (1919; repr. in *Abinger Harvest*, 1936).

2. *New York Times*, 23 May 1909, p. 11.

3. Lewis C. Strang, *Famous Actresses of the Day in America* (Boston: L. C. Page, 1902), p. 310.

4. "Creating the Role of Madame X," *Theatre Magazine*, January-June 1910, p. 71.

5. "Unconscious Suggestion—Part It Plays in Acting," *New York Times*, 13 February 1910, Section 10, p. 8.

6. *Ibid.*

7. *Ibid.*

8. *Ibid.*

9. *Ibid.*

10. *Philadelphia Record*, 19 September 1909, in Locke p. 90.

11. *Ibid.*

12. "Unconscious Suggestion—Part It Plays in Acting," *New York Times*, 13 February 1910, Section 10, p. 8.

13. *Ibid.*

14. "Creating the Role of Madame X," *Theatre Magazine*, January-June, 1910, p. 71.

15. *Michigan Sentinel*, 8 September 1907, in Locke, p. 66.

16. *Rochester Democrat*, 14 September 1909, in Locke p. 94.

17. *Rochester Post Express*, 14 September 1909, in Locke p. 94.

18. Arthur Hornblow, *A History of the Theatre in America* (Philadelphia: J. B. Lippincott, 1919) vol II, p. 300.

19. Alan Dale, "Two Kinds of Theater Goers," *Cosmopolitan*, May 1910, p. 756.

20. *Tips and Tales*, Locke, p. 94.

21. Gassner, *Best Plays of the Early American Theatre*, p. xxi.

22. Dorothy Donnelly, "Bad Women in Plays," *Green Book*, vol. II, no. 12, December 1909.

23. Charles de Forrest, "Madame X: A Novel Version by Charles de Forrest," *Green Book*, vol. III, no. 1, January 1910, in Locke, p. 103 ff.

24. Dale, "Two Kinds of Theater Goers," p. 756.

25. Locke, p. 90.

26. L. Blake Baldwin and Dorothy Donnelly, "Ether Drinking," *Chicago Sunday Tribune*, 31 October 1909, in Locke, p. 95 ff.

27. *New York Times*, Section 10, p. 8.

28. *San Francisco Chronicle*, 11 December 1910, p. 23.

29. Adolphe Klauber, *New York Times*, 3 February 1910, Section 9, p. 3.

30. Adolphe Klauber, "Plays of Emotion and the Acting in Them," *New York Times*, 6 February 1910, Section 10, p. 1.

31. Woollcott, "The Actress Who Became a Playwright," p. 114.

32. Dale, "Two Kinds of Theater Goers," p. 756.

33. "Unconscious Suggestion—Part It Plays in Acting," *New York Times*, 13 February 1910, Section 10, p. 8.

34. Hale, *The Actress*, p. 156.

35. O'Connor, "From Mde. X to Musical Comedy," p. 84.

36. *Ibid.*

37. *Ibid.*

38. Eaton, "The Theatre: The First Night Ordeal," p. 402.

39. Quinn, *History of the American Drama*, pp. 89–90.

40. Eric Wollencott Barnes, *The Man Who Lived Twice* (New York: Charles Scribner's Sons, 1956), pp. 70–71.

41. Sheldon quoted in John Barrymore, *Confessions of an Actor* (New York: Arno, 1980), chapter IV, p. 2. This reprint is unpaginated.

42. Fahringer, taped reminiscences.

43. Barnes, *The Man Who Lived Twice*, p. 99.

44. Skinner, *Madame Sarah*, pp. 307–313.

45. Elliott Arnold, *Deep in My Heart* (New York: Duell, Sloan, and Pearce, 1949), p. 12. This book is not quite a biography—though it's the only one—but a story of the life of Sigmund Romberg based on an extensive interview between Arnold and Romberg in 1947.

46. O'Connor, "From Mde. X to Musical Comedy," p. 84.

47. Alexander Woollcott, "Second Thoughts on First Nights," *New York Times*, 27 December 1914, sec. XX, p. 2.

48. Thomas McCall, S.J., letter to author, 27 September 1988.

49. Henry Conway, quoted in Thomas McCall, S.J., letter to author, 6 December 1988.

50. *Theatre Magazine*, vol. 172, p. 223.

51. O'Conner, "From Mde. X to Musical Comedy," p. 84.

52. Jolo, *Variety Movie Guide* (New York: Prentice Hall General Reference, 1992), 21 January 1916, p. 582.

53. Joan L. Cohen, "Madame X," *Magill's Survey of Cinema*, Silent Films Part II (Englewood Cliffs, New Jersey: Salem, 1982), p. 686.

Chapter 7: Intermission

1. "Miss Dorothy Donnelly's Views on the Labor Question," *New York Telegram*, 26 November 1906, in Locke, p. 53.

2. *Ibid.*

3. Daniel C. Blum, *A Pictorial History of the American Theatre: 100 Years, 1860–1960* (Philadelphia: Chilton, 1960).

4. John Walker, ed., *Halliwell's Film Guide* (New York: Harper Collins, 1991), 8th edition, p. 694.

5. Maude Adams, quoted in Phyllis Robbins, *Maude Adams: an Intimate Portrait* (New York: G. P. Putnam's Sons, 1956), p. 82.

6. William Klein, quoted in "William Klein's Early Years with the Shuberts," Maryann Chach, ed. *The Passing Show*, Vol. 13/14, No. 2/1, Fall 1990/Spring 1991, p. 7.

7. Contract dated 20 July 1916, Shubert Archive.

8. *Historical Statistics of the United States* (Washington, D. C.: Bureau of the Census, 1975), Part 1, p. 168.

9. Dorothy Donnelly, quoted in Rohe, "All Women Feline, Few Real Cats," in Locke, p. 35.

10. Mabelle Gilman Corey, "Art and American Society," *Cosmopolitan*, March 1909, pp. 29–34.

11. Fahringer, taped reminiscences.

12. *Chicago Record*, 8 October 1909, in Locke, p. 94.

13. Fahringer, taped reminiscences.

14. Morehouse, *George M. Cohan*, p. 127.

15. *Literary Digest*, vol. 54, p. 1848.

16. *Ibid.*

17. Margaret McIvor-Tyndall, "What Women of the Theatre Are Doing for Uncle Sam," *National Service with the International Military Digest*, May 1919, p. 283.

18. *Literary Digest*, vol. 54, p. 1848.

19. Advertisement in the Fulton Theatre program, 2 December 1918, p. 12.

20. *Literary Digest*, vol. 54, p. 1849.

21. McIvor-Tyndall, "What Women of the Theatre Are Doing for Uncle Sam," p. 283.

22. Fahringer, taped reminiscences.

23. Edwin L. James, *New York Times*, 18 March 1919, sec. 2, p. 2.

24. Richard F. Cox, Military Reference Branch, Military Archive Division, letter to author, 27 May 1988.

25. Edwin L. James, "Y.M.C.A. Play at Coblenz," *New York Times*, 2 April 1919, sec. 3, p. 6.

26. Nancy Fahringer, in telephone conversation with author, 9 June 1988.

27. "Report of the Carry On Meeting of the Stage Women's War Relief," presented at the Bijou Theatre, New York, 19 March 1920, pp. 8–11.

Chapter 8: In the Wings

1. Alexander Woollcott, "The Actress Who Became a Playwright," p. 26.

2. *Chicago Journal*, 23 September 1908, Locke p. 76.

3. Locke, pp. 80-81.

4. O'Connor, "From Mde. X to Musical Comedy," p. 84.

5. C. A. Browne, *The Story of Our National Ballads* (New York: Thomas Y. Crowell, 1931), p. 298.

6. Alexander Woollcott, *New York Times*, 18 February 1917, II, sec. 6, p. 1.

7. J. Brooks McNamara, "The Shubert Brothers and the 'Box-Office' Play," *The Passing Show*, Vol. 15, No. 2. Fall 1992, p. 3.

8. Notes signed by "Dunbar," Shubert Archive.

9. Correspondence file #3030, 5 January 1918, Shubert Archive.

10. Correspondence file #3030, Shubert Archive.

11. Dorothy Donnelly, quoted by A. Toxen Worm, Shubert Press Department, n.d., Shubert Archive.

12. *Ibid.*

13. *Ibid.*

14. Morehouse, *Matinee Tomorrow*, p. 139.

15. Peters, *Bernard Shaw and the Actresses*, p. xii.

16. The glass ceiling based on gender discrimination was installed past the first quarter of the twentieth century. In 1947, Cheryl Crawford, founder of Group Theatre and Actor's Studio, became the first female producer to break through. On Broadway she produced *Brigadoon*, *The Rose Tattoo*, and *Paint Your Wagon*.

17. Alexander Woollcott, *New York Times*, 29 November 1917.

18. Woollcott, "The Actress Who Became a Playwright," p. 114.

19. *Ibid.*

20. O'Connor, "From Mde. X to Musical Comedy," p. 84.

21. Correspondence file #3030, Shubert Archive.

22. Ken Bloom, *American Song: The Complete Musical Theatre Collection* (New York: Facts on File, 1985), p. 2262.

23. Alexander Woollcott, *New York Times*, 22 December 1919, p. 19, col.1.

24. O'Connor, "From Mde. X to Musical Comedy," p. 84.

25. *Ibid.*

Chapter 9: Behind the Scenes

1. Macgowan, *Footlights Across America*, p. 68.

2. Correspondence File #3030, 10 January 1920, Shubert Archive.

3. Correspondence File #3030, 24 March 1920, Shubert Archive. The photostat copy of the letter is unsigned but initialed "JM/FC." Ms. Florence Cohen served as a secretary to J. J. Shubert.

4. Jerry Stagg, *The Brothers Shubert* (New York: Random House, 1968), p. 186.

5. Correspondence File #3030, 28 February 1919, Shubert Archive.

6. Bordman, *American Operetta: from H.M.S. Pinafore to Sweeney Todd* (New York: Oxford University Press, 1981), p. 124.

7. William Green, "Broadway Book Musicals: 1900–1969," *The American Theatre: a Sum of Its Parts*, (New York: Samuel French, 1971) p. 250.

8. Ethan Mordden, "A Critic at Large," *The New Yorker*, 3 July 1989, p. 20.

9. Gottfried, *Broadway Musicals*, p. 10.

10. Show Series, Box 93, Folder 3, Shubert Archive.

11. Charles O'Connell, *The Victor Book of the Symphony* (New York: Simon and Shuster, 1941), p. 429.

12. *Ibid.*, p. 438.

13. *Ibid.*, p. 429.

14. Richard Traubner, *Operetta: A Theatrical History* (New York: Doubleday, 1983) p. 424.

15. Stanley Green, *The World of Musical Comedy* (New York: A. S. Barnes, 1980), 4th edition, p. 41.

16. William Arlic Everett, *The Operettas of Sigmund Romberg: Blossom Time, The Student Prince, My Maryland, My Princess*, doctoral dissertation (University of Kansas: 1991), p. 13.

17. Cecil Michener Smith and Glenn Litton, *Musical Comedy in America* (New York: Theatre Arts Books, 1950) p. 139.

18. Sources for this biographical sketch of Sigmund Romberg include the articles under his name in the following reference texts: *Encyclopedia Americana, The New Oxford Companion to Music, The New Grove Dictionary of American Music, The New Grove Dictionary of Music and Musicians, Current Biography 1945, Guiness Encyclopedia of Popular Music*, David Ewen's *Panorama of American Popular Music*. See also Everett, *Operettas of Sigmund Romberg*, p. 15.

19. Alan Jay Lerner, *The Musical Theatre* (London: Collins, 1986), p. 71.

20. "Schubert's Magicry Fills '*Blossom Time*'," *New York Tribune*, 30 September 1921.

21. For a synopsis of the original libretto, as well as many other operettas, see Kurt Ganzl and Andrew Lamb, *Ganzl's Book of the Musical Theatre* (New York: Schimer, 1989), pp. 1046–1048.

22. Stagg, *The Brothers Shubert*, p. 188.

23. *Ibid.*

24. Everett, *Operettas of Sigmund Romberg*, p. 84.

25. Arnold, *Deep in My Heart*, p. 278.

26. Correspondence File #3030, Shubert Archive.

27. Charles Darnton, "'Blossom Time' Rich in Melodies," *Evening World*, 30 September 1921.

28. Ludwig Lewison, "Drama: Oasis," *The Nation*, vol. 113, no. 2937.

29. *Ibid.*

30. Press package for *Blossom Time*, Shubert Archive.

31. Arnold, *Deep in My Heart*, pp. 296–297.

32. Helen Hayes and Katherine Hatch, *My Life in Three Acts* (San Diego: Harcourt, Brace, Jovanovich, 1990) p. 61.

33. Fahringer, taped reminisences.

34. Hayes and Hatch, *My Life in Three Acts*, p. 61.

35. Lionel Barrymore, *We Barrymores* (New York: Appleton-Century-Crofts, 1951) pp. 158–159.

36. Gene Fowler, *Goodnight, Sweet Prince*, (New York: Viking, 1944) p. 149.

37. Denis Brian, *Tallulah, Darling* (New York: Macmillan, 1980), pp. 32-33.

38. *American Academic Encyclopedia* (Darlburg, Connecticut: Grolier, 1994), Vol. B, p. 97.

39. Morris, *Curtain Time*, p. 323.

40. Hayes and Hatch, *My Life in Three Acts*, p 61.

41. Barnes, *The Man Who Lived Twice*, p. 161.

42. Arnold, *Deep in My Heart*, pp. 296–297.

43. Fahringer, taped reminiscences.

44. Charles Eliot Norton, *Two Notebooks of Thomas Carlyle* (New York: Grolier, 1989), p. 136.

45. Available on microfilm at the University of California.

46. O'Connor, "From Mde. X to Musical Comedy," p. 84.

47. *Theatre Magazine*, 23 May 1923.

48. *New York Times*, 24 February 1924, sec. VII, p. 2, col. 8.

49. Fahringer, taped reminiscences.

50. J. J. Shubert to Dorothy Donnelly, August 1922, Shubert Archive.

51. Lee Shubert, unpublished autobiography, *The Passing Show*, Newsletter of the Shubert Archive, Fall 1990/Spring 1991, vol. 13/14, no. 2/1, p. 14.

52. *Ibid.*, p. 15.

53. *New York Times*, 9 December 1903, p. 6, col 1.

54. Richard Mansfield, quoted in Toby Cole and Helen Krich Chinoy, *Actors on Acting*, p. 371.

55. Arnold, *Deep in My Heart*, pp. 502 and 290.

56. Everett, *Operettas of Sigmund Romberg*, p. 130 ff.

57. Abe Laufe, *Broadway's Greatest Musicals* (New York: Funk and Wagnalls, 1969), p. 14.

58. For a more detailed synopsis, see Ganzl, pp. 583–586.

59. Correspondence File #3030, 21 August 1922, Shubert Archive.

60. Stagg, *The Brothers Shubert*, p. 227.

61. A. J. Liebling, "The Boys from Syracuse," *The New Yorker*, 18 November–2 December, 1939.

62. Sigmund Romberg, "A Peep into the Workshop of a Composer," *Theatre Magazine*, December 1928, p. 27.

63. *Ibid.*, p. 72.

64. *Ibid.*

65. Bordman, *American Operetta*, p. 116.

66. David Ewen, *The New Complete Book of the American Musical Theatre* (New York: Holt, Rhinehart and Winston, 1970), p. 513.

67. Stagg, *The Brothers Shubert*, p. 227.

68. Sigmund Romberg, quoted by Stanley Green, *The World of Musical Comedy*, as reprinted on the Columbia Records jacket cover of *The Student Prince*, 1963. See also Bordman, *American Operetta*, p. 116.

69. Stagg, *The Brothers Shubert*, p. 277. See also Gerald Martin Bordman, *American Musical Theatre: A Chronicle* (New York: Oxford University Press, 1986), p. 397.

70. Everitt, *Operettas of Sigmund Romberg*, p. 157 ff.

71. Correspondence File #3030, Shubert Archive.

72. Sigmund Romberg, quoted in "A Peep into the Workshop of a Composer," *Theatre Magazine*, December 1928, p. 72.

73. Arnold, *Deep in My Heart*, p. 329.

74. Fahringer, taped reminiscences.

75. Abel Green, *Variety*, 10 December 1924, p. 23. He also made note of the length of the performance: "8.20-11.25."

76. George S. Kaufman, *New York Times*, 3 December 1924, p. 25, col. 3.

77. Smith and Litton, *Musical Comedy in America*, p. 139.

78. Bordman, *American Operetta*, p. 115.

79. *The Definitive Broadway Collection*, (Winona, MN: Hal Leonard, 1988), pp. 83–84.

Chapter 10: Final Curtain

1. Correspondence File #3030, 11 December 1922, Shubert Archive.

2. Arnold, *Deep in My Heart*, p. 296 ff.

3. Fahringer, taped reminiscences.

4. Stone, *Herald Tribune*, 7 March 1925.

5. *Ibid.*

6. *Ibid.*

7. *Ibid.*

8. Woollcott, *Pictorial Review*, p. 26.

9. Fahringer, taped reminiscences.

10. Ryan, letter to author, 25 March 1988.

11. Fahringer, taped reminiscences.

12. For the history of these independent houses see Weldon B. Durham, *American Theatre Companies* (New York: Greenwood, 1987).

13. Cole and Chinoy, *Actors on Acting*, p. 539.

14. Henderson and Bowers, *Red, Hot & Blue*, p. 50.

15. Keene Sumner, "Sometimes You Fight Better if You're Driven to the Wall," *American Magazine*, October 1921, p. 81.

16. Arthur Schnizler, quoted in Bernard Sobel, *The Theatre Handbook and Digest of Plays* (New York: Crown, 1950), p. 692.

17. "Schnitzler's Romantic Tragedy," *New York Times*, 10 October 1925, sec. 10, p. 1.

18. George Jean Nathan, *House of Satan* (New York: Alfred A. Knopf, 1926) p. 190.

19. Dudley Digges, quoted in Theodore Strauss, *Theatre Arts Monthly*, October 1941, pp. 719–720.

20. J. Brooks Atkinson, "'Seventeen' to Music," *New York Times*, 13 January 1926.

21. Gerald Martin Bordman, *American Musical Theatre: A Chronicle*, p. 408.

22. Charles Higham, *Ziegfeld* (Chicago: Henry Regnery Company, 1972), p. 182.

23. *Ibid.*

24. "Dorothy Donnelly, Dramatist, Dies," *New York Times*, 4 January 1928.

25. Fahringer, taped reminiscences.

26. Dorothy Donnelly, undated letter to John A. McCall, courtesy Philip Fahringer.

27. Correspondence File #3030, Shubert Archive.

28. Leslie Carter enacted the title role in 1923, Pauline Fredericks in 1926 in California, Carroll McComas in 1926 on Broadway, and Marjorie Rambeau in 1929.

29. Bordman says Arthur Cunningham played Stonewall Jackson and spells "Casavant" with a double "s."

30. Bordman, *American Musical Theatre*, p. 428.

31. *Ibid.*, p. 425.

32. Ruth Hinman, "'My Maryland' Melodies Unique," *Atlanta Georgian*, 3 January 1928.

33. Stagg, *The Brothers Shubert*, p. 254.

34. J. Brooks Atkinson, "'My Maryland' Stirs with Martial Airs," *New York Times*, 13 September 1927.

35. Barnes, *The Man Who Lived Twice*, p. 161.

36. *Ibid.*

37. Everitt, p. 208 ff

38. Alexander Woollcott, "The Stage," *New York World*, 7 October 1927.

39. *New York Times*, 11 September 1927, sec. VIII, p. 1, col. 3.

40. Charles Brackett, *New Yorker*, 15 October 1929.

41. J. Brooks Atkinson, "The Play," *New York Times*, 9 October 1927, sec 7, p. 24, col. 2.

42. Bordman, *American Musical Theatre*, p. 430.

43. McCall, letter to author, 27 September 1988.

44. Ryan, letter to author, 25 May 1988, p. 3.

Chapter 11: Curtain Call

1. According to *The Value of a Dollar*, ed. Scott Derkes (Detroit: Gale Research, 1994), in 1925 the annual average per capita consumption amounted to $619.45 and few women earned more than $3500 a year.

2. Sally Donnelly Conway Ryan has possession of the painting, attributed to English artist C. Julian Thorpe.

3. Fahringer, taped reminiscences.

4. *Ibid.*

5. "Donnelly Estate $150,000," *New York Times*, 13 January 1928.

6. William Klein, letter to J. J. Shubert, 25 May 1938, Shubert Archive.

7. Thomas D. McCall, S.J., letter to author, 8 January 1991.

8. "Unconscious Suggestion—Part It Plays in Acting," *New York Times*, 13 February 1910, Sec. 10, p. 8.

9. Dorothy Donnelly, letter to Robinson Locke, 9 October 1906, in Locke, p. 48.

10. Locke p. 45.

11. Alice Kessler Harris, *Out to Work: A History of Wage-Earning Women in the U. S.*, 1982, Abstract, Electronic Collection A14199999.

12. Burns Mantle, editor, *Best Plays and Yearbook of Drama in America 1925–1926*, pp. 627–631.

13. About one third of the plays during the 1920s were written by women according to the *Oxford Companion to Women's Writings* (New York: Oxford University Press, 1995), p. 258.

14. Stone, *Herald Tribune*, 7 March 1925.

15. Carlotta Monti, *W. C. Fields and Me* (Englewood Cliffs, New Jersey: Prentice-Hall, 1971) p. 36.

16. W. C. Fields, "Anything for a Laugh," *American*, September 1934, pp. 129–130.

17. Stanley Green, *The World of Musical Comedy* (San Diego: A. S. Barnes, 1980), p. 163.

18. Howard Dietz, *Dancing in the Dark* (New York: Quadrangle/The New York Times, 1974), p. 65.

19. Thomas McCall, S. J., telephone conversation with author, 3 October 1988.

20. Bordman, *American Musical Theatre*, p. 409.

21. Ethan Mordden, *Broadway Babies: The People Who Made the American Musical* (New York: Oxford University Press, 1983), p. 206.

22. Bordman, *American Musical Theatre*, p. 409.

23. Steven Suskin, *Opening Night on Broadway* (New York: Schirmer, 1990), p. 94.

24. Brooks McNamara, *The Shuberts of Broadway* (New York: Oxford University Press, 1990), p. 143.

25. Little and Cantor, *The Playmakers*, p. 19.

26. Stagg, *The Brothers Shubert*, p. 141.

27. Dwight Blocker Bowers, *American Musical Theatre: Shows, Songs, and Stars* (Washington, D. C.: Smithsonian Collection of Recordings, 1989), p. 19.

28. *Variety Movie Guide* (New York: Prentice Hall General Reference, 1992), p. 582.

29. Joan L. Cohen, "The Student Prince," *McGill's Survey of Cinema III* (Englewood Cliffs, New Jersey: Salem, 1982), p. 1077.

30. Richard Traubner, *Operetta: A Theatrical History* (New York: Doubleday, 1983), p. 424.

31. Ethan C. Mordden, *Better Foot Forward* (New York: Oxford University Press, 1981), p. 93.

32. Everett, *Operettas of Sigmund Romberg*, p. 225.

33. *Ibid.*, p. 78.

34. *Ibid.*, p. 69.

35. William Green, *The New York Times Guide to Listening Pleasure* (New York: Macmillan, 1968), p. 253.

36. Robert Sherman, "Light Music," *The New York Times Guide to Listening Pleasure* (New York: Macmillan, 1968), p. 180.

37. Alfred Simon, "The Musical Theatre," *The New York Times Guide to Listening Pleasure* (New York: Macmillan, 1968), p. 147.

38. *Current Biography 1945* (New York: H. W. Wilson, 1946), p. 512.

39. Bernard Holland, "Revisiting the Scene of a Royal Heartbreak," *New York Times* n.d., pp. 13–15.

40. Bowers, *American Musical Theatre: Shows, Songs, and Stars*, p. 19.

41. Traubner, *Operetta*, p. 424.

Career Chronology

Actress—Stage Appearances

The New South 8/27/98 [Kate Fessenden]
Young Mrs. Winthrop 9/10/98 [maid]
The Pilt [Kitty]
Secret Services [Edith Varnay]
The Young Wife 10/3/98 [Barbara]
The Ticket of Leave Man 12/19/98 [Emily]
Ours 3/20/99 [Blanche Hope]
In Mizzoura 9/25/99
Madame Sans Gene 10/30/99 [Lady Ursula]
The Lottery of Love [*Les Surprises du Divorce*] 11/27/99
The Girl I Left Behind Me 12/11/99
Carmen 12/18/99 [title role]
Men and Women 12/26/99 [Kate Delafield]
The Wife 1/6/00 [Lucille Ferrant]
An Enemy to the King 1/15/00 [Jeannotte]
Never Again [*Le Truc de Seraphin*] 1/22/00 [Octavie]
Captain Letterblair 1/29/00 [Fanny Hadden]
The Private Secretary 2/12/00 [Edith Marsland]
Diplomacy 2/19/00 [Eleanor]
Lord Chumley 2/26/00
7-20-8 3/5/00
Peaceful Valley 3/14/00 [Virginia Rand]

Esmeralda 3/14/00 [Nora Desmond]
Squire Kate 3/26/00 [title role]
She Stoops to Conquer 5/21/00 [daughter]
Nancy and Company 5/29/00 [title role]
A Colonial Girl 9/17/00 [Molly Heddin]
Romeo and Juliet 10/31/00 [Juliet]
The Nominee [*Le Depute de Bombignac*] 11/5/00 [Mabel Medford]
The Princess and the Butterfly 11/13/90 [Fay Juliani]
Le Truc d'Arthur 11/27/90 [Gloriana]
The Gray Mare 12/10/90
Mistress Nell 1/23/01 [Nell Gwynne, title role]
The School for Scandal 2/4/01 [Lady Teazle]
A Midnight Ball 2/18/91 [schoolmarm]
The Adventure of Lady Ursula 3/5/91 [title role]
A Contented Woman 4/10/01 [Grace Holmes]
Fédora 4/26/01 [title role]
My Friend from India
The Dancing Girl
The Girl and the Judge
Ingomar [Parthenia]
> *Note:* The plays listed above were presented by the Murray Hill Theatre Company. Many of the playbills have been collected in a

single volume and donated as a gift of the Actor's Fund to the Billy Rose Theatre Collection of the New York Public Library.

New England Folks 11/11/01

Soldiers of Fortune 3/17/02 [Madame Alvarez]

The Countess Cathleen (Kathleen ni Houlihan) 6/3/03 [title role]

Candida 12/8/03 and on tour [title role]

The Man of Destiny 2/11/04; 9/26/04; and on tour [Strange Lady]

Friquet 1/31/05 [Madame Schlemmer]

When We Dead Awaken 3/7/05 [Maia Rubek]

The Proud Laird 4/24/05

Mrs. Battle's Bath 5/9/05 [title role]

On Satan's Mount 5/29/05

The Little Gray Lady 1/22/06 [Ruth Jordan]

The Masqueraders 4/30/06

Note: Although not individually reviewed, the following plays were also presented by the Harlem Stock Company in repertory: *Cousin Kate, Captain Jinks of the Horse Marines, The Gilded Fool, Sowing the Wind, Letty,* and *The Bauble Shop.*

Daughters of Men 11/11/06 and on tour [Louise Stolbeck]

The Movers [Marion Manners] 9/3/07

The Lion and the Mouse on tour [Shirley Rossmore]

The Sins of Society 4/14/09 in Chicago [Lady Marion Beaumont]

Madame X 10/2/10 [title role]

Disengaged 4/10/11 [Mrs. Jasper]

Princess Zim Zim 12/4/11 [Tessie Casey, title role]

The Right to Be Happy 3/26/12 [Janet van Roof]

The Garden of Allah on tour [Dominie Enfielden]

Maria Rosa 1/19/14 [title role]

Grand Maumee 3/30/14 [title role]

The Song of Songs 12/22/14 [Anna Markle]

Candida 5/18/15 in revival [title role]

The Bargain 10/5/15 [Sarah Lusskin]

The Golden Fleece 3/24/19 [Dulcie Larondie]

Actress—Screen Appearances

The Thief 10/12/14 [Marie Landau]

Sealed Valley 8/7/15 [Nahnya Crossfire]

Madame X 1/4/16 [title role]

Playwright

Flora Bella 9/11/16 (written in collaboration)

Johnny Get Your Gun 2/12/17 (written in collaboration)

Fancy Free 4/11/18 (written in collaboration)

The Riddle: Woman 10/23/18; 1/5/20; (written in collaboration)

The Melting of Molly 12/30/18 (written in collaboration)

Forbidden 12/20/19

The Proud Princess opened in Baltimore on 2/16/24

The Call of Life 10/9/25 (translation)

Producer

Six Months Option 11/29/17

Seven Keys to Baldpate produced in Coblenz, Germany

Librettist

Blossom Time 9/29/21

Poppy 9/3/23

The Student Prince 12/2/24

Hello, Lola 1/12/26

My Maryland 9/12/27
My Princess 10/6/27

Lyricist

Blossom Time
"In Old Vienna Town"—in Opening
"Keep It Dark"
"Let Me Awake"
"Lonely Hearts"
"Love Is a Riddle"
"Melody Triste"
"Moment Musical"
"My Springtime Thou Art"
"Only One Love Ever Fills the
   Heart"
"Serenade"
"Song of Love"
"Tell Me Daisy"
"Three Little Maids"
"Underneath the Lilac Tree"—in
   Opening
"Wait I Implore You"—in Finale Act
   I

Poppy
"Choose Your Partner, Please"
"The Dancing Lesson"
"Fortune Telling"
"The Girl I've Never Met"
"Hang Your Sorrows in the Sun"
"Kadoola Kadoola"
"On Our Honeymoon"
"Picnic Party with You"
"Poppy Dear"
"Stepping Around"
"Two Make a Home"
"When Men are Alone"
"When You Are in My Arms"
   Note: "When You Are in My
   Arms" was cut from the produc-
   tion but available in sheet music.

The Student Prince
"Birds Are Winging"
"By Our Beauty So Sedate"
"Carnival of Springtime"
"Come, Sir, Will You Join"

"Come Answer to Our Call"
"Come Boys, Let's All Be Gay, Boys"
"Come, Sir, Your Time Is Short"
"Deep in My Heart, Dear"
"Drinking Song"
"Farewell, Dear"
"Farewell to Youth"
"Farmer Jacob"
"The Flag That Flies Above Us"
"For You"*
"Garlands Bright"
"Gavotte"
"Golden Days"
"In the Park"
"In Heidelberg Fair"
"I'm Coming at Your Call"
"Just We Two"
"The Magic of Springtime"
"May I Come to See You, Dear"*
"Oh, Tell Me if Your Heart"
"Serenade" ["Overhead the Moon Is
   Beaming"]
"Sing a Little Song"
"Students' Life"
"Take Care"*
"There's No Joy but Love"*
"Thoughts Will Come To Me"
"To the Inn We're Marching"
"Waltz Ensemble"
"Welcome to the Prince"
"We're Off to Paris"
"What Memories"
"When the Spring Awakens Every-
   thing"
"You're in Heidelberg"
   Note: Songs marked by an asterisk
   were omitted from the production
   but published separately in sheet
   music. "Birds Are Winging" was
   cut during the tryout.

Hello, Lola
"Baxter's Party"
"Bread and Butter and Sugar"
"Don't Stop"
"Five-Foot-Two"
"Grau Brae Nicht"
"Hello, Cousin Lola"
"High Toned Trot"*

"I Know Something"
"In the Dark"
"Keep It Up"
"Little Boy Blue"
"Lullaby"
"My Baby Talk Lady"
"My Brother Willie"
"She Never Spent a Cent on Me"*
"Shush Katy"**
"Sophie"
"Step on the Gasoline"
"Story Book Land"**
"The Summertime"
"Swinging on the Gate"
"Take 'Em to the Door Blues"**
"That Certain Party"
"Water, Water, Wildflowers"
"While We Go Waltzing Around"*
  Note: Songs marked by a single asterisk were cut from the tryout in Newark on 16 November 1925. Songs marked by a double asterisk were cut from the tryout in Washington, D. C., on 29 November 1925.

June Days
"Take 'Em to the Door Blues"**
  Note: This song was cut from *Hello, Lola* and interpolated into the musical of *The Charm School*.

My Maryland
"Boys in Grey"
"Here's Someone that I Know You Will Like"
"Ker-choo!"

"The Mocking Bird"
"Mother"
"Mr. Cupid"
"My Land Is Your Land"
"Night Life"
"Old John Barleycorn"
"Please Do Not Prevent Us"
"The Same Silver Moon"
"Scottishe"
"Something Old, Something New"
"Song of Victory"
"Strawberry Jam"
"Strolling with the One I Love Best"
"The Three Musketeers"
"We Have Come to Call"
"When You're in Mexico"
"Won't You Marry Me"

My Princess
"Dear Girls, Goodbye"
"Eviva"
"Follow the Sun to the South"
"Gigolo"
"The Glorious Chase"
"Have You Anxiety"
"Here's How"
"The Hunting Dance"
"I Wonder Why"
"Kiss the Bride"
"The Moulin Rouge Girls"
"My Passion Flower"
"My Mimosa"
"Our Bridal Night"
"Prince Charming"
"The Steppe Sisters"
"When I Was a Girl Like You"

APPENDIX B
Professional Affiliations

Actors' Equity
Actors' Fund of America
Actors' Theatre
American Women's Club (London)
American Society of Composers,
    Authors, and Publishers
Author League of America
Dramatists Guild

New York Woman's Suffrage Associ-
    ation
Overseas League of Women
Speedwell Society
Stage Women's War Relief
State Society of New York
Twelfth Night Club
Women's Democratic Union

Bibliography

Musical Theatre

Alpert, Hollis. *Broadway! 125 Years of Musical Theatre.* New York: Museum of the City of New York, Arcade Publishers, 1991.

Bloom, Ken. *American Song: The Complete Musical Theatre Collection.* New York: Facts on File, 1985.

Bordman, Gerald Martin. *American Musical Theatre: A Chronicle.* New York: Oxford University Press, 1986

_____. *American Operetta: from H.M.S. Pinafore to Sweeney Todd,* New York: Oxford University Press, 1981.

Bowers, Dwight Blocker. *American Musical Theatre: Shows, Songs, and Stars.* Washington, D. C.: Smithsonian Collection of Recordings, 1989.

The Definitive Broadway Collection: The Most Comprehensive Collection of Broadway Music Ever Compiled into One Volume. Winona, MN: Hal Leonard Publishing Corporation, 1988.

Dietz, Howard. *Dancing in the Dark.* New York: Quadrangle/The New York Times Book Co., 1974.

Everett, William Arlie. *The Operettas of Sigmund Romberg: Blossom Time, The Student Prince, My Maryland, My Princess.* Doctoral dissertation, University of Kansas: 1991.

Ewen, David. *The New Complete Book of the American Musical Theatre.* New York: Holt, Rinehart, and Winston, 1970.

Ganzl, Kurt, and Andrew Lamb. *Ganzl's Book of the Musical Theatre.* New York: Schimer Books, 1989.

Gottfried, Martin. *Broadway Musicals.* New York: Harry N. Abrams, 1979.

Green, Stanley. 4th ed. *The World of Musical Comedy.* New York: A. S. Barnes & Company, Inc., 1980.

Guernsey, Jr., Otis L., ed. *Broadway Song and Story: Playwrights/Lyricists/Composers Discuss Their Hits.* New York: Dodd Mead, 1985.

Henderson, Amy, and Dwight Bowers. *Red, Hot & Blue.* Washington, D. C.: Smithsonian Institution Press, 1996.

Laufe, Abe. *Broadway's Greatest Musicals.* New York: Funk and Wagnalls, 1969.

Lerner, Alan Jay. *The Musical Theatre.* London: Collins, 1986.

Mordden, Ethan. *Better Foot Forward.* New York: Oxford University Press, 1981.

_____. *Broadway Babies: The People Who Made the American Musical*. New York: Oxford University Press, 1983.

Smith, Cecil Michener, and Glenn Litton. *Musical Comedy in America*. New York: Theatre Arts Books, 1950.

Traubner, Richard. *Operetta: A Theatrical History*. New York: Doubleday, 1983.

Histories of the Theatre

The American Theatre: A Sum of Its Parts. New York: Samuel French, Inc., 1971. Addresses delivered to a symposium, "The American Theater—A Cultural Process," sponsored by the American College Theater Festival.

Beckerman, Bernard, and Howard Siegman, eds. *Selected Theatre Reviews from the New York Times*. New York: Arno Press, 1973.

Best Plays of 1894–1899. New York: Dodd Mead, 1899.

Blum, Daniel C. *A Pictorial History of the American Theatre: 100 Years, 1860–1960*. Philadelphia: Chilton Co., Book Division, 1960.

Chapman, John Arthur. *Best Plays of 1894–1899*. New York: Random House, 1953.

Chinoy, Helen Krich, and Linda Walsh Jenkins. *Women in American Theatre*. New York: Theatre Communications Group, 1987.

Davidson, Cathy N., and Linda Wagner-Martin, eds. *Oxford Companion to Women's Writings*. New York: Oxford University Press, 1995.

Durham, Weldon B. *American Theatre Companies*. New York: Greenwood Press, 1987.

Gassner, John. *Best Plays of the Early American Theatre*. New York: Crown, 1967.

Hornblow, Arthur. *A History of the Theatre in America*. Philadelphia: J. B. Lippincott and Company, 1919. vol II.

Little, Stuart W., and Arthur Cantor. *The Playmakers*. New York: W. W. Norton & Company, Inc., 1970. A historical view of later twentieth-century producers.

Loney, Glenn. *20th Century Theatre*. New York: Facts on File, 1983, vol. 1.

MacGowen, Kenneth. *Footlights Across America*. New York: Harcourt, Brace, 1929.

Malvern, Gladys. *Curtain Going Up*. New York: Julian Messner, 1943.

Mantle, Burns, ed. *Best Plays and Yearbook of Drama in America 1925–1926*. New York: Dodd Mead, 1951–1952.

Morehouse, Ward. *Matinee Tomorrow: Fifty Years of Our Theater*. New York: McGraw-Hill, 1949.

Morris, Lloyd. *Curtain Time: The Story of the American Theater*. New York: Random House, 1953.

Nathan, George Jean. *House of Satan*. New York: Alfred A. Knopf, 1926.

Odell, George Clinton Densmore. *Annals of the New York Stage*. New York: AMS Press, 1970. Vol. 14.

Quinn, Arthur Hobson. *History of the American Drama*. New York: Harper and Brothers, 1927. Vols. 1 and 2.

Sobel, Bernard. *The Theatre Handbook and Digest of Plays*. New York: Crown, 1950.

Suskin, Steven. *Opening Night on Broadway*. New York: Schirmer Books, 1990.

Taubman, Hyman Howard. *The Making of the American Theatre*. New York: Coward McCann, 1965.

Wilmeth, Don B., and Tice L. Miller, eds. *Cambridge Guide to the American The-atre.* New York: Cambridge University Press, 1993.

Individual Actors

Barrymore, John. *Confessions of an Actor.* New York: Arno Press, 1980.
Barrymore, Lionel. *We Barrymores.* New York: Appleton-Century-Crofts, 1951.
Denis, Brian. *Tallulah, Darling.* New York: Macmillan, 1980. A biography of screen actress Tallulah Bankhead.
Cole, Toby, and Helen Krich Chinoy. *Actors on Acting.* New York: Crown, 1970.
Fowler, Gene. *Goodnight, Sweet Prince.* New York: Viking, 1944. A biography of John Barrymore.
Goldman, Herbert G. *Fanny Brice: The Original Funny Girl.* New York: Oxford University Press, 1992.
Hayes, Helen, and Katherine Hatch. *My Life in Three Acts.* San Diego: Harcourt, Brace, Javanovich, 1990.
Kobbe, Gustav. *Famous Actresses and Their Homes.* Boston: Little, Brown, 1905.
Kotsilibos-Davis, James. *Great Times, Good Times: The Odyssey of Maurice Bar-rymore.* Garden City, New York: Doubleday, 1977.
Locke, Robinson. *Robinson Locke Collection of Dramatic Scrapbooks*, Billy Rose Theatre Collection of the New York City Public Library, vol. 160.
McKay, Frederic Edward, and Charles E. L. Wingate, eds. *Famous American Actors of To-day.* New York: Thomas Y. Crowell, 1986.
Monti, Carlotta. *W. C. Fields and Me.* Englewood Cliffs, New Jersey: Prentice Hall, 1971.
Morehouse, Ward. *George M. Cohan: Prince of the American Theatre.* Westport, Connecticut: Greenwood, 1943.
Ormsbee, Helen. *Backstage with Actors.* New York: Thomas Y. Crowell, 1938.
Robbins, Phyllis. *Maude Adams: an Intimate Portrait.* New York: G. P. Putnam's Sons, 1956.
Skinner, Cornelia Otis. *Madame Sarah.* Boston: Houghton Mifflin, 1967. A biog-raphy of Sarah Bernhardt.
Strang, Lewis C. *Famous Actresses of the Day in America.* Boston: L. C. Page and Company, 1902.
Wilson, James Grant, and John Fiske, eds. *Appleton's Cyclopedia of American Biog-raphy.* Vol. 2. New York: Appleton, 1888.
Winter, William. *Life and Art of Richard Mansfield.* 2 vols. New York: Moffat, Yard, 1910.

Playwrights

Barnes, Eric Wollencott. *The Man Who Lived Twice.* New York: Charles Scrib-ner's Sons, 1956. Biography of Edward Sheldon.
Chappelow, Allan. *Shaw, the Villager and Human Being.* New York: Macmillan, 1962.
Coolidge, Olivia. *George Bernard Shaw.* Boston: Houghton Mifflin, 1968.

Ervine, St. John Greer. *Bernard Shaw: His Life, Work, and Friends.* New York: William Morrow, 1956.

Henderson, Archibald. *Bernard Shaw: Playboy and Prophet.* New York: D. Appleton, 1932.

_____. *George Bernard Shaw: His Life and Works.* Cincinnati: Stewart & Kidd, 1911.

_____. *George Bernard Shaw: Man of the Century.* New York: Appleton-Century-Crofts, 1959.

Langford, Gerald. *The Richard Harding Davis Years.* New York: Holt, Rinehart and Winston, 1961.

Pearson, Hesketh. *G.B.S.: A Full Length Portrait.* New York: Harper & Brothers, 1942.

Peters, Margot. *Bernard Shaw and the Actresses.* Garden City, New York: Doubleday, 1980.

Miscellaneous

Arnold, Elliott. *Deep in My Heart.* New York: Duell, Sloan, and Pearce, 1949.

Browne, C. A. *The Story of Our National Ballads.* New York: Thomas Y. Crowell, 1931.

Callan, Louise. *Society of the Sacred Heart in North America.* New York: Longmans, Green, and Company, 1937.

Current Biography 1945. New York: H. W. Wilson Company, 1946.

Derkes, Scott, ed. *The Value of a Dollar.* Detroit: Gale Research, 1994.

Elley, Derek, ed. *Variety Movie Guide.* New York: Prentice Hall General Reference, 1992.

Fahringer, Dorothy McCall. Tape-recorded reminiscences.

Felheim, Marvin. *The Theatre of Augustin Daly.* Cambridge: Harvard University Press, 1956.

Frohman, Daniel. *Memoirs of a Manager.* New York: Doubleday, Page, 1911.

Hale, Louise Closser. *The Actress.* New York: Harpers, 1909.

Harris, Alice Kessler. *Out to Work: A History of Wage-Earning Women in the U. S.* New York: Oxford University Press, 1982.

Higham, Charles. *Ziegfeld.* Chicago: Henry Regnery Company, 1972.

Historical Statistics of the United States. Washington, D. C.: Dept. of Commerce, Bureau of the Census, 1975. Part 1.

Luey, Beth. *Handbook for Academic Authors.* Cambridge: Cambridge University Press, 1987.

Norton, Charles Eliot, ed. *Two Notebooks of Thomas Carlyle, from 23d March 1822 to 16th May.* New York: Grolier, 1989.

Mcgill, Frank N., ed. *Mcgill's Survey of Cinema III.* Englewood Cliffs, New Jersey: Salem Press, 1982.

McNamara, Brooks. *The Shuberts of Broadway.* New York: Oxford University Press, 1990.

Miller, Kerby A. *Emigrants and Exiles.* New York: Oxford University Press, 1985.

O'Connell, Charles. *The Victor Book of the Symphony.* New York: Simon and Schuster, 1941.

Potter, George. *To the Golden Door.* Boston: Little Brown, 1960.

Stagg, Jerry. *The Brothers Shubert*. New York: Random House, 1968.

Taubman, Hyman Howard. *The New York Times Guide to Listening Pleasure*. New York: The Macmillan Company, 1968.

Walker, John, ed. 8th ed. *Halliwell's Film Guide*. New York: Harper Collins, 1991.

Wilson, Garff B. *A History of American Acting*. Bloomington: Indiana University Press, 1966.

Wittke, Carl. *We Who Built America*. New York: Prentice Hall, 1939.

Periodicals

American
American Magazine
Cosmopolitan
Literary Digest
Modern Maturity
The Nation
National Service with the International Military Digest
The New Yorker

The Passing Show (newsletter of the Shubert Archive)
Pictorial Review
The Playgoer (program of the Curran Theatre, San Francisco)
Theatre
Theatre Arts Monthly
Theatre Magazine

Index